Fors Clavigera. Letters to the Workmen and Labourers of Great Britain

John Ruskin L.L.D.

BIBLIOLIFE

FORS CLAVIGERA.

LETTERS

*TO THE WORKMEN AND LABOURERS
OF GREAT BRITAIN.*

BY

JOHN RUSKIN, LL.D.,

HONORARY STUDENT OF CHRIST CHURCH, AND SLADE PROFESSOR OF FINE ART.

VOL. V.

GEORGE ALLEN,
SUNNYSIDE, ORPINGTON, KENT.
1875

FORS CLAVIGERA.

FIRST SERIES.

CONTENTS OF VOL. V. (1875.)

LETTER

XLIX. FROM THE PROPHET, EVEN UNTO THE PRIEST.

L. AGNES' BOOK.

LI. HUMBLE BEES.

LII. VALE OF LUNE.

LIII. THESE BE YOUR GODS.

LIV. PLAITED THORNS.

LV. THE WOODS OF MURI.

LVI. TIME-HONOURED LANCASTER

LVII. MICHAL'S SCORN.

LVIII. THE CATHOLIC PRAYER.

LIX. SCHOOL BOOKS.

LX. STARS IN THE EAST.

FORS CLAVIGERA.

LETTER THE 49th.

FROM THE PROPHET EVEN UNTO THE PRIEST.

I WONDER if Fors will let me say any small proportion, this year, of what I intend. I wish she would, for my readers have every right to be doubtful of my plan till they see it more defined ; and yet to define it severely would be to falsify it, for all that is best in it depends on my adopting whatever good I can find, in men and things, that will work to my purpose ; which of course means action in myriads of ways that I neither wish to define, nor attempt to anticipate. Nay, I am wrong, even in speaking of it as a plan or scheme at all It is only a method of uniting the force of all good plans and wise schemes : it is a principle and tendency, like the law of form in a crystal ; not a plan. If I live, as I said at first, I will endeavour to show some small part of it in action , but it would be a poor design indeed, for the bettering of the world, which any man could see either quite round the outside, or quite into the inside of.

But I hope in the letters of this next year to spend less time in argument or attack ; what I wish the reader to know, of principle, is already enough proved, if only he take the pains to read the preceding letters thoroughly ; and I shall now, as far as Fors will let me, carry out my purpose of choosing and annotating passages of confirmatory classical literature ; and answering, as they occur, the questions of my earnest correspondents, as to what each of them, in their place of life, may immediately do with advantage for St. George's help

If those of my readers who have been under the impression that I wanted them to join me in establishing some model institution or colony, will look to the fifth page of Letter I., they will see that, so far from intending or undertaking any such thing, I meant to put my whole strength into my Oxford teaching ; and, for my own part, to get rid of begging letters and live in peace.

Of course, when I have given fourteen thousand pounds away in a year,* everybody who wants some money thinks I have plenty for *them.* But my having given fourteen thousand pounds is just the reason I have *not* plenty for them ; and, moreover, have no time to attend to them, (and generally, henceforward, my friends will please to note that I have spent my life in helping other

---

* Seven thousand to St. George's Company ; five, for establishment of Mastership in Drawing in the Oxford schools ; two, and more, in the series of drawings placed in those schools to secure their efficiency.

people, and am quite tired of it , and if they can now help me in my work, or praise me for it, I shall be much obliged to them , but I can't help them at theirs)

But this impression of my wanting to found a colony was founded on page 23 of Letter V., and page 15 of Letter VIII. Read them over again now, altogether.

If the help I plead for come, we will indeed try to make some small piece of English ground beautiful ; and if sufficient help come, many such pieces of ground ; and on those we will put cottage dwellings, and educate the labourers' children in a certain manner. But that is not founding a colony. It is only agreeing to work on a given system. Any English gentleman who chooses to forbid the use of steam machinery—be it but over a few acres,— and to make the best of them he can by human labour, or who will secure a piece of his mountain ground from dog, gun, and excursion party, and let the wild flowers and wild birds live there in peace ,—any English gentleman, I say, who will so command either of these things, is doing the utmost I would ask of him ;—if, seeing the result of doing so much, he felt inclined to do more, field may add itself to field, cottage rise after cottage, —here and there the sky begin to open again above us, and the rivers to run pure. In a very little while, also, the general interest in education will assuredly discover that healthy habits, and not mechanical drawing nor church catechism, are the staple of it ; and then, not in my model colony only, but as best it can be managed in any unmodelled place or way—girls will be taught to cook, boys to plough, and both to behave ; and that with the heart,—which is the first piece of all the body that has to be instructed.

A village clergyman, (an excellent farmer, and very kind friend of my earliest college days,) sent me last January a slip out of the 'Daily Telegraph,' written across in his own hand with the words "Advantage of Education" The slip described the eloquence and dexterity in falsehood of the Parisian Communist prisoners on their trial for the murder of the hostages. But I would fain ask my old friend to tell me himself whether he thinks instruction in the art of false eloquence should indeed receive from any minister of Christ the title of 'education' at all , and how far display of eloquence, instead of instruction in behaviour, has become the function, too commonly, of these ministers themselves.

I was asked by one of my Oxford pupils the other day why I had never said any serious word of what it might seem best for clergymen to do in a time of so great doubt and division.

I have not, because any man's becoming a clergyman in these days must imply one of two things—either that he has something to do and say for men which he honestly believes himself impelled to do and say by the Holy Ghost,—and in that case he is likely to see his way without being shown it,—or else he is one of the group of so-called Christians who, except with the outward ear, "have not so much as heard whether there *be* any Holy Ghost," and are practically lying, both to men and to God ;—persons to whom, whether they be foolish or wicked in their ignorance, no honest way can possibly be shown

The particular kinds of folly also which lead youths to become clergymen, uncalled, are especially intractable. That a lad just out of his teens, and not under the influence of any deep religious enthusiasm, should ever contemplate the possibility of his being set up in the middle of a mixed company of men and women of the world, to instruct the aged, encourage the valiant, support the weak, reprove the guilty, and set an example to all ; —and not feel what a ridiculous and blasphemous business it would be, if he only pretended to do it for hire ; and what a ghastly and murderous business it would be, if he did it strenuously wrong ; and what a marvellous and all but incredible thing the Church and its power must be, if it were possible for him, with all the good meaning in the world, to do it rightly ;—that any youth, I say, should ever have got himself into the state of recklessness, or conceit, required to become a clergyman at all, under these existing circumstances, must put him quite out of the pale of those whom one appeals to on any reasonable or moral question, in serious writing I went into a ritualistic church, the other day, for instance, in the West End. It was built of bad Gothic, lighted with bad painted glass, and had its Litany intoned, and its sermon delivered—on the subject of wheat and chaff—by a young man of, as far as I could judge, very sincere religious sentiments, but very certainly the kind of person whom one might have brayed in a mortar among the very best of the wheat with a pestle, without making his foolishness depart from him. And, in general, any man's becoming a clergyman in these days implies that, at best, his sentiment has overpowered his intellect ; and that, whatever the feebleness of the latter, the victory of his impertinent piety has been probably owing to its alliance with his conceit, and its promise to him of the gratification of being regarded as an oracle, without the trouble of becoming wise, or the grief of being so.

It is not, however, by men of this stamp that the principal mischief is done to the Church of Christ. Their foolish congregations are not enough in earnest even to be misled ; and the increasing London or Liverpool respectable suburb is simply provided with its baker's and butcher's shop, its alehouse, its itinerant organ-grinders for the week, and stationary organ-grinder for Sunday, himself his monkey, in obedience to the commonest condition of demand and supply, and without much more danger in their Sunday's entertainment than in their Saturday's. But the importunate and zealous ministrations of the men who have been strong enough to deceive themselves before they deceive others ;—who give the grace and glow of vital sincerity to falsehood, and lie for God from the ground of their heart, produce forms of moral corruption in their congregations as much more deadly than the consequences of recognizedly vicious conduct, as the hectic of consumption is more deadly than the flush of temporary fever. And it is entirely unperceived by the members of existing churches that the words, 'speaking lies in hypocrisy, having their conscience seared with a hot iron,' do not in the least apply to wilful and self-conscious hypocrites, but only to those who do not recognize themselves for such. Of wilful assumption of the appearance of piety, for promotion of their own interests, few, even of the basest men, are frankly capable : and to the average English gentleman, deliberate hypocrisy is impossible. And, therefore, all the fierce invectives of Christ, and of the prophets and apostles, against hypocrisy, thunder above their heads unregarded ; while all the while Annas and Caiaphas are sitting in Moses' seat for ever ; and the anger of God is accomplished against the daughter of His people, "for the sins of her prophets, and the iniquities of her priests, that have shed the blood of the just in the midst of her. They have wandered blind in the streets ; they have polluted themselves with blood, so that men could not touch their garments."*

Take, for example, the conduct of the heads of the existing Church respecting the two powers attributed to them in this very verse. There is certainly no Bishop now in the Church of England who would either dare in a full drawing-

* Lamentations v 13.

room to attribute to himself the gift of prophecy, in so
many words , or to write at the head of any of his sermons,
" On such and such a day, of such and such a month,
in such and such a place, the Word of the Lord came
unto me, saying" Nevertheless, he claims to have received the Holy Ghost himself by laying on of hands ;
and to be able to communicate the Holy Ghost to other
men in the same manner　And he knows that the office
of the prophet is as simply recognized in the enumeration of the powers of the ancient Church, as that of the
apostle, or evangelist, or doctor.　And yet he can neither
point out in the Church the true prophets, to whose
number he dares not say he himself belongs, nor the
false prophets, who are casting out devils in the name
of Christ, without being known by Him ;—and he contentedly suffers his flock to remain under the impression
that the Christ who led captivity captive, and received
gifts for men, left the gift of prophecy out of the group,
as one needed no longer

But the second word, ' priest,' is one which he finds it
convenient to assume himself, and to give to his fellow-
clergymen.　He knows, just as well as he knows prophecy to be a gift attributed to the Christian minister,
that priesthood is a function expressly taken away from
the Christian minister.*　He dares not say in the open

---

* As distinguished, that is to say, from other members of the Church
All are priests, as all are kings ; but the kingly function exists apart ; the
priestly, not so　The subject is examined at some length, and with a clearness

drawing-room that he offers sacrifice for any soul there ; —and he knows that he cannot give authority for calling himself a priest from any canonical book of the New Testament. So he equivocates on the sound of the word ' presbyter,' and apologizes to his conscience and his flock by declaring, " The priest I say,—the presbyter I mean," without even requiring so much poor respect for his quibble as would be implied by insistance that a so-called priest should at least *be* an Elder. And securing, as far as he can, the reverence of his flock, while he secretly abjures the responsibility of the office he takes the title of, again he lets the rebuke of his God fall upon a deafened ear, and reads that " from the Prophet unto the Priest, every one dealeth falsely," without the slightest sensation that his own character is so much as alluded to.

Thus, not daring to call themselves prophets, which they know they ought to be; but daring, under the shelter of equivocation, to call themselves priests, which they know they are not, and are forbidden to be ; thus admittedly, without power of prophecy, and only in stammering pretence to priesthood, they yet claim the power to forgive and retain sins. Whereupon, it is to be strictly asked of them, whose sins they remit ; and whose sins they retain. For truly, if they have a right to claim any authority or function whatever—this is it. Prophesy, they cannot ;—sacrifice, they cannot ;—in their hearts

which I cannot mend, in my old pamphlet on the ' Construction of Sheepfolds,' which I will presently reprint. See also Letter XIII., in ' Time and Tide.'

there is no vision—in their hands no victim   The work
of the Evangelist was done before they could be made
Bishops ; that of the Apostle cannot be done on a
Bishop's throne   there remains to them, of all possible
office of organization in the Church, only that of the
pastor,—verily and intensely their own ; received by them
in definite charge when they received what they call the
Holy Ghost ;—" Be to the flock of Christ, a shepherd,
not a wolf ;—feed them, devour them not."

Does any man, of all the men who have received this
charge in England, know what it *is* to be a wolf ?—recognize in himself the wolfish instinct, and the thirst for the
blood of God's flock ?   For if he does not know what is
the nature of a wolf, how should he know what it is to be
a shepherd ?   If he never felt like a wolf himself, does he
know the people who do ?   He does not expect them to
lick their lips and bare their teeth at him, I suppose, as
they do in a pantomime ?   Did he ever in his life see
a wolf coming, and debate with himself whether he should
fight or fly?—or is not rather his whole life one headlong
hireling's flight, without so much as turning his head to
see what manner of beasts they are that follow ?—nay,
are not his very hireling's wages paid him *for* flying
instead of fighting ?

Dares any one of them answer me—here from my
college of the Body of Christ I challenge every mitre
of them : definitely, the Lord of St. Peter's borough,
whom I note as a pugnacious and accurately worded

person, and hear of as an outspoken one, able and ready
to answer for his fulfilment of the charge to Peter : How
many wolves does he know in Peterborough—how many
sheep ?—what battle has he done—what bites can he
show the scars of ?—whose sins has he remitted in Peterborough—whose retained ?—has he not remitted, like his
brother Bishops, all the sins of the rich, and retained all
those of the poor ?—does he know, in Peterborough, who
are fornicators, who thieves, who liars, who murderers ?—
and has he ever dared to tell any one of them to his face
that he was so—if the man had over a hundred a year ?

"Have mercy upon all Jews, Turks, infidels, and
heretics, and so fetch them home, blessed Lord, to Thy
flock, that they may be saved among the remnant
of the true Israelites." Who *are* the true Israelites, my
lord of Peterborough, whom you can definitely announce
for such, in your diocese ? Or, perhaps, the Bishop of
Manchester will take up the challenge, having lately
spoken wisely—in generalities—concerning Fraud. Who
are the true Israelites, my lord of Manchester, on your
Exchange ? Do they stretch their cloth, like other
people ?—have they any underhand dealings with the
liable-to-be-damned false Israelites—Rothschilds and the
like ? or are they duly solicitous about those wanderers'
souls ? and how often, on the average, do your Manchester
clergy preach from the delicious parable, savouriest of all
Scripture to rogues, at least since the eleventh century,
when I find it to have been specially headed with golden

title in my best Greek MS., "of the Pharisee and Publican"—and how often, on the average, from those objectionable First and Fifteenth Psalms ?

For the last character in St. Paul's enumeration, which Bishops can claim, and the first which they are bound to claim, for the perfecting of the saints, and the work of the ministry, is that of the Doctor or Teacher.

In which character, to what work of their own, frank and faithful, can they appeal in the last fifty years of especial danger to the Church from false teaching ? On this matter, my challenge will be most fittingly made to my own Bishop, of the University of Oxford. He inhibited, on the second Sunday of Advent of last year, another Bishop of the English Church from preaching at Carfax. By what right ? Which of the two Bishops am I, their innocent lamb, to listen to ? It is true that the insulted Bishop was only a colonial one ;—am I to understand, therefore, that the Church sends her heretical Bishops out as Apostles, while she keeps her orthodox ones at home ? and that, accordingly, a stay-at-home Bishop may always silence a returned Apostle ? And, touching the questions which are at issue, is there a single statement of the Bishop of Natal's, respecting the Bible text, which the Bishop of Oxford dares to contradict before Professor Max Muller, or any other leading scholar of Europe ? Does the Bishop of Oxford himself believe every statement in the Bible ? If not,—which does he disbelieve, and why ? He suffers the whole collection of books to be spoken of—certainly by many clergymen in his diocese—as the Word of God. If he disbelieves any portion of it, that portion he is bound at once to inhibit them from so calling, till inquiry has been made concerning it ; but if he and the other orthodox home-Bishops,—who would very joyfully, I perceive, burn the Bishop of Natal at Paul's, and make Ludgate Hill safer for the omnibuses with the cinders of him,—if they verily believe all, or even, with a living faith, *any*, vital part of the Bible, how is it that we, the incredulous sheep, see no signs following them that believe ;—that though they can communicate the Holy Spirit, they cannot excommunicate the unholy one, and apologetically leave the healing of sick to the physician, the taking up of serpents to the juggler, and the moving of mountains to the railway-navvy ?

"It was never meant that any one should do such things literally, after St Paul's time."

Then what *was* meant, and what *is*, doctors mine ?

Challenge enough, for this time, it seems to me , the rather that just as I finish writing it, I receive a challenge myself, requiring attentive answer. Fors could not have brought it me at better time The reader will find it the first in the Notes and Correspondence of this year ; and my answer may both meet the doubts of many readers who would not so frankly have expressed them , and contain some definitions of principle which are necessary for our future work.

My correspondent, referring to my complaint that no matron nor maid of England had yet joined the St George's Company, answers, for her own part, first that her husband and family prevent her from doing it; secondly, that she has done it already; thirdly, that she will do it when I do it myself. It is only to the third of these pleas that I at present reply.

She tells me, first, that I have not joined the St. George's Company because I have no home. It is too true. But that is because my father, and mother, and nurse, are dead; because the woman I hoped would have been my wife is dying; and because the place where I would fain have stayed to remember all of them, was rendered physically uninhabitable to me by the violence of my neighbours;—that is to say, by their destroying the fields I needed to think in, and the light I needed to work by. Nevertheless, I have, under these conditions, done the best thing possible to me—bought a piece of land on which I could live in peace; and on that land, wild when I bought it, have already made, not only one garden, but two, to match against my correspondent's; nor that without help from children who, though not mine, have been cared for as if they were.

Secondly; my correspondent tells me that my duty is to stay at home, instead of dating from places which are a dream of delight to *her*, and which, therefore, she concludes, must be a reality of delight to me.

She will know better after reading this extract from

my last year's diary; (worth copying, at any rate, for other persons interested in republican Italy). " Florence, 20th September, 1874.—Tour virtually ended for this year I leave Florence to-day, thankfully, it being now a place of torment day and night for all loving, decent, or industrious people ; for every face one meets is full of hatred and cruelty, and the corner of every house is foul ; and no thoughts can be thought in it, peacefully, in street, or cloister, or house, any more And the last verses I read, of my morning's readings, are Esdras II., xv. 16, 17 · ' For there shall be sedition among men, and invading one another ; they shall not regard their kings nor princes, *and the course of their actions shall stand in their power.* A man shall desire to go into a city, and shall not be able.' "

What is said here of Florence is now equally true of every great city of France or Italy , and my correspondent will be perhaps contented with me when she knows that only last Sunday I was debating with a very dear friend whether I might now be justified in indulging my indolence and cowardice by staying at home among my plants and minerals, and forsaking the study of Italian art for ever. My friend would fain have it so ; and my correspondent shall tell me her opinion, after she knows—and I will see that she has an opportunity of knowing—what work I have done in Florence, and propose to do, if I can be brave enough.

Thirdly ; my correspondent doubts the sincerity of my

abuse of railroads because she suspects I use them. I do so constantly, my dear lady, few men more. I use everything that comes within reach of me If the devil were standing at my side at this moment, I should endeavour to make some use of him as a local black. The wisdom of life is in preventing all the evil we can, and using what is inevitable, to the best purpose. I use my sicknesses, for the work I despise in health ; my enemies, for study of the philosophy of benediction and malediction ; and railroads, for whatever I find of help in them—looking always hopefully forward to the day when their embankments will be ploughed down again, like the camps of Rome, into our English fields. But I am perfectly ready even to construct a railroad, when I think one necessary, and in the opening chapter of 'Munera Pulveris' my correspondent will find many proper uses for steam-machinery specified What is required of the members of St. George's Company is, not that they should never travel by railroads, nor that they should abjure machinery ; but that they should never travel unnecessarily, or in wanton haste ; and that they should never do with a machine what can be done with hands and arms, while hands and arms are idle

Lastly, my correspondent feels it unjust to be required to make clothes, while she is occupied in the rearing of those who will require them.

Admitting (though the admission is one for which I do not say that I am prepared) that it is the patriotic duty of every married couple to have as large a family as possible, it is not from the happy Penelopes of such households that I ask—or should think of asking—the labour of the loom. I simply require that when women belong to the St. George's Company they should do a certain portion of useful work with their hands, if otherwise their said fair hands would be idle ; and if on those terms I find sufficient clothing cannot be produced, I will use factories for them,—only moved by water, not steam.

My answer, as thus given, is, it seems to be, sufficient ; and I can farther add to its force by assuring my correspondent that I shall never ask any member of St George's Company to do more, in relation to his fortune and condition, than I have already done myself. Nevertheless, it will be found by any reader who will take the trouble of reference, that in recent letters I have again and again intimated the probable necessity, before the movement could be fairly set on foot, of more energetic action and example, towards which both my thoughts and circumstances seem gradually leading me ; and, in that case, I shall trustfully look to the friends who accuse me of cowardice in doing too little, for defence against the, I believe, too probable imputations impending from others, of folly in doing too much.

NOTES AND CORRESPONDENCE.

I. I hope my kind correspondent will pardon my publication of the following letter, which gives account of an exemplary life, and puts questions which many desire to have answered.

"My dear Mr. Ruskin,—I do not know if you have forgotten me, for it is a long time since I wrote to you; but you wrote so kindly to me before, that I venture to bring myself before you again, more especially as you write *to* me (among others) every month, and I want to answer something in these letters.

"I do answer your letters (somewhat combatively) every month in my mind, but all these months I have been waiting for an hour of sufficient strength and leisure, and have found it now for the first time. A family of eleven children, through a year of much illness, and the birth of another child in May, have not left me much strength for *pleasure*, such as this is.

"Now a little while ago, you asked reproachfully of English-women in general, why none of them had joined St. George's Company. I can only answer for myself, and I have these reasons.

"First. Being situated as I am, and as doubtless many others are more or less, I *cannot* join it. In my actions I am subject first to my husband, and then to my family. Any one who is entirely free cannot judge how impossible it is to make inelastic and remote rules apply to all the ever-varying and incalculable changes and accidents and personalities of life. They' are a disturbing element to us visionaries, which I have been *forced* to acknowledge and submit to, but which you have not. Having so many to consider and consult, it is all I can do to get through the day's work, I am obliged to take things as I find them, and to do the best I can, in haste; and I might constantly be breaking rules, and not able to help it, and indeed I should not have time to think about it. I do not want to be hampered more than I am. I am not straitened for money; but most people with families are so more or less, and this is another element of difficulty.

"Secondly. Although I do not want to be further bound by *rules,* I believe that as regards *principles* I am a member of St. George's Company already; and I do not like to make any further profession which would seem to imply a renunciation of the former errors of my way, and the beginning of a *new* life. I have never been conscious of any other motives or course of life than those which you advocate; and my children and all around me do not know me in any other light; and I find a gradual and unconscious conformation to them growing up round me, though I have no sort of *teaching* faculty. I cannot tell how much of them I owe to you, for some of your writings which fell in my way when I was very young made a deep impression on me, and I grew up embued with their spirit, but certainly I cannot now profess it for the first time.

"Thirdly (and this is wherein I fear to offend you), *I will join St. George's Company whenever you join it yourself.* Please pardon me for saying that I appear to be more a member of it than you are. My life is strictly bound and ruled, and within those lines I live. Above all things, you urge our duties to the land, the common earth of our country. It seems to me that the first duty any one owes to his country is *to live in it.* I go further, and maintain that every one is bound to have a home, and live in that. You speak of the duty of acquiring, if possible, and cultivating, the smallest piece of ground. But, (forgive the question,) where is your house and your garden? I know you have got *places*, but you do not stay there. Almost every month you date from some new place, a dream of delight to me; and all the time I am stopping at home, labouring to improve the place I live at, to keep the lives entrusted to me, and to bring forth other lives in the agony and peril of my own. And when I read your reproaches, and see where they date from, I feel as a soldier freezing in the trenches before Sebastopol might feel at receiving orders from a General who was dining at his club in London. If you would come and see me in May, I could show you as pretty a little garden of the spade as any you ever saw, made on the site of an old rubbish heap, where seven tiny pair of hands and feet have worked like fairies. Have you got a better one to show me? For the rest of my garden I cannot boast; because out-of-door work or pleasure is entirely forbidden me by the state of my health.

"Again, I agree with you in your dislike of railroads, but I suspect you use them, and sometimes go on them. *I never do.* I obey these laws and others, with whatever inconvenience or privation they may involve, but you do not, and that makes me revolt when you scold us.

"Again, I *cannot*, as you suggest, grow, spin, and weave the linen for myself and family. I have enough to do to get the clothes made. If you would establish factories where we could get pure woven cotton, linen, and woollen, I would gladly *buy* them there; and that would be a fair division of labour. It is not fair that the more one does, the more should be required of one.

"You see you are like a clergyman in the pulpit in your books: you can scold the congregation, and they cannot answer; behold the congregation begins to reply; and I only hope you will forgive me.   "Believe me,

"Yours very truly."

II. It chances, I see, while I print my challenge to the Bishop of my University, that its neighbouring clergymen are busy in expressing to him their thanks and compliments. The following address is worth preserving. I take it from the 'Morning Post' of December 16, and beneath it have placed an article from the 'Telegraph' of the following day, describing the results of clerical and episcopal teaching of an orthodox nature in Liverpool, as distinguished from 'Doctor' Colenso's teaching in Africa,

"THE INHIBITION OF BISHOP COLENSO.—The clergy of the rural deanery of Witney, Oxford, numbering thirty-four, together with the rural dean (the Rev F M. Cunningham), have sub-scribed their names to the following circular, which has been forwarded to the Bishop of Oxford:—'To the Right Rev. Father in God, John Fielder, by Divine permission Lord Bishop of Oxford.—We, the undersigned clergy of the rural deanery of Witney, in your Lordship's diocese, beg respectfully to offer to your Lordship our cordial sympathy under the painful circum-stances in which you have been placed by the invitation to the Right Rev Dr. Colenso to preach in one of the churches in your diocese Your firm and spontaneous refusal to permit Dr. Colenso to preach will be thankfully accepted by all con-sistent members of our Church as a protest much needed in these times against the teaching of one who has grievously offended many consciences, and has attempted as far as in him lay to injure the 'faith which was delivered to the saints.'[a] That your Lordship may long be spared to defend the truth, is the prayer of your Lordship's obedient and attached clergy."

([a] I append a specimen of the conduct of the Saints to whom our English clergymen have delivered the Faith.)

III. "Something startling in the way of wickedness is needed to astonish men who, like our Judges, see and hear the periodical crop of crime gathered in at Assizes; yet in two great cities of England, on Tuesday, expressions of amazement, shame, 'and disgust fell from the seat of Justice. At York, Mr. Justice Denman was driven to utter a burst of just indignation at the conduct of certain people in his court, who grinned and tittered while a witness in a disgraceful case was reluctantly repeating some indelicate language. 'Good God!' exclaimed his Lordship, 'is this a Christian country? Let us at least have decency in courts of justice. One does not come to be amused by filth which one is obliged to extract in cases that defame the land.' At Liverpool a sterner declaration of judicial anger was made, with even stronger cause. Two cases of revolting barbarism were tried by Mr. Justice Mellor—one of savage violence towards a man, ending in murder; the other of outrage upon a woman, so unspeakably shameful and horrible that the difficulty is how to convey the facts without offending public decency. In the first, a gang of men at Liverpool set upon a porter named Richard Morgan, who was in the company of his wife and brother, and because he did not instantly give them sixpence to buy beer they kicked him completely across the street, a distance of thirty feet, with such ferocity, in spite of all the efforts made to save him by the wife and brother, that the poor man was dead when he was taken up. And during this cruel and cowardly scene the crowd of bystanders not only did not attempt to rescue the victim, but hounded on his murderers, and actually held back the agonized wife and the brave brother from pursuing the homicidal wretches. Three of them were placed at the bar on trial for their lives, and convicted; nor would we intervene with one word in their favour, though that word might save their vile necks. This case might appear bad enough to call forth the utmost wrath of Justice; but the second, heard at the same time and place, was yet more hideous. A tramp-woman, drunk, and wet to the skin with rain, was going along a road near Burnley, in company with a navvy, who by-and-by left her helpless at a gate. Two out of a party of young colliers coming from work found her lying there, and they led her into a field. They then sent a boy named Slater to·fetch the remaining eight of their band, and, having thus gathered many spectators, two of them certainly, and others of the number in all probability, outraged the hapless creature, leaving her after this infernal treatment in such plight that next day she was found lying dead in the field. The two in question—Durham, aged twenty, and Shepherd, aged sixteen— were arraigned for murder; but that charge was found difficult to make good, and the minor indictment for rape was alone pressed against them. Of the facts there was little or no doubt; and it may well be thought that in stating them we have accomplished the saddest portion of our duty to the public.

"But no! to those who have learned how to measure human nature, we think what followed will appear the more horrible portion of the trial—if more horrible could be. With a strange want of insight, the advocate for these young men called up the companions of their atrocity to swear—what does the public expect?—to swear *that they did not think the tramp-woman was ill-used,* nor fhat *what was done was wrong.* Witness after witness, present at the time, calmly deposed to his personal view of the transaction in words like those of William Bracewell, a collier, aged nineteen. Between this precious specimen of our young British working man and the Bench, the following interchange of questions and answers passed. 'You did not think there was anything wrong in it?'—'No.' 'Do you mean to tell me you did not think there was anything wrong in outraging a drunken woman?'—'She never said nothing.' 'You repeat you think there was nothing wrong—that there was no harm in a lot of fellows outraging a drunken woman is that your view of the thing?'—'Yes.' And, in reply to further questions by Mr. Cottingham, this fellow Bracewell said he only 'thought the matter a bit of fun. None of them interfered to protect the woman.' Then the boy Slater, who was sent to bring up the laggards, was asked what he thought of his errand Like the others, 'he hadn't seen anything very wrong in it.' At this point the Judge broke forth, in accents which may well ring through England. His Lordship indignantly exclaimed : 'I want to know how it is possible in a Christian country like this that there should be such a state of feeling, even among boys of thirteen, sixteen, and eighteen years of age. It is outrageous. If there are missionaries wanted to the heathen, there are heathens in England who require teaching a great deal more than those abroad.' (Murmurs of 'Hear, hear,' from the jury box, and applause in court.) His Lordship continued. 'Silence ! It is quite shocking to hear boys of this age come up and say these things.' How, indeed, is it possible ? that is the question which staggers one Murder there will be—manslaughter, rape, burglary, theft, are all unfortunately recurring and common crimes in every community Nothing in the supposed nature of 'Englishmen' can be expected to make our assizes maiden, and our gaol deliveries blank But there was thought to be something in the blood of the race which would somehow serve to keep us from seeing a Liverpool crowd side with a horde of murderers against their victim, or a gang of Lancashire lads making a ring to see a woman outraged to death. A hundred cases nowadays tell us to discard that idle belief, if it ever was true, it is true no longer. The most brutal, the most cowardly, the most pitiless, the most barbarous deeds done in the world, are being perpetrated by the lower classes of the English people—once held to be by their birth, however lowly, generous, brave, merciful, and civilized. In all the pages of Dr Livingstone's experience among the negroes of Africa, there is no single instance approaching this Liverpool story, in savagery of mind and body, in bestiality of heart and act. Nay, we wrong the lower animals by using that last word the foulest among the beasts which perish is clean, the most ferocious gentle, matched with these Lancashire pitmen, who make sport of the shame and slaying of a woman, and blaspheme nature in their deeds, without even any plea whatever to excuse their cruelty."

The clergy may vainly exclaim against being made responsible for this state of things. They, and chiefly their Bishops, are wholly responsible for it; nay, are efficiently the causes of it, preaching a false gospel for hire. But, putting all questions of false or true gospels aside, suppose that they only obeyed St Paul's plain order in 1st Corinthians v. 11. Let them determine as distinctly what covetousness and extortion are in the rich, as what drunkenness is, in the poor. Let them refuse, themselves, and order their clergy to refuse, to go out to dine with such persons; and still more positively to allow such persons to sup at God's table. And they would soon know what fighting wolves meant; and something more of their own pastoral duty than they learned in that Consecration Service, where they proceeded to follow the example of the Apostles in. Prayer, but carefully left out the Fasting.

Accounts.

The following Subscriptions have come in since I made out the list in the December number, but that list is still incomplete, as I cannot be sure of some of the numbers till I have seen my Brantwood note-book :—

		£	s	d
31.	"In Memoriam"	5	0	0
32.	(The tenth of a tenth) . . .	1	1	0
33.	Gift	20	0	0
34.	An Old Member of the Working Men's College.			
	Gift	5	0	0
35.	H. T. S.	9	0	0
36.	. . . . . .	5	0	0
7.	Second Donation . . .	5	0	0
15.	,, ,, . . .	5	0	0
		£55	1	0

FORS CLAVIGERA.

A FRIEND, in whose judgment I greatly trust, remonstrated sorrowfully with me, the other day, on the desultory character of Fors ; and pleaded with me for the writing of an arranged book instead

But he might as well plead with a birch-tree growing out of a crag, to arrange its boughs beforehand The winds and floods will arrange them according to their wild liking ; all that the tree has to do, or can do, is to grow gaily, if it may be , sadly, if gaiety be impossible ; and let the black jags and scars rend the rose-white of its trunk where Fors shall choose

But I can well conceive how irritating it must be to any one chancing to take special interest in any one part of my subject—the life of Scott for instance,—to find me, or lose me, wandering away from it for a year or two , and sending roots into new ground in every direction : or (for my friend taxed me with this graver error also) needlessly re-rooting myself in the old

And, all the while, some kindly expectant people are

waiting for 'details of my plan.' In the presentment
of which, this main difficulty still lets me ; that, if I told
them, or tried to help them definitely to conceive, the
ultimate things I aim at, they would at once throw the
book down as hopelessly Utopian ; but if I tell them
the immediate things I aim at, they will refuse to do
those instantly possible things, because inconsistent with
the present vile general system. For instance—I take
(see Letter V.) Wordsworth's single line,

" We live by admiration, hope, and love,"

for my literal guide, in all education. My final object,
with every child born on St. George's estate, will be to
teach it what to admire, what to hope for, and what to
love : but how far do you suppose the steps necessary
to such an ultimate aim are immediately consistent with
what Messrs. Huxley and Co. call ' Secular education '?
Or with what either the Bishop of Oxford, or Mr.
Spurgeon, would call ' Religious education '?

What to admire, or wonder at! Do you expect a
child to wonder at—being taught that two and two
make four—(though if only its masters had the sense to
teach *that*, honestly, it would be something)—or at the
number of copies of nasty novels and false news a
steam-engine can print for its reading ?

What to hope ? Yes, my secular friends—What ? That
it shall be the richest shopman in the street ; and be
buried with black feathers enough over its coffin ?

What to love—Yes, my ecclesiastical friends, and who is its neighbour, think you ? Will you meet these three demands of mine with your three Rs, or your catechism ?

And how would I meet them myself ? Simply by never, so far as I could help it, letting a child read what is not worth reading, or see what is not worth seeing ; and by making it live a life which, whether it will or no, shall enforce honourable hope of continuing long in the land—whether of men or God.

And who is to say what is worth reading, or worth seeing ? sneer the Republican mob. Yes, gentlemen, you who never knew a good thing from a bad, in all your lives, may well ask that !

Let us try, however, in such a simple thing as a child's book. Yesterday, in the course of my walk, I went into a shepherd-farmer's cottage, to wish whoever might be in the house a happy new year. His wife was at home, of course, and his little daughter, Agnes, nine years old ; both as good as gold, in their way.

The cottage is nearly a model of those which I shall expect the tenants of St. George's Company, and its active members, to live in ,—the entire building, parlour, and kitchen, (in this case one, but not necessarily so,) bedrooms and all, about the size of an average dining-room in Grosvenor Place or Park Lane The conversation naturally turning to Christmas doings and havings.—and I, as an author, of course inquiring whether Agnes had any new books, Agnes brought me her library—consisting chiefly in a good pound's weight of the literature which cheap printing enables the pious to make Christmas presents of for a penny. A full pound, or it might be, a pound and a half, of this instruction, full of beautiful sentiments, woodcuts, and music. More woodcuts in the first two ounces of it I took up, than I ever had to study in the first twelve years of my life. Splendid woodcuts, too, in the best Kensington style, and rigidly on the principles of high, and commercially remunerative, art, taught by Messrs Redgrave, Cole, and Company.

Somehow, none of these seem to have interested little Agnes, or been of the least good to her. Her pound and a half of the best of the modern pious and picturesque is (being of course originally boardless) now a crumpled and variously doubled-up heap, brought down in a handful, or lapful, rather ; most of the former insides of the pamphlets being now the outsides ; and every form of dog's ear, puppy's ear, cat's ear, kitten's ear, rat's ear, and mouse's ear, developed by the contortions of weary fingers at the corners of their didactic and evangelically sibylline leaves. I ask if I may borrow one to take home and read. Agnes is delighted ; but undergoes no such pang of care as a like request would have inflicted on my boyish mind, and needed generous stifling of ;— nay, had I asked to borrow the whole heap, I am not sure whether Agnes' first tacit sensation would not have been one of deliverance.

Being very fond of pretty little girls, (not, by any

means, excluding pretty—tall ones,) I choose, for my own
reading, a pamphlet* which has a picture of a beautiful
little girl with long hair, lying very ill in bed, with her
mother putting up her forefinger at her brother, who
is crying, with a large tear on the side of his nose ,
and a legend beneath : 'Harry told his mother the
whole story' The pamphlet has been doubled up by
Agnes right through the middle of the beautiful little
girl's face, and no less remorselessly through the very
middle of the body of the 'Duckling Astray,' charmingly
drawn by Mr. Harrison Weir on the opposite leaf But
my little Agnes knows so much more about real ducklings than the artist does, that her severity in this case
is not to be wondered at.

I carry my Children's Prize penny's-worth home to
Brantwood, full of curiosity to know "the whole story."
I find that this religious work is edited by a Master of
Arts—no less—and that two more woodcuts of the
most finished order are given to Harry's story,—representing Harry and the pretty little girl, (I suppose so,
at least , but, alas, now with her back turned to me,—
the cuts came cheaper so,) dressed in the extreme of
fashion, down to her boots,—first running with Harry, in
snow, after a carriage, and then reclining against Harry's
shoulder in a snowstorm.

I arrange my candles for small print, and proceed to
read this richly illustrated story.

* The Children's Prize No. XII. December, 1873 Price one penny

Harry and his sister were at school together, it appears, at Salisbury ; and their father's carriage was sent, in a snowy day, to bring them home for the holidays. They are to be at home by five ; and their mother has invited a children's party at seven. Harry is enjoined by his father, in the letter which conveys this information, to remain inside the carriage, and not to go on the box.

Harry is a good boy, and does as he is bid ; but nothing whatever is said in the letter about not getting out of the carriage to walk up hills. And at ' two-mile hill ' Harry thinks it will be clever to get out and walk up it, without calling to, or stopping, John on the box. Once out himself, he gets Mary out ;—the children begin snowballing each other ; the carriage leaves them so far behind that they can't catch it ; a snowstorm comes on, etc, etc, ; they are pathetically frozen within a breath of their lives , found by a benevolent carter, just in time , warmed by a benevolent farmer, the carter's friend ; restored to their alarmed father and mother , and Mary has a rheumatic fever, " and for a whole week it was not known whether she would live or die," which is the Providential punishment of Harry's sin in getting out of the carriage.

Admitting the perfect appositeness and justice of this Providential punishment ; I am, parenthetically, desirous to know of my Evangelical friends, first, whether from the corruption of Harry's nature they could have expected anything better than his stealthily getting out of the carriage to walk up the hill?—and, secondly, whether the merits of Christ, which are enough to save any murderer or swindler from all the disagreeable consequences of murder and swindling, in the next world, are not enough in this world, if properly relied upon, to save a wicked little boy's sister from rheumatic fever? This, I say, I only ask parenthetically, for my own information, my immediate business being to ask what effect this story is intended to produce on my shepherd's little daughter Agnes?

Intended to produce, I say, what effect it *does* produce, I can easily ascertain, but what do the writer and the learned editor expect of it? Or rather, to touch the very beginning of the inquiry, for what class of child do they intend it? 'For all classes,' the enlightened editor and liberal publisher doubtless reply. 'Classes, indeed! In the glorious liberty of the Future, there shall be none!'

Well, be it so; but in the inglorious slavery of the Past, it has happened that my little Agnes's father has not kept a carriage; that Agnes herself has not often seen one, is not likely often to be in one, and has seen a great deal too much snow, and had a great deal too much walking in it, to be tempted out,—if she ever has the chance of being driven in a carriage to a children's party at seven,—to walk up a hill on the road. Such is our benighted life in Westmoreland. In the future, do my pious and liberal friends suppose that all little Agneses are to drive in carriages ? That is *their* Utopia. Mine, so much abused for its impossibility, is only that a good many little Agneses who at present drive in carriages, shall have none.

Nay, but perhaps, the learned editor did not intend the story for children 'quite in Agnes's position.' For what sort did he intend it, then ? For the class of children whose fathers keep carriages, and whose mothers dress their girls by the Paris modes, at three years old ? Very good ; then, in families which keep carriages and footmen, the children are supposed to think a book is a prize, which costs a penny ? Be that also so, in the Republican cheap world ; but might not the cheapeners print, when they are about it, prize poetry for their penny ? Here is the 'Christmas Carol,' set to music, accompanying this moral story of the Snow.

> " Hark, hark, the merry pealing,
>   List to the Christmas chime,
> Every breath and every feeling
>   Hails the good old time ;
> Brothers, sisters, homeward speed,
>   All is mirth and play ;
> Hark, hark, the merry pealing,—
>   Welcome Christmas Day.
>
> Sing, sing, around we gather,
>   Each with something new,

Cheering mother, cheering father,
    From the Bible true ;
Bring the holly, spread the feast,
    Every heart to cheer,
Sing, sing, a merry Christmas,
    A happy, bright New Year "

Now, putting aside for the moment all questions touching the grounds of the conviction of the young people
for whom these verses are intended of the truth of the
Bible ; or touching the propriety of their cheering their
fathers and mothers by quotations from it ; or touching
the difficultly reconcilable merits of old times and new
things , I call these verses bad, primarily, because they
are not rhythmical. I consider good rhythm a moral
quality. I consider the rhythm in these stanzas de-
moralized, and demoralizing. I quote, in opposition to
them, one of the rhymes by which my own ear and mind
were educated in early youth, as being more distinctly,
and literally 'moral,' than that Christmas carol

      " Dame Wiggins of Lee
      Was a worthy old soul,
      As e'er threaded a nee-
      Dle, or washed in a bowl
      She held mice and rats
      In such antipa-thy,
      That Seven good Cats
      Kept Dame Wiggins of Lee."

Putting aside also, in our criticism of these verses, the very debateable question, whether Dame Wiggins kept the Seven Cats, or the Seven Cats Dame Wiggins ; and giving no judgment as to the propriety of the license taken in pronunciation, by the accent on the last syllable of ' anti-pathy,' or as to the evident plagiarism of the first couplet from the classical ballad of King Cole, I aver these rhymes to possess the primary virtue of rhyme,—that is to say, to be rhythmical, in a pleasant and exemplary degree. And I believe, and will venture also to assert my belief, that the matter contained in them, though of an imaginative character, is better food for a child's mind than either the subject or sentiment of the above quoted Christmas Carol.

The mind of little Agnes, at all events, receives from story, pictures, and carol, altogether, no very traceable impression ; but, I am happy to say, certainly no harm. She lives fifteen miles from the nearest manufacturing district,—sees no vice, except perhaps sometimes in the village on Sunday afternoons ,—hears, from week's end to week's end, the sheep bleat, and the wind whistle,— but neither human blasphemy, nor human cruelty of command Her shepherd father, out on the hills all day, is thankful at evening to return to his fireside, and to have his little daughter to look at, instead of a lamb. She suffers no more from schooling than serves to make her enjoy her home ,—knows already the mysteries of butter-making and poultry-keeping ;—curtsies to me with-

out alarm when I pass her door, if she is outside of it ,—
and, on the whole, sees no enemy but winter and rough
weather.

But what effect this modern Christmas carol *would* have
had on her mind, if she had had the full advantage of
modern education in an advanced and prosperous town,
—the following well written letter,—happily sent me by
Fors at the necessary moment,—enables me at once to
exhibit :—

'10th *January*, 1874.

Dear Mr. Ruskin,

Your appendix to the Fors this month contains a
chapter on what some will assert is very exceptional
——shire brutality. After nine years' residence in a
——shire village, I am compelled to believe that the
vileness which horrified Judge Mellor is everywhere in-
grained where factory and colliery rule prevails.

Could you but hear the blasphemous and filthy language
our rosy village bairns use as soon as they are out of the
parson's earshot, even when leaving the Sabbath School!

Yet we have a rural dean as incumbent, an excellent schoolmaster, and model school. The Government
Inspector is highly satisfied, and there are the usual
edifying tea parties, prize-givings, and newspaper puffs,
yearly.

I know that the children are well taught six days a
week, yet there is little fruit of good behaviour among
them, and an indecency of speech which is amazing in

rural children. On Christmas morn a party of these children, boys and girls, singing carols, encountered my young daughter going alone to the church service. The opportunity was tempting, and as if moved by one vile spirit, they screamed at her a blast of the most obscene and profane epithets that vicious malice could devise. She knew none of them ; had never harmed them in her life. She came home with her kind, tender heart all aghast. 'Why do they hate me so?' she asked.

Yet a short time after the same children came into the yard, and began, with the full shrill powers of their young lungs,

'Why do I love Jesus?'
the refrain,

'Because He died for me,'
with especial gusto. My husband, ignorant of their previous conduct, gave them a bright shilling, which evoked three more hymns of similar character. What does all this mean ?

Our Bishop says that we have a model parish, a model school, and a model parson—yet we have children like this Our parson knows it, and says to me that he can do nothing to prevent it.

More than this. It is almost incredible ; but my own horrified ears have borne witness of it. Young boys will threaten girls of their own age, in the vilest terms, with outrage like that at Burnley. I have heard it again and again. Had Judge Mellor had nine years' experience of

——shire life, he would not have been surprised at the utter brutality of mind exhibited.

Yet we are not criminal compared with other districts Bastardy and drunkenness are at present the darkest shades we can show ; but there is perhaps some better influence at work from the vicinage of two great squires, which secures us pure air and wide fields.

I am glad to read that you purpose vexing yourself less with the sins of the times during the coming summer. It is too great a burthen for a human mind to bear the world's sins in spirit, as you do. If you mean to preserve yourself for the many thousands whose inner heart's bitterness your voice has relieved, you must vex yourself less about this age's madness

The sure retribution is at hand already " *

' What does all this mean ? ' my correspondent asks, in wise anxiety

National prosperity, my dear Madam, according to Mr. Goschen, the ' Times,' and ' Morning Post ',—national prosperity carried to the point of not knowing what to do with our money. Enlightenment, and Freedom, and orthodox Religion, and Science of the superbest and trustworthiest character, and generally the Reign of Law, answer the Duke of Argyll and Professor Huxley. Ruin —inevitable and terrible, such as no nation has yet suffered,—answer God and the Fates.

* Yes, I know that , but am I to be cheerfuller therefor ?

Yes—inevitable. England has to drink a cup which cannot pass from her—at the hands of the Lord, the cup of His fury;—surely the dregs of it, the wicked of the earth shall wring them and drink them out.

For let none of my readers think me mad enough or wild enough to hope that any effort, or repentance, or change of conduct, could now save the country from the consequences of her follies, or the Church from the punishment of her crimes. This St. George's Company of ours is mere raft-making amidst irrevocable wreck—the best we can do, to be done bravely and cheerfully, come of it what may.

Let me keep, therefore, to-day wholly to definite matters, and to little ones. What the education we now give our children leads to, my correspondent's letter shows. What education they should have, instead, I may suggest perhaps in some particulars.

What should be done, for instance, in the way of gift-giving, or instruction-giving, for our little Agnes of the hill-side? Would the St. George's Company, if she were the tenant, only leave her alone,—teach her nothing?

Not so ; very much otherwise than so. This is some part of what should be done for her, were she indeed under St. George's rule.

Instead of the "something new," which our learned Master of Arts edits for her in carolling, she should learn by heart, words which her fathers had known, many and many a year ago. As, for instance, these two little carols of grace before meat :—

> What God gives, and what we take,
> 'Tis a gift for Christ His sake ;
> Be the meale of Beanes and Pease,
> God be thanked for those and these.
> Have we flesh, or have we fish,
> All are Fragments from His dish :
> He His. Church save ; and the King ;
> And our Peace here, like a Spring,
> Make it ever flourishing.

> Here, a little child, I stand
> Heaving up my either hand ;
> Cold as Paddocks though they be,
> Here I lift them up to Thee.
> For a Benizon to fall,
> On our meat, and on us all.

These verses, or such as these, Agnes should be able to say, and sing ; and if . on any state occasion it were desired of her to say grace, should be so mannered as to say obediently, without either vanity or shame. Also, she should know other rhymes for her own contentment such as she liked best, out of narrow store offered to her, if *she chose* to learn to read. Reading by no means being enforced upon her—still less, writing; nothing enforced on her but household help to her mother; instant obedience to her father's or mother's word; order and cleanliness in her own departments and person, and gentleness to all inoffensive creatures—paddocks as well as lambs and chickens.

Further, instead of eighteen distinct penny Children's Prizes, containing seventy-two elaborate woodcuts of 'Ducklings Astray,' and the like, (which I should especially object to, in the case of Agnes, as too personal, she herself being little more at present than a duckling astray,) the St. George's Company would invest for her at once, the 'ridiculously small sum of eighteenpence,' in one coloured print—coloured by hand, for the especial decoration of her own chamber. This colouring by hand is one of the occupations which young women of the upper classes, in St. George's Company, will undertake as a business of pure duty; it was once a very wholesome means of livelihood to poorer art students. The plates of Sibthorpe's Flora Græca, for instance, cost, I am informed, on their first publication, precisely the sum in question,—eighteenpence each,—for their colouring by hand :—the enterprising publisher who issued the more recent editions, reducing, in conformity with modern views on the subject of economy, the colourist's remuneration to thirty shillings per hundred. But in the St. George's Company, young ladies who have the gift of colouring will be taught to colour engravings simply as well as they can do it, without any reference whatever to pecuniary compensation ; and such practice I consider to be the very best possible elementary instruction for themselves, in the art of watercolour painting.

And the print which should be provided and thus coloured for little Agnes' room should be no less than the best engraving I could get made of Simon Memmi's St. Agnes in Paradise ; of which—(according to the probable notions of many of my readers, absurd and idolatrous)—image, little Agnes should know the legend as soon as she was able to understand it ; though, if the St. George's Company could manage it for her, she should be protected from too early instruction in the meaning of that legend, by such threats from her English playfellows as are noticed in my correspondent's letter.

Such should be some small part of her religious education. For beginning of secular education, the St. George's Company would provide for her, above and before all things, a yard or two square of St. George's ground, which should be wholly her own ; together with instruments suited to her strength, for the culture, and seeds for the sowing, thereof. On which plot of ground, or near it, in a convenient place, there should be a beehive, out of which it should be considered a crowning achievement of Agnes' secular virtues if she could produce, in its season, a piece of snowy and well-filled comb. And, (always if she chose to learn to read,)

L.]   5 books should be given her containing such information respecting bees, and other living creatures, as it appeared to the St. George's Company desirable she should possess. But touching the character of this desirable information, what I have to say being somewhat lengthy, must be deferred to my March letter.

CASTLETON, PEAK OF DERBYSHIRE,
27th January.

Since finishing this letter, I have driven leisurely through the midland manufacturing districts, which I have not traversed, except by rail, for the last ten years. The two most frightful things I have ever yet seen in my life are the south-eastern suburb of Bradford, (six miles long,) and the scene from Wakefield bridge, by the chapel; yet I cannot but more and more reverence the fierce courage and industry, the gloomy endurance, and the infinite mechanical ingenuity of the great centres, as one reverences the fervid labours of a wasp's nest, though the end of all is only a noxious lump of clay.

NOTES AND CORRESPONDENCE.

In my last December's letter, I promised, for January, some statement of real beginning of operations by our Company; but, as usual, was hindered from fulfilling my promise at the time I intended. And the hindrance lay, as in all useful business it is pretty sure in some measure to lie, in the state of British law. An acre of ground, with some cottages on it, has been given me for our Company; but it is not easy to find out how the Company is to lay hold of it. I suppose the conveyancing will cost us, in the end, half a dozen times the value of the land, and in the meantime I don't care to announce our possession of it, or say what I mean to do with it. I content myself for the present with reprinting, and very heartily, as far as my experience holds, ratifying, the subjoined portions of a letter sent me the other day out of a country paper. The writer is speaking, at the point where my quotation begins, of the difficulty of getting a good bankruptcy act passed :—

"The reason alleged is that almost any lawyer is ready to help any lying and false-trading person to drive his coach and four through any Act, however good in intention it may be. This is a sad state of things, and is wasteful of more things than money or good temper. It is, however, on the matter of conveyancing that we wish to say a few words. . . .

"We are accustomed to look at the matter as a very simple one. We have before us the deeds of our dwelling-house.

The real point is, why can we not sell these papers to, say John Smith, for £1,000, if John is satisfied that our little cottage, with all its admirable rooms so well arranged, is worth that amount ? Why can't we sell him this matter in a simple and clear way ? Or, for a case the least bit complicated, take our six shops in the chief street. Why can't we sell one each to Brown, Jones, Robinson, Thompson, Atkinson, or Williams, their respective and respectable tenants, in an equally simple way? The English law steps in and says that we must have a cumbrous deed prepared for each case, and the total cost to all of us, without stamps, would be about one hundred pounds, at a reasonable computation. What do we get for this large sum ? Absolutely nothing but jargon on parchment, instead of plain and simple English, which all the Smiths and Browns might understand, and get for a tenth of the cost. This is all the more irritating, because sensible people are agreed that our present plan is a cumbrous farce, and, moreover, nobody laughs at it but the lawyers who get the picking. Any six honest, clear-headed, educated men could devise a system in a month which would put an end to the needless and costly worry entailed by the existing legal paraphernalia. We have never yet seen any tangible objections to the simple system, nor any salient and satisfactory reasons for retaining the present circumlocutory, wasteful, and foolish one.

" Another monstrous anomaly is that we might sell each of our before-mentioned shops in our chief street, and yet retain the original deed untouched ; so that after drawing cash from each of our present tenants, we could mortgage the whole block again, and clear off with the double cash.*

---

* I don't vouch for the particular statements in this letter. It seems to me incredible that any practical absurdity so great as this should exist in tenure of property.

"But even the present system might be made endurable, and herein lies its greatest blame, namely—that you never know what you are going to pay for the foolish and needless work you are having done. You are entirely at the mercy of the lawyer. When we consider that this so-called difficult and skilful work is always managed in the best offices by a mere clerk, and seldom, if ever, by the principal, we have a reasonable ground of complaint against the enormous and unfair charges usually made for work so done by wholesale.

"We will conclude with a practical suggestion or two. Building clubs have been a great boon to the saving element in our community. It is the wish of most people to have a house of their own, and these clubs find, for hundreds, the readiest means to that end. They have made easy the borrowing and the paying back of money, and they have been the means of simplifying mortgage deeds which, for clubs, are only £2 ,, 5s., and if got up simpler, and printed, instead of being written, might easily and profitably be done for a guinea. Could not they confer a still greater boon on the community by combining, and compelling by a strong voice, the lawyers to systematise and cheapen the present mode of conveyancing? This would be a great work, and might be done. Still better would it be to combine to send up suggestions to Parliament for a simpler and better plan, such as would lead to the passing of an Act for the embodiment of this great and much-needed reform."

Accounts.

The following additional subscriptions complete the account of receipts for St George's Fund to 15th January, 1875

		£	s	d
25.	Gift	5	0	0
26	Gift	1	13	4
30	Gift	0	2	6
37	Gift .	5	0	0
38	Annual (1875)	1	1	0
39	Gift (on condition of being immediately used)	25	0	0
40.	Gift	2	0	0
41.	Gift	5	0	0
44.	Third Donation (1874)	10	0	0
		£54	16	10

FORS CLAVIGERA.

HUMBLE BEES

HERNE HILL, *9th Feb.*, 1875

I HAVE been so much angered, distressed, and defeated, by many things, during these last autumn and winter months, that I can only keep steadily to my business by insisting to myself on my own extreme value and importance to the world ; and quoting, in self-application, the most flattering texts I can find, such as, " Simon, Simon, Satan hath desired to have you," and so on ; hoping that at least a little more of my foolishness is being pounded out of me at every blow ; and that the dough I knead for Fors may be daily of purer wheat.

I wish I could raise it with less leaven of malice ; but I dislike some things and some people so much, that, having been always an impetuous, inconsiderate, and weakly communicative person, I find it impossible to hold my tongue in this time of advanced years and petulance. I am thankful, to-day, to have one most

pleasant thing first to refer to ;—the notable speech,
namely, of Mr. Johnson, the President of the Manchester
Chamber of Commerce, on the immorality of cheapness ;
the first living words respecting commerce which I have
ever known to be spoken in England, in my time ;—on
which, nevertheless, I can in no wise dilate to-day, but
most thankfully treasure them for study in a future
letter ; having already prepared for this one, during my
course of self-applause taken medicinally, another passage
or two of my own biography, putting some of the
reasons for my carelessness about Agnes' proficiency in
reading or writing, more definitely before the reader.

Until I was more than four years old, we lived in
Hunter Street, Brunswick Square, the greater part of
the year ; for a few weeks in the summer breathing
country air by taking lodgings in small cottages (real
cottages, not villas, so-called) either about Hampstead, or
at Dulwich, at ' Mrs. Ridley's,' the last of a row in a
lane which led out into the Dulwich fields on one side,
and was itself full of buttercups in spring, and black-
berries in autumn.   But my chief remaining impressions
of those days are attached to Hunter Street.   My
mother's general principles of first treatment were, to
guard me with steady watchfulness from all avoidable
pain or danger ; and, for the rest, to let me amuse
myself as I liked, provided I was neither fretful nor
troublesome.   But the law was, that I should find my
own amusement.   No toys of any kind were at first

allowed ,—and the pity of my Croydon aunt for my monastic poverty in this respect was boundless On one of my birthdays, thinking to overcome my mother's resolution by splendour of temptation, she bought the most radiant Punch and Judy she could find in all the Soho bazaar—as big as a real Punch and Judy, all dressed in scarlet and gold, and that would dance, tied to the leg of a chair. I must have been greatly impressed, for I remember well the look of the two figures, as my aunt herself exhibited their virtues. My mother was obliged to accept them ; but afterwards quietly told me it was not right that I should have them ; and I never saw them again

Nor did I painfully wish, what I was never permitted for an instant to hope, or even imagine, the possession of such things as one saw in toyshops. I had a bunch of keys to play with, as long as I was capable only of pleasure in what glittered and jingled ; as I grew older, I had a cart, and a ball ; and when I was five or six years old, two boxes of well-cut wooden bricks. With these modest, but, I still think, entirely sufficient possessions, and being always summarily whipped if I cried, did not do as I was bid, or tumbled on the stairs, I soon attained serene and secure methods of life and motion , and could pass my days contentedly in tracing the squares and comparing the colours of my carpet ,—examining the knots in the wood of the floor, or counting the bricks in the opposite houses , with

rapturous intervals of excitement during the filling of
the water-cart, through its leathern pipe, from the drip-
ping iron post at the pavement edge; or the still
more admirable proceedings of the turncock, when he
turned and turned till a fountain sprang up in the
middle of the street. But the carpet, and what patterns
I could find in bed covers, dresses, or wall-papers to be
examined, were my chief resources, and my attention
to the particulars in these was soon so accurate, that
when at three and a half I was taken to have my
portrait painted by Mr. Northcote, I had not been ten
minutes alone with him before I asked him why there
were holes in his carpet. The portrait in question
represents a very pretty child with yellow hair, dressed
in a white frock like a girl, with a broad light-blue
sash and blue shoes to match; the feet of the child
wholesomely large in proportion to its body; and the
shoes still more wholesomely large in proportion to the
feet

These articles of my daily dress were all sent to
the old painter for perfect realization; but they appear
in the picture more remarkable than they were in my
nursery, because I am represented as running in a field
at the edge of a wood with the trunks of its trees
striped across in the manner of Sir Joshua Reynolds,
while two rounded hills, as blue as my shoes, appear
in the distance, which were put in by the painter at
my own request; for I had already been once, if not

twice, taken to Scotland , and my Scottish nurse having
always sung to me as we approached the Tweed or Esk,—

" For Scotland, my darling, lies full in my view,
 With her barefooted lassies, and mountains so blue,"

I had already generally connected the idea of distant hills with approach to the extreme felicities of
life, in my (Scottish) aunt's garden of gooseberry bushes,
sloping to the Tay.

But that, when old Mr. Northcote asked me (little
thinking, I fancy, to get any answer so explicit) what
I would like to have in the distance of my picture, I
should have said " blue hills " instead of " gooseberry
bushes," appears to me—and I think without any morbid
tendency to think overmuch of myself—a fact sufficiently curious, and not without promise, in a child of
that age.

I think it should be related also that having, as
aforesaid, been steadily whipped if I was troublesome,
my formed habit of serenity was greatly pleasing to
the old painter , for I sat contentedly motionless, counting the holes in his carpet, or watching him squeeze
his paint out of its bladders,—a beautiful operation,
indeed, it seemed to me ; but I do not remember
taking any interest in Mr. Northcote's applications of
the pigments to the canvas ; my ideas of delightful
art, in that respect, involving indispensably the possession of a large pot, filled with paint of the

brightest green, and of a brush which would come out of it soppy. But my quietude was so pleasing to the old man that he begged my father and mother to let me sit to him for the face of a child which he was painting in a classical subject ; where I was accordingly represented as reclining on a leopard skin, and having a thorn taken out of my foot by a wild man of the woods.

In all these particulars, I think the treatment, or accidental conditions, of my childhood, entirely right, for a child of my temperament ; but the mode of my introduction to literature appears to me questionable, and I am not prepared to carry it out in St. George's schools without much modification. I absolutely declined to learn to read by syllables ; but would get an entire sentence by heart with great facility, and point with accuracy to every word in the page as I repeated it. As, however, when the words were once displaced, I had no more to say, my mother gave up, for the time, the endeavour to teach me to read, hoping only that I might consent, in process of years, to adopt the popular system of syllabic study. But I went on, to amuse myself, in my own way, learnt whole words at a time, as I did patterns ;—and at five years old was sending for my 'second volumes' to the circulating library.

This effort to learn the words in their collective aspect, was assisted by my real admiration of the look of printed type, which I began to copy for my pleasure, as other children draw dogs and horses. The following inscription, facsimile'd from the fly leaf of my 'Seven Champions of Christendom,' I believe, (judging from the independent views taken in it of the character of the letter L, and the relative elevation of G,) to be an extremely early art study of this class; and as, by the will of Fors, the first lines of the note written the other day underneath my copy of it, in direction to Mr. Burgess, presented some notable points of correspondence with it, I thought it well he should engrave them together, as they stood.

The noble knight like a bowl and daring hero then entered the valley where the Dragon had his abode who no sooner had sight of him but his leathern throat sent forth a sound more

Bolton Abbey

Dear Arthur   24th Jan. 75

Will you kindly facsimile with moderate care, the above piece of ancient manuscript for Fors.

It would be difficult to give more distinct evidence than is furnished by these pieces of manuscript, of the incurably desultory character which has brought on me the curse of Reuben, "Unstable as water, thou shalt not excel." But I reflect, hereupon, with resolute self-complacency, that water, when good, is a good thing, though it be not stable; and that it may be better sometimes to irrigate than excel. And of the advantage, in many respects, of learning to write and read, if at all, in the above pictorial manner, I have much to say on some other occasion; but, having to-day discoursed enough about myself, will assume that Agnes, wholly at her own sweet will, has made shift to attain the skill and temper necessary for the use of any kind of good book, or bible. It is, then, for the St. George's Company to see that all the bibles she has, whether for delight or instruction, shall be indeed holy bibles; written by persons, that is to say, in whom the word of God dwelt, and who spoke or wrote according to the will of God; and, therefore, with faithful purpose of speaking the truth touching what they had to tell, or of singing, rhyming, or what not else, for the amusement whether of children or grown-up persons, in a natural, modest, and honest manner, doing their best for the love of God and men, or children, or of the natural world; and not for money, (though for the time necessary to learn the arts of singing or writing, such honest minstrels and authors, manifestly possessing talent for their business, should be allowed to claim daily moderate maintenance, and for their actual toil, in performance of their arts, modest reward, and daily bread).

And, passing by for the present the extremely difficult and debateable question, by what kind of entertaining and simple bibles Agnes shall be first encouraged in the pursuits of literature, I wish to describe to-day more particularly the kind of book I want to be able to give her about her bees, when she is old enough to take real charge of them. For I don't in the least want a book to tell her how many species of bees there are ; nor what grounds there may be for suspecting that one species is another species ; nor why Mr. B—— is convinced that what Mr. A—— considered two species are indeed one species ; nor how conclusively Mr. C—— has proved that what Mr. B—— described as a new species is an old species. Neither do I want a book to tell her what a bee's inside is like, nor whether it has its brains in the small of its back, or nowhere in particular, like a modern political economist ; nor whether the morphological nature of the sternal portion of the thorax should induce us, strictly, to call it the prosternum, or may ultimately be found to present no serious inducement of that nature. But I want a book to tell her, for instance, how a bee buzzes ; and how, and by what instrumental touch, its angry buzz differs from its pleased or simple busy buzz.* Nor have I any objection to the

---

* I am not sure, after all, that I should like her to know even so much as this. For on inquiring, myself, into the matter, I find (Ormerod, quoting Dr. H. Landois) that a humble bee has a drum in its stomach, and that one half of this drum can be loosened and then drawn tight again, and that the bee breathes through the slit between the loose half and tight half

child's learning, for good and all, such a dreadful word
as 'proboscis,' though I don't, myself, understand why
in the case of a big animal, like an elephant, one should
be allowed, in short English, to say that it takes a bun
with its trunk ; and yet be required to state always,
with severe accuracy, that a bee gathers honey with its
proboscis. Whatever we were allowed to call it, however, our bee-book must assuredly tell Agnes and me,
what at present I believe neither of us know,—certainly
I don't, myself,—how the bee's feeding instrument differs
from its building one, and what either may be like

I pause, here, to think over and put together the little
I do know , and consider how it should be told Agnes.
For to my own mind, it occurs in a somewhat grotesque
series of imagery, with which I would not, if possible,
infect hers The difference, for instance, in the way of
proboscis, between the eminent nose of an elephant, and
the not easily traceable nose of a bird : the humorous,
and, it seems to me, even slightly mocking and cruel
contrivance of the Forming Spirit, that we shall always,
unless we very carefully mind what we are about, think
that a bird's beak is its nose :—the, to me, as an epicure,
greatly disturbing, question, how much, when I see that

and that in this slit there is a little comb, and on this comb the humble
bee plays while it breathes, as on a Jew's harp and can't help it But
a honey bee hums with its "thoracic spiracles," not with its stomach
On the whole—I don't think I shall tell Agnes anything about all this
She may get through her own life, perhaps, just as well without ever
knowing that there's any such thing as a thorax, or a spiracle.

a bird likes anything, it likes it at the tip of its bill, or somewhere inside. Then I wonder why elephants don't build houses with their noses, as birds build nests with their faces ;—then, I wonder what elephants' and mares' nests are like, when they haven't got stables, or dens in menageries ; finally, I think I had better stop thinking, and find out a fact or two, if I can, from any books in my possession, about the working tools of the bee.

And I will look first whether there is any available account of these matters in a book which I once all but knew by heart, ' Bingley's Animal Biography,' which, though it taught me little, made me desire to know more, and neither fatigued my mind nor polluted it, whereas most modern books on natural history only cease to be tiresome by becoming loathsome.

Yes,—I thought I had read it, and known it, once. " They " (the worker bees) " are so eager to afford mutual assistance " (bestial, as distinct from human competition, you observe), " and for this purpose so many of them crowd together, that their individual operations can scarcely be distinctly observed." (If I re-write this for Agnes, that last sentence shall stand thus . ' that it is difficult to see what any one is doing.') " It has, however, been discovered that their two jaws are the only instruments they employ in modelling and polishing the wax. With a little patience we perceive cells just begun, we likewise remark the quickness with which a bee moves its teeth against a small portion of the cell , this portion the animal, by repeated strokes on each side, smooths, renders compact, and reduces to a proper thinness."

Here I pause again,—ever so many questions occurring to me at once,—and of which, if Agnes is a thoughtful child, and not frightened from asking what she wants to know, by teachers who have been afraid they wouldn't be able to answer, she may, it is probable, put one or two herself. What are a bee's teeth like? are they white or black? do they ever ache? can it bite hard with them? has it got anything to bite? Not only do I find no satisfaction in Mr. Bingley as to these matters, but in a grand, close-printed epitome of entomology* lately published simultaneously in London, Paris, and New York, and which has made me sick with disgust by its descriptions, at every other leaf I opened, of all that is horrible in insect life, I find, out of five hundred and seventy-nine figures, not one of a bee's teeth, the chief architectural instruments of the insect world. And I am the more provoked and plagued by this, because, my brains being, as all the rest of me, desultory and ill under control, I get into another fit of thinking what a bee's lips can be like, and of wondering why whole meadows-full of flowers are called "cows' lips" and none called "bees' lips." And finding presently, in Cassell, Petter, and Galpin, something really interesting about bees' tongues, and that they don't suck, but lick up honey, I go on wondering

---

* "The Insect World." Cassell, Petter, and Galpin.

how soon we shall have a scientific Shakespeare printed for the use of schools, with Ariel's song altered into

'Where the bee licks, there lurk I,'

and "the singing masons building roofs of gold," explained to be merely automatic arrangements of lively viscera.

Shaking myself at last together again, I refer to a really valuable book—Dr. Latham Ormerod's 'History of Wasps'—of which, if I could cancel all the parts that interest the Doctor himself, and keep only those which interest Agnes and me, and the pictures of wasps at the end,—I would make it a standard book in St. George's Library, even placing it in some proper subordinate relation to the Fourth Georgic but as it is, I open in every other page on something about 'organs,' a word with which I do not care for Agnes's associating any ideas, at present, but those of a Savoyard and his monkey.

However, I find here, indeed, a diagram of a wasp's mouth, but as it only looks like what remains of a spider after being trodden on, and, as I find that this "mandibulate form of mouth" consists of

" *a*, the labium, with the two labial palpi ,

b, the maxilla, whose basilar portions bear at one end the cardo, at the other the hairy galea and the maxillary palpas ,

c, the labrum, and *d*, the mandible,"

Agnes and I perceive that for the present there is an end of the matter for us ; and retreat to our Bingley, there to console ourselves with hearing how Mr. Wildman, whose remarks on the management of bees are well known, possessed a secret by which " he could at any time cause a hive of bees to swarm upon his head, shoulders, or body, in a most surprising manner. He has been seen to drink a glass of wine, having at the same time the bees all over his head and face more than an inch deep : several fell into the glass, but they did not sting him. He could even act the part of a general with them, by marshalling them in battle array upon a large table. There he divided them into regiments, battalions, and companies, according to military discipline, waiting only for his word of command. The moment he uttered the word 'march !' they began to march in a regular manner, like soldiers. To these insects he also taught so much politeness, that they never attempted to sting any of the numerous company."

Agnes, on reading this, is sure to ask me 'how he taught them?' Which is just what, as a student of new methods of education, I should like to know myself; and not a word is said on the matter · and we are presently pushed on into the history of the larger animal which I call a humble, but Agnes, a bumble, bee. Not, however, clearly knowing myself either what the ways of this kind are, or why they should be called humble, when I always find them at the top of a thistle rather than the bottom, I spend half my morning in hunting through my scientific books for information on this matter, and find whole pages of discussion whether the orange-tailed bee is the same as the white-tailed bee, but nothing about why either should be called humble or bumble :—at last I bethink me of the great despiser of natural history ; and find that stout Samuel, with his good editor Mr. Todd, have given me all I want , but there is far more and better authority for ' bumble ' than I thought. However ,—this first guess of Johnson's own assuredly touches one popular, though it appears mistaken, reason for the Shakespearian form. " The humble bee is known to have no sting. The Scotch call a cow without horns a 'humble cow.' " But truly, I have never myself yet had clear faith enough in that absence of sting to catch a humble bee in my fingers , * only I suppose Bottom would have warned Cobweb against that danger, if there had been such, as well as against being overflown with the honey bag † Red-hipped, Bottom calls them , and yet I find nothing about their red hips anywhere in my books.

---

* Alas, that incredulity, the least amiable of the virtues, should often be the most serviceable ! Here is a pleasant little passage to fall in with, after Dr Johnson's " it is well known " ! I find it in Ormerod, discussing the relative tenability of insects between the fingers for the study of their voices. " Wasps are obviously ill fitted for this purpose, and humble bees are no better ; they are so strong and so slippery that they need all our attention to prevent their putting their long stings through our gloves while we are examining them. '

† Foolish of me a cobweb may be overthrown, but cannot be stung

We have not done with the name yet, however. It is from the Teutonic 'hommolen,' bombum edere : (in good time, some years hence, Agnes shall know what Teutons are,—what bombs are,—shall read my great passage in 'Unto this Last' about bombshells and peaches ; and shall know how distinct the Latin root of Edition and Editor is from that of Edification).

Next,—Chaucer, however, uses 'humbling' in the sense of humming or muttering "like to the humblinge after the clap of a thunderinge." So that one might classically say—a busy bee hums and a lazy bee humbles ; only we can't quite rest even in this ; for under Bumblebee in Johnson, I find a quantity of other quotations and branched words, going off into silk and bombazine ; —of which I shall only ask Agnes to remember—

"The Bittern, with his bump,
The crane, with his trump,"

and Chaucer's single line,

"And as a bytorne bumblith in the mire."

This, however, she should write out carefully, letter by letter, as soon as she had learned to write ; and know at least that the image was used of a wife telling her husband's faults—and, in good time, the whole story of Midas. Meanwhile, we remain satisfied to teach her to call her large brown friends, humble bees, because Shakespeare does, which is reason enough : and then the next thing I want to know, and tell her, is, why they

are so fond of thistles. Before she can know this, I
must be able to draw a thistle-blossom rightly for her ;
and as my botany has stood fast for some years at the
point where I broke down in trying to draw the separate
tubes of thistle-blossom, I can't say any more on that
point to-day but, going on with my Bingley, I
find four more species of bees named, which I should
like to tell Agnes all I could about · namely, the Mason
Bee , the Wood-piercing Bee ; and the one which Bingley
calls the Garden Bee , but which, as most bees are to be
found in gardens, I shall myself call the Wool-gathering
Bee ; the Leaf-cutting Bee

1. The mason bee, it appears, builds her nest of
sand, which she chooses carefully grain by grain ; then
sticks, with bee-glue, as many grains together as she
can carry, (like the blocks of brick we see our builders
prepare for circular drains)—and builds her nest like a
swallow's, in any angle on the south side of a wall ,
only with a number of cells inside, like—a monastery,
shall we say ?—each cell being about the size of a
thimble. But these cells are not, like hive bees', regularly placed, but anyhow—the holes between filled up
with solid block building ;—and this disorder in the
architecture of mason bees seems to be connected with
moral disorder in their life ; for, instead of being 'so
eager to afford mutual assistance' that one can't see
what each is doing, these mason bees, if they can,
steal each other's nests, just like human beings, and

fight, positively, like Christians. "Sometimes the two
bees fly with such rapidity and force against each other
that both fall to the ground "; and the way their cells
are built—back of one to side of the other, and so on,
is just like what a friend was telling me only the
day before yesterday of the new cottages built by a
speculative builder, who failed just afterwards, on some
lots of land which a Lord of the Manor, near my friend,
had just stolen from the public common and sold.

2. The wood-piercing bee cuts out her nest in decayed
wood; the nest being a hollow pipe like a chimney,
or a group of such pipes, each divided by regular floors,
into cells for the children; one egg is put in each cell,
and the cell filled with a paste made of the farina of
flowers mixed with honey, for the young bee to eat
when it is hatched. Now this carpentering work, I find,
is done wholly by the wood-piercing bee's strong jaws;
but here again is no picture of her jaws, or the teeth
in them; though the little heaps of sawdust outside
where she is working "are of grains nearly as large
as those produced by a handsaw"; and she has to
make her floors of these grains, by gluing them in
successive rings from the outside of her cell to the
centre. Yes; that's all very well; but then I want
to know if she cuts the bits of any particular shape,
as, suppose, in flattish pieces like tiles, and if then
she glues these sideways or edgeways in their successive
rings.

But here is the prettiest thing of all in her work. It takes, of course, a certain time to collect the farina with which each cell is filled, and to build the floor between it and the nest ; so that the baby in the room at the bottom of the pipe will be born a day or two before the baby next above, and be ready to come out first ; and if it made its way upwards, would disturb the next baby too soon. So the mother puts them all upside down, with their feet—their tails, I should say—uppermost ; and then when she has finished her whole nest, to the last cell at the top, she goes and cuts a way at the bottom of it, for the oldest of the family to make her way out, as she naturally will, head foremost, and so cause the others no discomfort by right of primogeniture

3. The wool-gathering bee is described by White of Selborne, as "frequenting the Garden Campion, for the sake of its Tomentum." I lose half an hour in trying to find out the Garden Campion among the thirty-two volumes of old Sowerby : I find nothing but the sort of white catchfly things that grow out of hollow globes, (which Mary of the Giessbach, by the way, spoken of in a former letter, first taught me to make pops with). I vainly try to find out what "Campion" means. Johnson fails me this time. "Campion, the name of a plant." I conjecture it must be simple for champion, "keeper of the field,"—and let that pass, but lose myself again presently in the derivation of Tomentum, and its relation

to Tome, in the sense of a volume. Getting back out
of all that, rather tired, I find at last in Bingley that the
Garden Campion is Agrostemma Coronaria of Linnæus;
and I look in my Linnæus, and find it described as
Tomentosum; and then I try my two Sowerbys, ancient
and modern, where I find nothing under Agrostemma
but the corn-cockle, and so have to give in at last; but
I can tell Agnes, at least, that there's some sort of pink
which has a downy stem, and there's some sort of bee
which strips off the down from the stalk of this pink,
"running from the top to the bottom of a branch, and
shaving it bare with all the dexterity of a hoop-shaver."

Hoop-shaver? but I never saw so much as a hoop-
shaver! Must see one on the first chance, only I
suppose they make hoops by steam now

"When it has got a bundle almost as large as itself
it flies away, holding it secure between its chin and
forelegs."

Chin?—what is a bee's chin like?

Then comes a story about a knight's finding the key
wouldn't turn in the lock of his garden gate; and
there being a wool-gathering bee's nest inside and it
seems she makes her cells or thimbles of this wool,
but does not fill them with honey inside; so that I
am in doubt whether the early life of the young bees
who live in wood, and have plenty to eat, be not
more enviable than the lot of those who live in wool
and have no larders. I can't find any more about

the wool-gatherer ; and the fourth kind of bee, most interesting of all, must wait till next Fors' time, for there's a great deal to be learnt about her.

'And what of the St. George's Company meanwhile'?

Well, if I cannot show it some better method of teaching natural history than has been fallen upon by our recent Doctors, we need not begin our work at all. We cannot live in the country without hunting animals, or shooting them, unless we learn how to look at them

NOTES AND CORRESPONDENCE.

————————

"THE PARSONAGE, WERRINGTON, PETERBOROUGH. *Feb.* 12*th* 1875.

"MY DEAR SIR,—In your 'Fors' published last month you have charged the Pastors, and especially the Chief Pastors of our Church, with 'preaching a false gospel for hire,' and thus becoming responsible for the hideous immorality which prevails.

It is very painful to be told this by *you*, of whom some of us have learned so much.

I have been reading your words to my conscience, but—is it my unconscious hypocrisy, my self-conceit, or my sentiment overpowering intellect which hinders me from hearing the word 'Guilty'?

The gospel I endeavour with all my might to preach and embody is this—Believe on, be persuaded by, the Lord Jesus Christ; let His life rule your lives, and you shall be 'safe and sound' now and everlastingly.

Is this 'a false gospel preached for hire'? If not, what other gospel do you refer to?

"I am very faithfully yours,

"JOHN RUSKIN, Esq. EDWARD Z. LYTTEL."

The gospel which my correspondent preaches (or, at the least, desires to preach)—namely, "Let His life rule your lives," is eternally true and salutary. The "other gospel which I refer to" is the far more widely preached one, "Let His life be in the stead of your lives," which is eternally false and damnatory.

The rest of my correspondent's letter needs, I think, no other reply than the expression of my regret that a man of his amiable character should be entangled in a profession, respecting which the subtle questions of conscience which he proposes can be answered by none but himself, nor by himself with security.

I do not know if, in modern schools of literature, the name of Henry Fielding is ever mentioned; but it was of repute in my early days, and I think it right, during the discussion of the subjects to which Fors is now approaching, to refer my readers to a work of his which gives one of the most beautiful types I know of the character of English clergymen, (the 'Vicar of Wakefield' not excepted). His hero is thus introduced "He was a perfect master of the Greek and Latin languages, to which he added a great share of knowledge in the Oriental tongues, and could read and translate French, Italian, and Spanish. He had applied many years to the most severe study, and had treasured up a fund of learning rarely to be met with in a university.* He was besides a man of good sense, good parts, and good-nature,—his virtue, and his other qualifications, as they rendered him equal to his office, so they made him an agreeable and valuable companion, and had so much endeared and well recommended him to a Bishop, that, at the age of fifty, he was provided with a handsome income of twenty-three pounds a year, which, however, he could not make any great figure with, because he lived in a dear country, and was a little encumbered with a wife and six children"

* His debate with Barnabas, on the occasion of the latter's visit to the wounded Joseph, throws some clear light on the questions opened in Mr Lyttel's letter.

Of course, in our present estimate of the good Bishop's benevolence, we must allow for the greater value of money in those times·—nevertheless, it was even then to be obtained in considerable sums, as it is now, by persons who knew the right channels and proper methods of its accumulation, as our author immediately afterwards shows us by the following account of part of the economy of an English gentleman's estate :—

"Joseph had not quite finished his letter when he was summoned downstairs by Mr. Peter Pounce to receive his wages, for, besides that out of eight pounds a year, he allowed his father and mother four, he had been obliged, in order to furnish himself with musical instruments," Mr. Fielding countenances my own romantic views respecting the propriety of the study of music even by the lower classes, and entirely approves of these apparently extravagant purchases,) "to apply to the generosity of the aforesaid Peter, who on urgent occasions used to advance the servants their wages, not before they were due, but before they were payable,—that is, perhaps half a year after they were due, and this at the moderate premium of fifty per cent, or a little more; by which charitable methods, together with lending money to other people, and even to his own master and mistress, the honest man had, from nothing, in a few years amassed a small sum of twenty thousand pounds or thereabouts."

Of the character of the modern English country clergyman, from my own personal knowledge, I could give some examples quite deserving place with the Fielding and Goldsmith type;— but these have influence only in their own villages, and are daily diminishing in number; while another type, entirely modern, is taking their place, of which some curious illustration has been furnished me by the third Fors as I was looking over the Christmas books of last year to see if I could find a prize or two for Agnes and some other of my younger cottage friends. Among them, I get two books on natural history, by a country clergyman, who takes his children out on beach and moorland expeditions, and puts a charming portrait of himself, in his best coat, and most elegant attitude of instruction, for the frontispiece. His little daughter has been taught to express herself in such terms as the following :—

(Of a jelly-fish.)   " Let me look.   If you hold it up to the light, you see it is nearly transparent, and the surface is marked with numerous angular spaces "

(Of a sand-worm.)   " Oh—in this respect the little Pectinaria resembles the fresh-water Melicerta we find abundantly on the weeds in the canal at home "

(Of a sea-mouse.)   " Oh, papa, I do think here is a sea-mouse lying on the shore.   Bah ! I don't much like to touch it."

The childish simplicity and ladylike grace of these expressions need no comment ; but the clergyman's education of his children in *gentleness* is the point peculiarly striking to me in the books, collated with my own experience in the case of the boy and the squirrel.   The following two extracts are sufficiently illustrative —

" ' Well, papa,' said Jack, ' I am tired of sitting here ; let us now go and hunt for peewits' eggs.'   ' All right, Jack, and if you find any you shall each have one for your breakfast in the morning.   When hard-boiled and cold, a peewit's egg is a very delicious thing, though I think the peewits are such valuable birds, and do so much good, that I should not like to take many of their eggs.   We had better separate from each other, so as to have a better chance of finding a nest.'   Soon we hear a shout from Willy, whose sharp eyes had discovered a nest with four eggs in it ; so off we all scamper to him.   See how the old bird screams and flaps, and how near she comes to us ; she knows we have found her eggs, and wishes to lure us away from the spot ; so she pretends she has been wounded, and tries to make us follow after her.   ' Now, Jack, run and catch her.   Hah ! hah !

There they go I will back the peewit against the boy. So you have given up the chase, have you? Well, rest again, and take breath.'"

"' Well, Mr. Parry Evans, how many salmon have you counted in the pool?' 'There are seven or eight good fish in, sir, this time; and one or two will be ten or eleven pounds each' Look at the dog 'Jack'; he is evidently getting a little impatient, as he sees in the retiring water of the pool every now and then a salmon darting along. And now Mr Evans takes the silver collar off, and sets 'Jack' free; and in a second he is in the middle of the pool. Now for the fun ! Willy and Jack * tuck up their trousers, take off their shoes and stockings, and with nets in their hands enter the water Bah ! it is rather cold at first, but the excitement soon warms them. There goes a salmon, full tilt, and 'Jack' after him. What a splashing in the water, to be sure ! There is another dog learning the trade, and 'Jack' is his tutor in the art; he is a brown retriever, and dashes about the water after the salmon as if he enjoyed the fun immensely, but he has not yet learned how to catch a slippery fish. There ! there ! see ! see! good dog, now you have him ! No ! off again ! well done, salmon ! Now, dog ! have at him !

" How immensely rapid is the motion of a frightened salmon ! ' Quick as an arrow' is hardly a figure of speech. Bravo, ' Jack,' bravo ! Do you see? He has caught the salmon firmly by the head. Good dog ! Mr Parry Evans is immediately on the spot, and takes the fish from old ' Jack,' whom he kindly pats on the back, holds the salmon aloft for us all to see, and consigns him to the basket which his man is guarding on the shore. See, see, again ! off they go, dogs and men, and soon another salmon is captured ; and there is lots of fun, meanwhile, in catching the mackerel and garfish. Well, the sport of catching

---

* Some ambiguity is caused in this passage by the chance of both dog and boy having the same name, as well as the same instincts

the various fish in the pool—there were nine salmon, averaging
about five pounds each—lasted about half an hour. 'Jack'
behaved admirably, it was wonderful to see his skill in the
pursuit, he generally caught hold of the salmon by the head, on
which he gave one strong bite, and the fish was rendered helpless
almost instantaneously Sometimes he would catch hold of the
back fin. When the sport was finished, we went to survey the
spoils, and a nice 'kettle of fish' there was. I bought one
salmon and the gurnard; the rest were soon disposed of by Mr.
Evans to his numerous visitors, all of whom were much pleased
with the sport. But wait a little; some of the fish lie on the
sand. I will look for parasites. Here, on this salmon, is a
curious parasite, with a body an inch long, and with two long
tail-like projections three times the length of the creature itself.
It is a crustacean, and related to the *Argulus foliaceus* '

The reverend and learned author will perhaps be surprised to
hear that the principal effect of these lively passages on me has
been slightly to diminish my appetite for salmon, no less than
for sea-side recreations I think I would rather attend my pious
instructor, in discourse on the natural history of the Land I get
his 'Country Walks of a Naturalist,' therefore, in which I find a
graceful preface, thanking Mr. Gould for permission to copy his
Birds of England; and two very gummy and shiny copies (so-
called) adorning the volume.

Now there was boundless choice for the pleasing of children
in Gould's marvellous plates. To begin with, the common
sparrow's nest, in the ivy, with the hen sitting:

> The sparrow's dwelling, which, hard by.
> My sister Emmeline and I
> Together visited
> She looked at it as if she feared it —
> Still wishing, dreading to be near it,
> Such heart was in her

But the reverend naturalist will none ¯of this. Sparrows indeed ! are not five sold for two farthings ? Shall any note be taken of them in our modern enlightened science ? No; nor yet of the dainty little Bramble Finch, couched in her knotty hollow of birch trunk ; though England, and mainland Europe, and Asia Minor, Persia, China, and Japan, all know the little Brambling,—and though in the desolate region of the Dovrefeldt,[*] too high for the Chaffinch, she decorates the outer walls of her nest with flat pieces of lichen and other materials,—though she is attractive in her winter dress ; and in her summer costume, " no pencil can do her justice," clerical taste and propriety will none of her ;—no, nor even of the dear little fellow who looks so much like the properest of clergymen himself, in the sprucest of white ties—the Stone-Chat,—preaching, or chattering, or chatting, from the highest twig of his furze-bush ;—no, nor of the Fire-crested Wren, poised on long spray of larch with purple buds , nor even, though she, at least might, one would have thought, have provided some 'fun' for the ecclesiastical family, the long-tailed Tit, or Bottle-tit, with her own impatient family of six Bottle-tits, every one with a black eye, as if to illustrate the sympathy of their nature with bottle-tits of the human species, and every one with its mouth open , and the nest, of their mother's exquisite building, with the pale sides of the lichens always turned to the light, and 2,000 feathers used in its lining, and these, nothing to the amount of " invisible cobwebs " taken to attach the decorative pieces of lichen to the outside. All this is contemptible to my religious author , but he hunts Mr. Gould's whole book through, to find the horriblest creature in it—the Butcher-bird ! transfixing mice on the spines of the blackthorn, and tearing their flesh from them as they hang, 'invariably breaking the skull,' with farther parental direction of the youthful mind. 'Do you see that great

* I don't put inverted commas to all Mr Gould's words, having necessarily to mix up mine with them in a patchwork manner ; but I don't know anything worth telling, whatever, about—so much as a sparrow,—but what he tells me

tit on a branch of this poplar? He is actually at work doing a bit of butchering on a small warbler. See how he is beating the poor little fellow about the head; he wants to get at his brains." This—for one of his two plates, besides the frontispiece, of the back of his own head and its hat; with his two children 'wanting to get at'—something in his hand—and his only remaining plate is of the heron, merely because it is big; for his miserable copyist has taken care to change every curve of the bird's neck and body, so as to destroy every gracious character it has in Mr. Gould's plate, to an extent so wonderful that I mean to impale the two together—on the stem of a blackthorn—in my Oxford schools.

I have much to say, eventually, about this extraordinary instinct for the horrible, developing itself at present in the English mind. The deep root of it is cruelty, indulged habitually by the upper classes in their sports, till it has got into the blood of the whole nation, then, the destruction of beautiful things, taking place ever since the sixteenth century, and of late ending in utter blackness of catastrophe. and ruin of all grace and glory in the land; so that sensation *must* be got out of death, or darkness, or frightfulness, else it cannot be had at all—while it is daily more and more demanded by the impatient cretinism of national dotage.

And the culmination of the black business is, that the visible misery drags and beguiles, to its help, all the enthusiastic simplicity of the religious young, and the honest strength of the really noble type of English clergymen, and swallows them as Charybdis would lifeboats. Courageous and impulsive men, with just sense enough to make them soundly practical, and therefore complacent in immediate business; but not enough to enable them to see what the whole business comes to, when done, are sure to throw themselves desperately into the dirty work, and die like lively moths in candle-grease. Here is one of them at this instant—" dangerously ill of scarlet fever,"—alas! his whole generous life having been but one fit of scarlet fever,—and all aglow in vain.

The London correspondent of the *Brighton Daily News* writes :—' On Sunday morning Mr. Moncure Conway, preaching his usual sermon in his chapel in Finsbury, made a strong attack upon the National Church, but subsequently modified it so far as to admit that it was possible for some clergymen of the Church to be of use in their day and generation ; and he referred especially to the rector of a neighbouring parish, whom he did not name, but who was evidently Mr. Septimus Hansard, rector of Bethnal-green, who is now lying dangerously ill of scarlet fever. This is the third perilous illness he has had since he has been in this parish ; each time it was caught while visiting the sick poor. On one occasion he fell down suddenly ill in his pulpit. It was found that he was suffering from small-pox, and he at once said that he would go to an hospital. A cab was brought to take him there, but he refused to enter it, lest he should be the means of infecting other persons ; and, a hearse happening to pass, he declared that he would go in that, and in it he went to the hospital—a rare instance this of pluck and self-devotion. His next illness was typhus fever, and now, as I have said, he is suffering from a disease more terrible still. Five hundred a year (and two curates to pay out of it) is scarcely excessive payment for such a life as that."

For such a life—perhaps not. But such a death, or even perpetual risk of it, it appears to me, is dear at the money.

" But have I counted the value of the poor souls he has saved in Bethnal ? "

No—but I am very sure that while he was saving one poor soul in Bethnal, he was leaving ten rich souls to be damned, at Tyburn,—each of which would damn a thousand or two more by their example—or neglect.

The above paragraph was sent me by a friend, of whose accompanying letter I venture to print a part together with it.

"I send you a cutting from a recent *Times*, to show you there are some faithful men left. I have heard of this Mr. Hansard before, and how well he works. I want to tell you, too, that I am afraid the coarseness and shamelessness you write about, in Fors, is not wholly caused by the neighbourhood of large manufacturing towns, for in the lonely villages I used to know long ago, it was exactly the same. I don't mean that brutal crimes, such as you speak of, were heard of or even possible; but the conversation of men and women, working in the fields together, was frequently such that no young girl working with them could keep modesty. Nor if a girl had what they termed a 'misfortune,' was she one bit worse off for it. She was just as certain to be married as before. Reform in all these things—*i.e.*, immodest conversation—ought to begin with women. If women in cottages, and indeed elsewhere, were what they ought to be, and kept up a high tone in their households, their sons would not dare to speak in their presence as I know they often do, and their daughters would feel they fell away from much more than they do now, when they go wrong. Men are, I fancy, very much what women make them, and seem to like them to be; and if women withdrew from those who hurt their sense of what is right, I do believe they would try to be different, but it seems very difficult to preserve a high tone of maidenly dignity in poor girls, who, from youth up, hear every possible thing usually left unspoken of freely discussed by fathers and mothers and brothers, and sometimes very evil deeds treated as jests. This is the case painfully often."

Though my notes, for this month, far exceed their usual limits, I cannot close them without asking my readers to look back, for some relief of heart, to happier times. The following piece of biography, printed only for private circulation, is so instructive that I trust the friend who sent it me will forgive my placing it in broader view ; and the more because in the last section of the ' Queen of the Air,' my readers will find notice of this neglected power of the tide. I had imagined this an idea of my own, and did not press it,—being content to press what is already known and practically proved to be useful; but the following portion of a very interesting letter, and the piece of biography it introduces, show the tide-mill to be in this category

" My father, who began life humbly, dates the prosperity of his family to the time when—being the tenant of a small *tide-mill*—he laboured with spade and barrow (by consent of the Earl of Sheffield) to enclose an increased area—overflowed by the tide—in order to lay under contribution as motive power this wasted energy of rising and falling waters. He thereby nearly quadrupled the power of the mill, and finally became its possessor."

" William Catt was the son of Mr. John Catt, a Sussex farmer, who married the daughter of a yeoman named Willett, living on a small estate at Buxted. He was born in the year 1780, and soon after that date his parents removed to the Abbey Farm at Robertsbridge. There he passed his early years, and there obtained such education as a dame's school could afford This of course was limited to very rudimentary English. He was not a particularly apt scholar he hated his books—but liked cricket.

" When little more than nineteen, he married a daughter of Mr Dawes, of Ewhurst. Farming in the Weald of Sussex was then, as now, a laborious and unremunerative occupation : and as an interesting record of the habits of his class at that period, it may be stated, *that* on the morning of his wedding-day he went

* Italics mine throughout

into a wood with his father's team for a load of hop-poles, was after-wards married in a white ' round-frock,' and returned to his usual work the next morning. He commenced business at Stonehouse, in Buxted, a farm of between 100 and 200 acres. Banking was in those days in its infancy, and travelling notoriously unsafe ; * so his good and prudent mother sewed up beneath the lining of his waistcoat the one-pound notes which he carried from Robertsbridge to Buxted to meet the valuation of his farm. When settled in his little homestead, his household arrange-ments were of the simplest kind One boy, one girl, and one horse, formed his staff, yet he throve and prospered. And no wonder: for *both himself and his young wife often rose at three in the morning; he to thrash by candlelight in his barn, she to feed or prepare her poultry for the market.* His principle was—' earn a shilling. and spend elevenpence ,' and hence, no doubt, his subsequent success.

" After two years' farming he took a small mill at Lamberhurst, where a journeyman miller, Saunders Ditton, gave him all the instruction that he ever received in the manufacture and business in which he was afterwards so extensively engaged Hard work was still a necessity , the mill by night, the market and his cus-tomers by day, demanded all his time , and on one occasion, overcome by cold and fatigue, he crept for warmth into his meal-bin, where he fell asleep, and would certainly have been suffocated but for the timely arrival of Ditton. This worthy man afterwards followed his master to Bishopston, and survived him—a pensioner in his old age.

" At this time the Bishopston Tide-mills were in the occupation of Messrs Barton and Catt. The former exchanged with Mr. Catt, of Lamberhurst, who went into partnership with his cousin Edmund. The power of the mill was then only five pair of

---

* Nowadays the travelling is of course ' notoriously safe ' ! but what shall we say of the banking ?

stones, though he ultimately increased it to sixteen.* In this much more important sphere the same habits of industry still marked his character, amidst all disadvantages. It was war time; corn was of inferior quality and high price; and privateering prevented trading by water. His cousin and he were not suited to each other, and dissolved partnership, but, by the aid of a loan from his worthy friends and neighbours, Mr. Cooper, of Norton, and Mr. Farncombe, of Bishopston, he was enabled to secure the whole of the business to himself. Subsequently Mr. Edmund Cooper, the son of his friend, became his partner in the mills, and the business was for many years carried on under the title of Catt and Cooper.

"During this partnership *a lease was obtained*, from the Earl of Sheffield, *of the waste lands between the Mills and Newhaven harbour.* This was embanked and reclaimed as arable land at first, and subsequently partly used as a reservoir of additional water power. Mr. Catt took great interest in the work; *laboured at it himself with spade and barrow;* and to it he always referred as the main cause of his success in life. In the third year a crop of oats was grown on the arable portion, which repaid the expenses of reclamation and induced him to increase the power of the mill as mentioned above. Mr. Cooper retired from the concern by agreement, and afterwards, under the firm of William Catt and Sons, in conjunction with his children, Mr. Catt completed fifty years of business at Bishopston. During a considerable portion of those years he had also a large stake with other sons in West Street Brewery, Brighton.

"His faithful wife died in 1823, leaving him the responsible legacy of eleven children—the youngest being not an hour old.

---

* The oldest *wind*mill on record in this country (I speak under correction) stood in this parish, and was given by Bishop Seffrid to the see of Chichester about the year 1199. The largest *water* mill ever constructed in Sussex was that of Mr. Catt.

This bereavement seemed to stimulate him to renewed exertion and to extraordinary regard for little savings. *He would always stop to pick up a nail or any scrap of old iron that lay in the road, and in the repeated enlargements and construction of his mills he was his own architect and surveyor,* he was always pleased with the acquisition of a bit of wreck timber, any old materials from Blatchington barracks, or from the dismantled mansion of Bishopston Place, formerly the seat of the Duke of Newcastle. Yet he was ever bountiful as a host, liberal to his neighbours, and charitable to his dependants and the deserving poor.

"To a man of Mr. Catt's experience in life, ordinary amusements would have few charms. His business was his pleasure, yet he delighted in his garden, and the culture of pears afforded him much recreation. A more bleak and unpromising place of horticulture than the Bishopston Mills could hardly exist; but by the aid of good walls, and the observation of wind effects, he was eminently successful, and no garden in Sussex produced a greater variety, or finer specimens, of that pleasant fruit. His maxim on this subject was, '*Aim to get a good pear all the year round.*'

"In the latter years of his life, Mr. Catt retired from active business and resided at Newhaven, where he died in 1853, in the seventy-third year of his age, leaving behind him not only the good name which an honourable life deserves, but a substantial fortune for his somewhat numerous descendants."

FORS CLAVIGERA.

I MUST steadily do a little bit more autobiography in every Fors, now, or I shall never bring myself to be of age before I die——or have to stop writing,——for which last turn of temper, or fortune, my friends, without exception, (and I hope——one or two of my enemies,) are, I find, praying with what devotion is in them.

My mother had, as she afterwards told me, solemnly devoted me to God before I was born ; in imitation of Hannah.

Very good women are remarkably apt to make away with their children prematurely, in this manner : the real meaning of the pious act being, that, as the sons of Zebedee are not, (or at least they hope not,) to sit on the right and left of Christ, in His kingdom, their own sons may perhaps, they think, in time be advanced to that respectable position in eternal life ; especially if they ask Christ very humbly for it every day ;——and they always forget in the most naive way that the position is not His to give !

'Devoting me to God,' meant, as far as my mother knew herself what she meant, that she would try to send me to college, and make a clergyman of me : and I was accordingly bred for 'the Church.' My father, who—rest be to his soul—had the exceedingly bad habit of yielding to my mother in large things and taking his own way in little ones, allowed me, without saying a word, to be thus withdrawn from the sherry trade as an unclean thing ; not without some pardonable participation in my mother's ultimate views for me. For, many and many a year afterwards, I remember while he was speaking to one of our artist friends, who admired Raphael, and greatly regretted my endeavours to interfere , with that popular taste,—while my father and he were condoling with each other on my having been impudent enough to think I could tell the public about Turner and Raphael,—instead of contenting myself, as I ought, with explaining the way of their souls' salvation to them—and what an amiable clergyman was lost in me,—" Yes," said my father, with tears in his eyes— (true and tender tears—as ever father shed,) " he would have been a Bishop."

Luckily for me, my mother, under these distinct impressions of her own duty, and with such latent hopes of my future eminence, took me very early to church ,—where, in spite of my quiet habits, and my mother's golden vinaigrette, always indulged to me there, and there only, with its lid unclasped that I might see the wreathed open pattern above the sponge, I found the bottom of the pew so extremely dull a place to keep quiet in, (my best story-books being also taken away from me in the morning,) that—as I have somewhere said before—the horror of Sunday used even to cast its prescient gloom as far back in the week as Friday—and all the glory of Monday, with church seven days removed again, was no equivalent for it.

ͻNotwithstanding, I arrived at some abstract in my own mind of the Rev. Mr. Howell's sermons; and occasionally—in imitation of him—preached a sermon at home over the red sofa cushions;—this performance being always called for by my mother's dearest friends, as the great accomplishment of my childhood. The sermon was—I believe—some eleven words long;—very exemplary, it seems to me, in that respect—and I still think must have been the purest gospel, for I know it began with ' People, be good '

We seldom had company, even on week days; and I was never allowed to come down to dessert, until much later in life—when I was able to crack nuts neatly. I was then permitted to come down to crack other people's nuts for them; (I hope they liked the ministration)—but never to have any myself, nor anything else of dainty kind, either then or at other times. Once, at Hunter Street, I recollect my mother's giving me three raisins, in the forenoon— out of the store cabinet; and I remember perfectly the first time I tasted custard, in our lodgings in Norfolk Street—where we had gone while the house was being painted, or cleaned, or something. My father was dining in the front room, and did not finish his custard ; and my mother brought me the bottom of it into the back room.

I've no more space for garrulity in this letter, having several past bits of note to bring together.

BOLTON BRIDGE, 24*th January,* 1875.

I have been driving by the old road* from Coniston here, through Kirby Lonsdale, and have seen more ghastly signs of modern temper than I yet had believed possible.

The valley of the Lune at Kirby is one of the loveliest scenes in England—therefore, in the world. Whatever moorland hill, and sweet river, and English forest foliage can be at their best, is gathered there ; and chiefly seen from the steep bank which falls to the stream side from the upper part of the town itself. There, a path leads from the churchyard out of which

---

* Frightened, (I hear it was guessed in a gossiping newspaper,) by the Shipton accident, and disgusted afterwards by unexpected expenses. The ingenious British public cannot conceive of anybody's estimating danger before accidents as well as after them, or amusing himself by driving from one place to another, instead of round the Park. There was some grain of truth in the important rumour, however. I have posted, in early days, up and down England (and some other countries) not once nor twice ; and I grumbled. in Yorkshire. at being charged twenty-pence instead of eighteen-pence a mile. But the pace was good, where any trace of roads remained under casual outcasting of cinders and brickbats.

Turner made his drawing of the valley, along the brow of the wooded bank, to open downs beyond ; a little bye footpath on the right descending steeply through the woods to a spring among the rocks of the shore. I do not know in all my own country, still less in France or Italy, a place more naturally divine, or a more priceless possession of true " Holy Land."

Well, the population of Kirby cannot, it appears, in consequence of their recent civilization, any more walk, in summer afternoons, along the brow of this bank, without a fence. I at first fancied this was because they were usually unable to take care of themselves at that period of the day : but saw presently I must be mistaken in that conjecture, because the fence they have put up requires far more sober minds for safe dealing with it than ever the bank did ; being of thin, strong, and finely sharpened skewers, on which if a drunken man rolled heavily, he would assuredly be impaled at the armpit. They have carried this lovely decoration down on both sides of the woodpath to the spring, with warning notice on ticket,—" This path leads only to the Ladies'* well—all trespassers will be prosecuted "—and the iron rails leave so narrow footing that I myself scarcely ventured to go down, —the morning being frosty, and the path slippery,— lest I should fall on the spikes. The well at the bottom was choked up and defaced, though ironed all

* "Our Lady's," doubtless, once.

round, so as to look like the 'pound' of old days for strayed cattle : they had been felling the trees too ; and the old wood had protested against the fence in its own way, with its last root and branch,—for the falling trunks had crashed through the iron grating in all directions, and left it in already rusty and unseemly rags, like the last refuse of a railroad accident, beaten down among the dead leaves

Just at the dividing of the two paths, the improving mob* of Kirby had got two seats put for themselves —to admire the prospect from, forsooth. And these seats were to be artistic, if Minerva were propitious,— in the style of Kensington. So they are supported on iron legs, representing each, as far as any rational con- jecture can extend—the Devil's tail pulled off, with a goose's head stuck on the wrong end of it Thus :

and what is more—two of the geese-heads are without eyes (I stooped down under the seat and rubbed the frost off them to make sure,) and the whole symbol is perfect, therefore,—as typical of our English populace, fashionable and other,

* I include in my general term 'mob,' lords, squires clergy, parish beadles, and all other states and conditions of men concerned in the pro- ceedings described

which seats itself to admire prospects, in the present day.

Now, not a hundred paces from these seats there is a fine old church, with Norman door, and lancet east windows, and so on ; and this, of course, has been duly patched, botched, plastered, and primmed up ; and is kept as tidy as a new pin. For your English clergyman keeps his own stage properties, nowadays, as carefully as a poor actress her silk stockings. Well, all that, of course, is very fine ; but, actually, the people go through the churchyard to the path on the hill-brow, making the new iron railing an excuse to pitch their dust-heaps, and whatever of worse they have to get rid of, crockery and the rest,—down *over the fence* among the primroses and violets to the river,—and the whole blessed shore underneath, rough sandstone rock throwing the deep water off into eddies among shingle, is one waste of filth, town-drainage, broken saucepans, tannin, and mill-refuse.

The same morning I had to water my horses at the little village of Clapham, between Kirby and Settle. There is another exquisite rocky brook there ; and an old bridge over it. I went down to the brook-side to see the bridge ; and found myself instantly, of course, stopped by a dunghill,—and that of the vilest human sort ; while, just on the other side of the road,—not twenty yards off,—were the new schools, with their orthodox Gothic belfry—all spick and span—and the children playing fashionably at hoop, round them, in a narrow paved yard—like debtor children in the Fleet, in imitation of the manners and customs of the West End. High over all, the Squire's house, resplendent on the hillside, within sound alike of belfry, and brook.

I got on here, to Bolton Bridge, the same day; and walked down to the Abbey in the evening, to look again at Turner's subject of the Wharfe shore. If there is one spot in England, where human creatures pass or live, which one would expect to find, in *spite* of their foul existence, still clean—it is Bolton Park But to my final and utter amazement, I had not taken two steps by the waterside at the loveliest bend of the river below the stepping-stones, before I found myself again among broken crockery, cinders, cockle-shells, and tinkers' refuse ;—a large old gridiron forming the principal point of effect and interest among the pebbles The filth must be regularly carried past the Abbey, and across the Park, to the place.

But doubtless, in Bolton Priory, amiable school teachers tell their little Agneses the story of the white doe ;— and duly make them sing, in psalm tune, "As the hart panteth after the waterbrooks."

Very certainly, nevertheless, the young ladies of Luneside and Wharfedale don't pant in the least after their waterbrooks , and this is the saddest part of the business to me. Pollution of rivers!—yes, that is to be considered also ,—but pollution of young ladies' minds to the point of never caring to scramble by a riverside, so long as they can have their church-curate and his altar-cloths to their fancy—*this* is the horrible thing, in my own wild way of thinking. That shingle of the Lune, under Kirby, reminded me, as if it had been yesterday, of a summer evening by a sweeter shore still the edge of the North Inch of Perth, where the Tay is wide, just below Scone ; and the snowy quartz pebbles decline in long banks under the ripples of the dark clear stream.

My Scotch cousin Jessie, eight years old, and I, ten years old, and my Croydon cousin, Bridget, a slim girl of fourteen, were all wading together, here and there, and of course getting into deep water as far as we could,—my father and mother and aunt watching us,— till at last, Bridget, having the longest legs, and, taking after her mother, the shortest conscience,—got in so far and with her petticoats so high, that the old people were obliged to call to her, though hardly able to call, for laughing , and I recollect staring at them, and wondering what they were laughing at. But alas, by Lune shore, now, there are no pretty girls to be seen holding their petticoats up. Nothing but old saucepans and tannin— or worse—as signs of modern civilization.

' But how fine it is to have iron skewers for our fences ; and no trespassing, (except by lords of the manor on poor men's ground,) and pretty legs ex- hibited where they can be so without impropriety,

and with due advertisement to the public beforehand;
and iron legs to our chairs, also, in the style of
Kensington!' Doubtless; but considering that Kensington is a school of natural Science as well as Art,
it seems to me that these Kirby representations of the
Ophidia are slightly vague. Perhaps, however, in con-
veying that tenderly sagacious expression into his serpent's head, and burnishing so acutely the brandished
sting in his tail, the Kirby artist has been under the
theological instructions of the careful Minister who has
had his church restored so prettily,—only then the
Minister himself must have been, without knowing it,
under the directions of another person, who had an
intimate interest in the matter For there is more than
failure of natural history in this clumsy hardware It is
indeed a matter of course that it should be clumsy, for
the English have always been a dull nation in decorative art: and I find, on looking at things here afresh
after long work in Italy, that our most elaborate English
sepulchral work, as the Cockayne tombs at Ashbourne
and the Dudley tombs at Warwick, (not to speak of
Queen Elizabeth's in Westminster!) are yet, compared
to Italian sculpture of the same date, no less barbarous
than these goose heads of Kirby would appear beside
an asp head of Milan But the tombs of Ashbourne
or Warwick are honest, though blundering, efforts to
imitate what was really felt to be beautiful; whereas
the serpents of Kirby are ordered and shaped by the

" least erected spirit that fell," in the very likeness of himself !

For observe the method and circumstance of their manufacture. You dig a pit for ironstone, and heap a mass of refuse on fruitful land ; you blacken your God-given sky, and consume your God-given fuel, to melt the iron ; you bind your labourer to the Egyptian toil of its castings and forgings ; then, to refine his mind you send him to study Raphael at Kensington ; and with all this cost, filth, time, and misery, you at last produce—the devil's tail for your sustenance, instead of an honest three-legged stool.

You do all this that men may live—think you ? Alas —no ; the real motive of it all is that the fashionable manufacturer may live in a palace, getting his fifty per cent. commission on the work which he has taken out of the hands of the old village carpenter, who would have cut two stumps of oak in two minutes out of the copse, which would have carried your bench and you triumphantly,—to the end of both your times.

However, I must get back to my bees' heads and tails, to-day ;—what a serpent's are like in their true type of Earthly Injustice, it may be worth our while to see also, if we can understand the " sad-eyed justice " first.

Sad-eyed ! Little did Shakespeare think, I fancy, how many eyes the sad-eyed Justice had ! or how ill she saw with them. I continually notice the bees at

Brantwood flying rapturously up to the flowers on my wall paper, and knocking themselves against them, again and again, unconvinceable of their fallacy; and it is no compliment to the wall paper or its artist, neither—for the flowers are only conventional ones, copied from a radiant Bishop's cloak of the fifteenth century.

It is curious too, that although before coming to the leaf-cutting bee, Bingley expatiates on the Poppy bee's luxurious tapestry, cut from the scarlet poppy, he never considers whether she could *see* it, or not, underground—(unless by help of the fiery glowworms' eyes)—and still less, how long the cut leaves would remain scarlet. Then I am told wonderful things of the clasping of the curtains of her little tabernacle;—but when the curtains dry, and shrink, what then?

Let us hear what he tells us of the Rose bee, however—in full

" These bees construct cylindrical nests of the leaves of the rose and other trees. These nests are sometimes of the depth of six inches, and generally consist of six or seven cells, each shaped like a thimble.* They are formed with the convex end of one fitting into the open end of another. The portions of the leaf of which they are made are not glued together,† nor are they any otherwise fastened, than in the nicety of their adjust-

* They are round at the end, but do not taper.

† An Indian one, patiently investigated for me by Mr. Burgess, was fastened with glue which entirely defied cold water, and yielded only to the kettle.

ment to each other; and yet they do not admit the liquid honey to drain through them. The interior surface of each cell consists of three pieces of leaf, of equal size, narrow at one end, but gradually widening to the other, where the width equals half the length. One side of each of these pieces, is the serrated margin of the leaf. In forming the cell, the pieces of leaf are made to lap one over the other, (the serrated side always outermost,) till a tube is thus formed, coated with three or four, or more layers. In coating these tubes, the provident little animal is careful to lay the middle of each piece of leaf over the margins of others, so as, by this means, both to cover and strengthen the junctions. At the closed or narrow end of the cell, the leaves are bent down so as to form a convex termina-tion. When a cell is formed, the next care of the Bee is to fill it with honey and pollen, which being collected chiefly from the thistles, form a rose-coloured paste. With these the cell is filled to within about half a line of its orifice; and the female then deposits in it an egg, and closes it with three perfectly circular pieces of leaf, which coincide so exactly with the walls of the cylindrical cell, as to be retained in their situation without any gluten.* After this covering is fitted in, there still remains a hollow, which receives the convex end of the succeeding cell. In this manner the patient

* She bites them round the edge roughly enough ; but pushes them down with a tucked-up rim, quite tight, like the first covering of a pot of preserve

and indefatigable animal proceeds, till her whole cylinder of six or seven cells is completed.

"This is generally formed under the surface of the ground,* in a tubular passage, which it entirely fills, except at the entrance. If the labour of these insects be interrupted, or the edifice be deranged, they exhibit astonishing perseverance in setting it again to rights.

"Their mode of cutting pieces out of the leaves for their work, deserves particular notice. When one of these Bees selects a rose-bush with this view, she flies round or hovers over it for some seconds, as if examining for the leaves best suited to her purpose. When she has chosen one, she alights upon it, sometimes on the upper, and sometimes on the under surface, or not unfrequently on its edge, so that the margin passes between her legs. Her first attack, which is generally made the moment she alights, is usually near the footstalk, with her head turned towards the point. As soon as she begins to cut, she is wholly intent on her labour; nor does she cease until her work is completed. The operation is performed by means of her jaws, with as much expedition as we could exert with a pair of scissors. As she proceeds, she holds the margin of the detached part between her legs, in such a manner that the section keeps giving way to her, and does not interrupt her progress. She makes her incision in a curved line, approaching the

* Or in old wood.

midrib of the leaf at first ; but when she has reached
a certain point, she recedes from this towards the
margin, still cutting in a curve When she has nearly
detached from the leaf the portion she has been employed upon, she balances her little wings for flight,
lest its weight should carry her to the ground , and
the very moment it parts, she flies off in triumph,
carrying it in a bent position between her legs, and
perpendicularly to her body."

Now in this account, the first thing I catch at is
the clue to the love of bees for thistles " Their
pollen makes a rose-coloured paste with their honey ; "
(I think some of my Scottish friends might really
take measures to get some pure thistle honey made
by their bees. I once worked all the working hours I
had to spare for a fortnight, to clear a field of thistles
by the side of the Tummel under Schehallien : perhaps
Nature meant, all the while, its master and me to let
it alone, and put a hive or two upon it)

Secondly. The description of the bee's tubular house,
though sufficiently clear, is only intelligible to me,
though I know something of geometry, after some
effort ,—it would be wholly useless to Agnes, unless
she were shown how to be a leaf-cutting bee herself,
and invited to construct, or endeavour to construct, the
likeness of a bee's nest with paper and scissors.

What—in school-hours ?

Yes, certainly,—in the very best of school-hours ·

this would be one of her advanced lessons in Geometry.

For little Agnes should assuredly learn the elements of Geometry, but she should at first call it 'Earth measuring'; and have her early lessons in it, in laying out her own garden.

Her older companions, at any rate, must be far enough advanced in the science to attempt this bee problem ; of which you will find the terms have to be carefully examined, and somewhat completed. So much, indeed, do they stand in need of farther definition, that I should have supposed the problem inaccurately given, unless I had seen the bee cut a leaf myself.   But I have seen her do it, and can answer for the absolute accuracy of the passage describing her in that operation.

The pieces of leaf, you read, are to be narrow at one end, but gradually widen to the other, where the width equals half the length

And we have to cut these pieces with curved sides ; for one side of them is to be the serrated edge of a rose leaf, and the other side is to be cut in a curved line beginning near the root of the leaf.   I especially noticed this curved line as the bee cut it ; but like an ass, as often I have been on such occasions, I followed the bee instead of gathering the remnant leaf, so that I can't draw the curve with certainty.

Now each of my four volumes of Bingley has five

or more plates in it These plates are finished line engravings, with, in most cases, elaborate landscape backgrounds ; reeds for the hippopotamus, trees for the monkeys, conical mountains for the chamois, and a magnificent den with plenty of straw for the lioness and cubs, in frontispiece.

Any one of these landscape backgrounds required the severe labour of the engraver's assistant for at least three days to produce it,—or say two months' hard work, for the whole twenty and odd plates. And all the result of two months' elaborate work put together, was not worth to me, nor would be to any man, woman, or child, worth—what an accurate outline of a leaf-cutting bee's segment of leaf would have been, drawn with truth and precision. And ten minutes would have been enough to draw it , and half an hour to cut it.

But not only I cannot find it in my old book, but I know it is not in the grand modern Cuvier, and I don't believe it is findable anywhere I won't go on with Agnes's lesson at guess, however, till I get some help from kind Dr. Gray, at the British Museum. To-day, I must content myself with a closing word or two about zoological moralities.

After having, to my best ability, thus busied and informed little Agnes concerning her bees and their operations, am I farther to expatiate on the exemplary character of the bee ? Is she to learn " How doth," etc. (and indeed there never was a country in which more than in her own, it was desirable that shining hours should be taken advantage of when they come)? But above all, am I to tell her of the Goodness and Wisdom of God in making such amiable and useful insects?

Well, before I proceed to ask her to form her very important opinions upon the moral character of God, I shall ask her to observe that all insects are not equally moral, or useful.

It is possible she may have noticed—beforehand—some, of whose dispositions she may be doubtful; something, hereafter, I shall have to tell her of locust and hornet, no less than of bee; and although in general I shall especially avoid putting disagreeable or ugly things before her eyes, or into her mind, I should certainly require her positively, once for all, to know the sort of life led by creatures of at least alloyed moral nature,—such, for instance, as the 'Turner Savage' which, indeed, "lives in the haunts of men, whom it never willingly offends; but is the terror of all smaller insects. It inhabits holes in the earth on the side of hills and cliffs; and recesses that it forms for itself in the mud-walls of cottages and outhouses The mud wall of a cottage at Peterborough, in Northamptonshire, was observed to be frequented by these creatures, and on examination it was found to be wrought, by their operations, into the appearance of Honeycomb."

The appearance only, alas! for although these creatures

thus like to live in the neighbourhood of a Bishop, and though "there are none which display more affection for their offspring,"—they by no means live by collection of treasures of sweet dew. "They are excessively fierce, and, without hesitation, attack insects much larger than themselves. Their strength is very great, their jaws are hard and sharp, and their stings are armed with poison, which suddenly proves fatal to most of the creatures with which they engage. The 'Sphex' (generic name of the family) seizes, with the greatest boldness, on the creature it attacks, giving a stroke with amazing force, then falling off, to rest from the fatigue of the exertion, and to enjoy the victory. It keeps, however, a steady eye on the object it has struck, until it dies, and then drags it to its nest for the use of its young. The number of insects which this creature destroys, is almost beyond conception, fifty scarcely serving it for a meal. The mangled remains of its prey, scattered round the mouth of its retreat, sufficiently betray the sanguinary inhabitant. The eyes, the filament that serves as a brain, and a small part of the contents of the body, are all that the Sphex devours."

I cannot, therefore, insist, for the present, upon either pointing a moral, or adorning a tale, for Agnes, with entomological instances ; but the name of the insect, at which the (insect) world might grow pale, if it were capable of pallor,—might be made, at least, memorable, and not uninstructive, to the boys in the Latin

class, by making them first understand the power
of the preposition ' ex,' in the two pleasant senses of
examen, and the one unpleasant sense of ' examiner '—
and then observe, (carefully first distinguishing between
play with letters and real derivation,) that if you put
R for Right, before ex, you have ' Rex ' ; if you put L,
for Love, before ex, you have ' lex ' ; if you put G, for
George, and R, for Rural, before ex, you have ' grex ' ,
and then if you put S, for Speculation, P, for Pecu-
lation, and H, the immortal possessor of Pie, before ex,
you have ' Sphex ' ; pleasing and accurate type of the
modern carnivorous Economist, who especially discerns
of his British public, ' the eyes and small filament that
serves as a brain.'

NOTES AND CORRESPONDENCE.

·THE PARSONAGE, WERRINGTON PETERBOROUGH,
· *March* 4. 1875.

"MY DEAR SIR,—I have no doubt you know better than I do what Gospel is the more widely preached, for while you have been wandering, freer than a bee, from place to place, and from church to church, I have been 'entangled' from day to day in stuffy rooms among ignorant and immoral people, in crowded parishes in London and elsewhere, and on Sundays have listened chiefly to the gathered voices of the same ignorant people, led by my own.

"But, not to move from the ground of ascertained fact, I have a right to say that I *know* that the morality of the parishes best known to me has been made better, and not worse, by the shepherding of the Pastors.

"I have heard and read a good deal, in clerical circles, and clerical books, of doctrines of 'substitution' and 'vicarious righteousness,' such as you rightly condemn as immoral, but if all the sermons preached in the English Church on any given Sunday were fully and fairly reported, I question if a dozen would contain the least trace of these doctrines.

"Amidst all the isms and dogmas by which Clerics are entangled, I find the deep and general conviction getting clearer and clearer utterance, that the one supremely lovely, admirable and adorable thing,—the one thing to redeem and regenerate human life, the one true Gospel for mankind,—is the Spirit and Life of Jesus Christ

"As to your terrible charge against the Pastors, that they preach for hire, I need only quote your own opinion in this month's Fors, that all honest minstrels and authors, manifestly possessing talent for their business, should be allowed to claim 'for their actual toil, in performance of their arts, modest reward, and daily bread.'

"Surely the labourer who spends his life in *speaking* salutary truth is not less worthy of his hire than he who sings or writes it?

"The reward offered to most Pastors is 'modest' enough.

"I am very faithfully yours,

"EDWARD Z. LYTTEL.

"JOHN RUSKIN, Esq."

I willingly insert my correspondent's second letter, but will not at present answer it, except privately. I wonder, in the meantime, whether he will think the effect of the ministry of Felix Neff on the mind of the sweet English lady whose letter next follows, moral, or immoral? A portion of whose letter, I should have said, its opening touches on household matters little to her mind, to which her first exclamation refers.

"How sorrowful it all is! Yet, I don't feel so naughty about it as I did on Saturday, because yesterday I read the life of Felix Neff, who went to live by his own wish at that dismal Dormilleuse in the high Alps, amongst the wretched people who were like very unclean animals, and for whom he felt such sublime pity that he sacrificed himself to improve them : and as I read of that terrible Alpine desert, with eight months' hopeless dreariness, and of the wretched food and filthy hovels in which the miserable people lived, I looked up at my good fire and clean room, with dear white Lily lying so soft on my lap, and the snowdrops outside the window, and I really did feel ashamed of having felt so grumbly and discontented as I did on Saturday. So good Felix Neff's good work is not done yet, and he will doubtless help others as long as the world lasts."

The following letter is an interesting and somewhat pathetic example of religious madness; not a little, however, connected with mismanagement of money. The writer has passed great part of his life in a conscientious endeavour to teach what my correspondent Mr. Lyttel would, I think, consider "salutary truth"; but his intense egotism and absence of imaginative power hindered him from perceiving that many other people were doing the same, and meeting with the same disappointments. Gradually he himself occupied the entire centre of his horizon; and he appoints himself to "judge the United States in particular, and the world in general."

The introductory clause of the letter refers somewhat indignantly to a representation I had irreverently made to him that a prophet should rather manifest his divine mission by providing himself miraculously with meat and drink, than by lodging in widows' houses without in anywise multiplying their meal for them; and then leaving other people to pay his bill.

"So long as you deliberately refuse to help in any way a man who (you have every reason to know) possesses more of the righteousness of God than yourself, (when you have ample means to do so,) how can you be said *to* ' *do* the will of your Father which is in Heaven'? or how can you expect to receive understanding to 'know of the doctrine' of the Saviour, (or of my doctrine,) 'whether it be of God, or whether I speak of myself'? If you possessed a *genuine* 'faith,' you would exercise humanity towards such a man as myself, and leave the result with God; and not presumptuously decide that it was 'wrong' to relieve 'a righteous man' in distress, lest you should encourage him in delusions which you choose to suppose him to be labouring under.

"People seem to suppose that it is the Saviour who will judge the world, if any one does. He distinctly declares that He will not. 'If any one hear my words, and believe not, *I judge him not; for I came not to judge the world, but to save the world.* He that rejecteth me, and receiveth not my words, *hath one that judgeth him the word that I have spoken, the same shall judge him in the last day.'* John xii. 47, 48. I represent that 'WORD' which the Saviour spoke, and I have already judged, and condemned, this country, and the United States, in particular, and Christendom, and the World in general I have for twenty years been a preacher of 'the Righteousness of God' to this generation (as Noah was for a hundred years to his generation), and *I have proved* by actual experiment that none among the men of this generation can be induced to 'enter the kingdom of heaven' until the predicted 'time of trouble, such as was not since there was a nation,' comes suddenly, and compels those who are ready to enter the kingdom of God, to do so at once, and I know not how soon after I leave this country the 'trouble' will come; perhaps immediately, perhaps in about a year's time; but come it must; and the sooner it comes, the sooner it will be over, I suppose.

"Yours faithfully."

The following specimen of the kind of letters which the "judge of the United States in particular, and the World in general," leaves the people favoured by his judgment to send to his friends, may as well supplement his own letter :—

"Mr. (J of U. S in p. and the W. in g)'s name will, I trust, excuse me to you for writing; but my house entirely failed me, and I, with my child, are now really in great want. I write trusting that, after your former kindness to me, you will feel disposed to send me a little assistance.

" I would not have written, but I am seriously in need.

" Please address to me," etc.

Whether, however, the judge of the world in general errs most in expecting me to pay the necessary twopences to his hosts, or the world in general itself, in expecting me to pay necessary twopences to its old servants when it has no more need of them, may be perhaps questionable. Here is a paragraph cut out of an application for an hospital vote, which I received the other day :—

Mr. A., aged seventy-one, has been a subscriber to the Pension Fund forty-five years, the Almshouse Fund eighteen years, and the Orphan Fund four years. He is now, in consequence of his advanced age, and the infirmities attendant on a dislocated shoulder, asthma, and failing sight, incapable of earning sufficient for a subsistence for himself and wife, who is afflicted with chronic rheumatic gout. He was apprenticed to Mr. B, and has worked for Mr. C. D forty years, and his earnings at present are very small.

Next, here is a piece of a letter disclosing another curious form of modern distress, in which the masters and mistresses become dependent for timely aid on their servants. This is at least as old, however, as Miss Edgeworth's time ; I think the custom is referred to at the toilette of Miss Georgiana Falconer in ' Patronage.'

" Every day makes me bitterly believe more and more what you say about the wickedness of working by fire and steam, and the harm and insidious sapping of true life that comes from large mills and all that is connected with them. One of my servants told my sister to day (with an apology) that her mother had told her in her letter to ask me if I would sell her my children s old clothes, etc.—that indeed many ladies did—her mother had often bought things   Oh ! it made me feel horrible. We try to buy strong clothes, and mend them to the last, and then sometimes *give* them away ; but *selling* clothes to poor people seems to me dreadful.   I never thought ladies and gentlemen would sell their clothes even to shops—till we came to live here, and happened to know of its being done   It surely must be wrong and bad, or I should not feel something in me speaking so strongly against it, as mean and unholy."

A piece of country gossip on bees and birds, with a humiliating passage about my own Coniston country, may refresh us a little after dwelling on these serious topics :—

" A humble cow is I fancy more properly a humbled cow—it is so called in Durham—a cow whose horn is no longer set up on high.   A humble or bumble bee is there called a ' bumbler.'   To bumble in Durham means to go buzzing about ; a fussy man would be called a great bumbler.   But don't believe it has no sting : it can sting worse than a honey bee, and all but as badly as a wasp.   They used to tell us as children that ' bumblers ' did not sting, but I know from experience that they do   We used as children to feel that we knew that the little yellow mason bee (?) did not sting, but I have no true knowledge on that point.   Do you care to have the common village names of birds?   I am afraid I can only remember one or two, but they are universally used in the north

" The wren which makes the hanging nest lined with feathers is called the feather poke , yellow-hammer, yellow-yowley ; golden-crested wren, Christian wren ; white-throat, Nanny white-throat ; hedge-sparrow, Dickey Diky.   I could find more if you cared for them.   To wind up, I will send you an anecdote I find among father's writings, and which refers to *your* country.   He is speaking of some time early in 1800 'Cock-fighting was then in all its glory. When I was in the neighbourhood of Ulverston, in 18—,* I was told that about the time of which I am writing, a grave ecclesiastical question had been settled by an appeal to a battle with cocks. The chapelry of Pennington was vacant, but there was a dispute who should present a clerk to the vacant benefice,—the vicar of Ulverston, the mother-church, the church-wardens, the four-and-twenty, or the parishioners at large,—and recourse was had to a Welsh Main.'"

Finally, the following letter is worth preserving It succinctly states the impression on the minds of the majority of booksellers that they ought to be able to oblige their customers at my expense. Perhaps in time, the customers may oblige the booksellers by paying them something for their trouble, openly, instead of insisting on not paying them anything unless they don't know how much it is.

"MR. GEORGE ALLEN.

SIR,—We will thank you to send us Ruskin's

Aratra Pentelici . . .	£0	19	0
The Eagle's Nest . .	0	9	6
Relations between Angelo and Tintoret	0	1	0
	£1	9	6
And continue Account next year Fors			
Clavigera	0	7	0
Cheque enclosed.	£1	16	6

"It cannot be too frequently referred to by the trade,—the unjustifiable mode Ruskin has adopted in the sale of his books.

* He does not give the date.

It may be profitable to you (as we hope it is), but to the general trade it is nothing but a swindle. Our customer, for instance (whom we cannot afford to disoblige), pays us for this order just £1 16s. 6d ; and we must come back on him for expense of remitting, else we shall lose by the transaction.

" Your obedient Servant."

FORS CLAVIGERA.

THESE BE YOUR GODS

BRANTWOOD, *Good Friday* 1875.

I AM ashamed to go on with my own history to-day,
for though, as already seen, I was not wholly unacquainted
with the practice of fasting, at times of the year when
it was not customary with Papists, our Lent became to
us a kind of moonlight Christmas, and season of reflected
and soft festivity. For our strictly Protestant habits of
mind rendering us independent of absolution, on Shrove
Tuesday we were chiefly occupied in the preparation of
pancakes,—my nurse being dominant on that day over
the cook in all things, her especially nutritive art of
browning, and fine legerdemain in turning, pancakes,
being recognised as inimitable. The interest of Ash-
Wednesday was mainly—whether the bits of egg
should be large or small in the egg-sauce,—nor do
I recollect having any ideas connected with the day's
name, until I was puzzled by the French of it when
I fell in love with a Roman Catholic French girl, as
hereafter to be related —only, by the way, let me
note, as I chance now to remember, two others of my

main occupations of an exciting character in Hunter Street : watching, namely, the dustmen clear out the ash-hole, and the coalmen fill the coal-cellar through the hole in the pavement, which soon became to me, when surrounded by its cone of débris, a sublime repre-sentation of the crater of a volcanic mountain. Of these imaginative delights I have no room to speak in this Fors ; nor of the debates which used to be held for the two or three days preceding Good Friday, whether the hot-cross-buns should be plain, or have carraway seeds in them. For, my nurse not being here to provide any such dainties for me, and the black-plague wind which has now darkened the spring for five years,* veiling all the hills with sullen cloud, I am neither in a cheerful nor a religious state of mind ; and am too much in the temper of the disciples who forsook Him, and fled, to be able to do justice to the childish innocence of belief, which, in my mother, was too constant to need resusci-tation, or take new colour, from fast or festival.

Yet it is only by her help, to-day, that I am able to do a piece of work required of me by the letter printed in the second article of this month's corre-spondence. It is from a man of great worth, conscientious-ness, and kindliness ; but is yet so perfectly expressive of the irreverence, and incapacity of admiration, which

* See my first notice of it in the beginning of the Fors of August 1871 ; and further account of it in appendix to my Lecture on Glaciers, given at the London Institution this year.

maintain and, in great part, constitute, the modern liberal temper, that it makes me feel, more than anything I ever yet met with in human words, how much I owe to my mother for having so exercised me in the Scriptures as to make me grasp them in what my correspondent would call their ' concrete whole '; and above all, taught me to reverence them, as transcending all thought, and ordaining all conduct.

This she effected, not by her own sayings or personal authority ; but simply by compelling me to read the book thoroughly, for myself. As soon as I was able to read with fluency, she began a course of Bible work with me, which never ceased till I went to Oxford. She read alternate verses with me, watching, at first, every intonation of my voice, and correcting the false ones, till she made me understand the verse, if within my reach, rightly, and energetically. It might be beyond me altogether . *that* she did not care about; but she made sure that as soon as I got hold of it at all, I should get hold of it by the right end.

In this way she began with the first verse of Genesis and went straight through to the last verse of the Apocalypse ; hard names, numbers, Levitical law, and all ; and began again at Genesis the next day ; if a name was hard, the better the exercise in pronunciation,—if a chapter was tiresome, the better lesson in patience,—if loathsome, the better lesson in faith that there was some use in its being so outspoken. After our chapters, (from two to three a day, according to their length, the first thing after breakfast, and no interruption from servants allowed,—none from visitors, who either joined in the reading or had to stay up-stairs,—and none from any visitings or excursions, except real travelling,) I had to learn a few verses by heart, or repeat, to make sure I had not lost, some-thing of what was already known ; and, with the chapters above enumerated, (Letter XLII.*), I had to learn the whole body of the fine old Scottish paraphrases, which are good, melodious, and forceful verse ; and to which, together with the Bible itself, I owe the first cultivation of my ear in sound.

It is strange that of all the pieces of the Bible which my mother thus taught me, that which cost me most to learn, and which was, to my child's mind, chiefly repulsive—the 119th Psalm—has now become of all the most precious to me, in its overflowing and glorious passion of love for the Law of God : " Oh, how love I Thy law ! it is my meditation all the day ; I have refrained my feet from every evil way, that I might keep Thy word " ,—as opposed to the ever-echoing words of the modern money-loving fool : " Oh, how hate I thy law ! it is my abomination all the day ; my feet are swift in running to mischief, and I have done all the

---

* Will the reader be kind enough, in the last two lines of page 128, to put, with his pen, a semicolon after ' age,' a comma after ' unclean,' and a semicolon after ' use '? He will find the sentence thus take a different meaning.

things I ought not to have done, and left undone all I ought to have done , have mercy upon me, miserable sinner,—and grant that I, worthily lamenting my sins and acknowledging my wretchedness, may obtain of Thee, the God of all mercy, perfect remission and forgiveness,—and give me my long purse here and my eternal Paradise there, all together, for Christ's sake, to whom, with Thee and the Holy Ghost, be all honour and glory," etc. And the letter of my liberal correspondent, pointing out, in the defence of usury (of which he imagines himself acquainted with the history!) how the Son of David hit his father in the exactly weak place, puts it in my mind at once to state some principles respecting the use of the Bible as a code of law, which are vital to the action of the St. George's Company in obedience to it.

All the teaching of God, and of the nature He formed round Man, is not only mysterious, but, if received with any warp of mind, deceptive, and intentionally deceptive. The distinct and repeated assertions of this in the conduct and words of Christ are the most wonderful things, it seems to me, and the most terrible, in all the recorded action of the wisdom of Heaven. "To *you*" (His disciples) "it is given to know the mysteries of the Kingdom,—but to others, in parables, that, hearing, they might *not* understand" Now this is written not for the twelve only, but for all disciples of Christ in all ages,—of whom the sign is one and unmistakable : " They have forsaken *all* that they have" ; while those who "say they are Jews and are not, but do lie," or who say they are Christians and are not, but do lie, try to compromise with Christ,—to give Him a part, and keep back a part ;—this being the Lie of lies, the Ananias lie, visited always with spiritual death.*

There is a curious chapter on almsgiving, by Miss Yonge, in one of the late numbers of the 'Monthly Packet,' (a good magazine, though, on the whole, and full of nice writing,) which announces to *her* disciples, that "at least the tenth of their income is God's part." Now, in the name of the Devil, and of Baal to back him,—are nine parts, then, of all we have—our own? or theirs? The tithe may, indeed, be set aside for some special purpose—for the maintenance of a priesthood—or as by the St. George's Company, for distant labour, or any other purpose out of their own immediate range of action. But to the Charity or Alms of men—to Love, and to the God of Love, *all* their substance is due— and all their strength—and all their time. That is the first commandment : Thou shalt love the Lord with all thy strength and soul. Yea, says the false disciple— but not with all my money. And of these it is written, after that thirty-third verse of Luke xiv. : " Salt is good ; but if the salt have lost his savour, it is neither fit for the land nor the dunghill. He that hath ears to hear, let him hear."

* Isaiah xxviii. 17 and 18.

Now in Holbein's great sermon against wealth, the engraving, in the Dance of Death, of the miser and beggar, he chose for his text the verse: "He that stoppeth his ears at the cry of the poor, he also shall cry himself, and shall not be heard." And he shows that the ear is thus deafened by being filled with a murmuring of its own: and how the ear thus becomes only as a twisted shell, with the sound of the far-away ocean of Hell in it for ever, he teaches us, in the figure of the fiend which I engraved for you in the seventh of these letters,* abortive, fingerless, contemptible, mechanical, incapable;—blowing the winds of death out of its small machine: Behold, *this* is your God, you modern Israel, which has brought you up out of the land of Egypt in which your fathers toiled for bread with their not abortive hands; and set your feet in the large room, of Usury, and in the broad road to Death!

Now the moment that the Mammon devil gets his bellows put in men's ears,—however innocent they may be, however free from actual stain of avarice, they become literally deaf to the teaching of true and noble men. My correspondent imagines himself to have read Shakespeare and Goethe;—he cannot understand a sentence of them, or he would have known the meaning of the Merchant of Venice,† and of the vision of Plutus,

---

* The whole woodcut is given in facsimile in the fifth part of 'Ariadne Florentina.'

† See 'Munera Pulveris,' pp 99 to 103, and 'Ariadne Florentina,' Lecture VI.

and speech of Mephistopheles on the Emperor's paper-
money* in the second part of Faust, and of the continual under-current of similar teaching in it, from its
opening in the mountain sunrise, presently commented
on by the Astrologer, under the prompting of Mephistopheles,—" the Sun itself is pure Gold,"—to the ditch-
and-grave-digging scene of its close.   He cannot read
Xenophon, nor Lucian,—nor Plato, nor Horace, nor

* " NARR.
Funftausend Kronen waren mir zu Handen.

MEPH.
Zweibeiniger Schlauch, bist wieder auferstanden?

NARR.
Da seht nur her, ist das wohl Geldes werth?

MEPH.
Du hast dafür was Schlund und Bauch begehrt?

NARR.
Und kaufen kann ich Acker, Haus und Vieh?

MEPH.
Versteht sich! biete nur, das fehlt dir nie!

NARR.
Und Schloss mit Wald und Jagd, und Fischbach?

MEPH.
Traun!
Ich mochte dich gestrengen Herrn wohl schaun.

NARR
Heute Abend wieg' ich mich im Grundbesitz. (*ab*)

MEPH. (*solus*)
Wer zweifelt noch an unsres Narren Witz."

Pope,—nor Homer, nor Chaucer—nor Moses, nor David. All these are mere voices of the Night to him; the bought bellows-blower of the 'Times' is the only piper who is in tune to his ear.

And the woe of it is that all the curse comes on him merely as one of the unhappy modern mob, infected by the rest; for he is himself thoroughly honest, simple-hearted, and upright; only mischance made him take up literature as a means of life; and so brought him necessarily into all the elements of modern insolent thought: and now, though David and Solomon, Noah, Daniel, and Job, altogether say one thing, and the correspondent of the 'Times' another, it is David, Solomon, and Daniel who are Narrs to him.

Now the Parables of the New Testament are so constructed that to men in this insolent temper, they are *necessarily* misleading. It is very awful that it should be so; but that is the fact. Why prayer should be taught by the story of the unjust judge; use of present opportunity by that of the unjust steward; and use of the gifts of God by that of the hard man who reaped where he had not sown,—there is no human creature wise enough to know;—but there are the traps set; and every slack judge, cheating servant, and gnawing usurer may, if he will, approve himself in these.

"Thou knewest that I was a hard man." Yes—and if God were also a hard God, and reaped where *He* had not sown—the conclusion would be true that earthly usury was right. But which of God's gifts to us are *not* His own?

The meaning of the parable, heard with ears unbe-sotted, is this:—"*You*, among hard and unjust men, yet suffer their claim to the return of what they never gave; you suffer *them* to reap, where they have not strawed—But to me, the Just Lord of your life—whose is the breath in your nostrils, whose the fire in your blood, who gave you light and thought and the fruit of earth and the dew of heaven,—to me, of all this gift, will you return no fruit but only the dust of your bodies, and the wreck of your souls?"

Nevertheless, the Parables have still their living use, as well as their danger; but the Psalter has become practically dead; and the form of repeating it in the daily service only deadens the phrases of it by famili-arity. I have occasion to-day, before going on with any work for Agnes, to dwell on another piece of this writing of the father of Christ,—which, read in its full meaning, will be as new to us as the first-heard song of a foreign land.

I will print it first in the Latin, and in the letters and form in which it was read by our Christian sires.

The Eighth Psalm. Thirteenth Century Text *

Domine dominus noster q̄m
admirabile est nomen tuum
in universa terra. Quoniam ele
bata est magnificentia tua super
celos. Ex ore infantium ɪ lacten
cium p̄fecisti laudem ꝓpter mi
micos tuos ut destruas inimicū
ɪ ultorem. Quoniam videbo celos
tuos opeɪa digitor. tuor. lunam ɪ
stellas que tu fundasti Quid est
quod memor es ejus, aū filius hois
quia bisitas eum. Minuisti enm
paulominu; ab angelis, gloria ɪ ho
nore coronasti eum ɪ ɔstituisti eum
super opera manuum tuar. Omia
subjecisti sub pedibs ejus, obes ɪ bo
bes unibsas, insupeɪ t pecoɪa cam
pi. Volucres celi ɪ pisces maris q̄
ꝑambulant semitas maris. Domi
ne dominus noster quam admi
rabile est nomen tuum ɪn unibsa
terra.

---

* I have written it out from a perfect English psalter of early thirteenth
century work, with St. Edward, and St. Edmund, and St. Cuthbert in its
calendar; it probably having belonged to the cathedral of York. The
writing is very full, but quick; meant for service more than beauty;
illuminated sparingly, but with extreme care. Its contractions are curiously
varied and capricious thus, here in the fifth verse, c in constituisti stands
for 'con' merely by being turned the wrong way. I prefer its text, nevertheless,
to that of more elaborate MSS., for when very great attention is paid to the
writing, there are apt to be mistakes in the words. In the best thirteenth-
century service-book I have, 'tuos' in the third verse is written 'meos.'

I translate literally ; the Septuagint confirming the Vulgate in the differences from our common rendering, several of which are important.

" 1. Oh Lord, our own Lord, how admirable is thy Name in all the earth !

2. Because thy magnificence is set above the heavens.

3. Out of the mouth of children and sucklings thou hast perfected praise, because of thine enemies, that thou mightest scatter the enemy and avenger.

4. Since I see thy heavens, the work of thy fingers, the moon and the stars which thou hast founded,

5. What is man that thou rememberest him, or the son of man, that thou lookest on him ?

6. Thou hast lessened him a little from the angels; thou hast crowned him with glory and honour, and hast set him over all the works of thy hands.

7. Thou hast put all things under his feet ; sheep, and all oxen—and the flocks of the plain.

8. The birds of the heaven and the fish˙ of the sea, and all that walk in the paths of the sea.

9. Oh Lord, our own Lord, how admirable is thy Name in all the earth !

Note in Verses 1 and 9—Domine, Dominus noster ; our *own* Lord ; Κύριε, ὁ Κύριος ἡμῶν ; claiming thus the Fatherhood. The 'Lord our Governor' of the Prayer Book entirely loses the meaning. How *admirable* is Thy

Name! θαυμαστόν, 'wonderful,' as in Isaiah, " His name shall be called Wonderful, the Counsellor" Again our translation 'excellent' loses the meaning.

Verse 2.—Thy magnificence. Literally, ' thy greatness in working' (Gk μεγαλοπρέπεια—splendour in aspect), distinguished from mere 'glory' or greatness in fame.

Verse 3.—Sidney has it :

" From sucklings hath thy honour sprung,
Thy force hath flowed from babies' tongue."

The meaning of this difficult verse is given by implication in Matt. xxi 16. And again, that verse, like all the other great teachings of Christ, is open to a terrific misinterpretation ;—namely, the popular evangelical one, that children should be teachers and preachers,—(" cheering mother, cheering father, from the Bible true"). The lovely meaning of the words of Christ, which this vile error hides, is that children, *remaining children*, and uttering, out of their own hearts, such things as their Maker puts there, are pure in sight, and perfect in praise *

Verse 4.—The moon and the stars which thou hast founded—'fundasti'—ἐθεμελίωσας. It is much more than ' ordained ' : the idea of stable placing in space being the main one in David's mind. And it remains to this day

---

* Compare the 'Crown of Wild Olive,' p. 57 ; and put in the fifth line of that page, a comma after 'heaven,' and in the eighth line a semicolon after ' blessing '

the wonder of wonders in all wise men's minds. The earth swings round the sun,—yes, but what holds the sun? The sun swings round something else Be it so, —then, what else?

Sidney —

> "When I upon the heavens do look,
> Which all from thee their essence took,
> When moon and stars my *thought* beholdeth,
> Whose life no life but of thee holdeth."

Verse 5 —That thou lookest on him , ἐπισκέπτῃ αὐτόν, 'art a bishop to him' The Greek word is the same in the verse "I was sick and ye *visited* me."

Verse 6.—Thou hast lessened him ;—perhaps better, thou hast made him but by a little, less, than the angels . ἠλάττωσας αὐτὸν βραχύ τι. The inferiority is not of present position merely, but of scale in being.

Verse 7 —Sheep, and all oxen, and the *flocks of the plain*. κτήνη τοῦ πεδίου. Beasts for service in the plain traversing great spaces,—camel and horse. 'Pecora,' in Vulgate, includes all 'pecunia,' or property in animals.

Verse 8.—In the Greek, "that walk the paths of the seas" is only an added description of fish, but the meaning of it is without doubt to give an expanded sense—a generalization of fish, so as to include the whale, seal, tortoise, and their like. Neither whales nor seals, however, from what I hear of modern fishing, are likely to walk the paths of the sea much longer; and Sidney's verse becomes mere satire :—

> " The bird, free burgesse of the aire,
> The fish, of sea the native heire,
> And what things els of waters traceth
> The unworn pathes, his rule embraceth.
> Oh Lord, that rul'st our mortal lyne,
> How through the world thy name doth shine ! "

These being as far as I can trace them, the literal meanings of each verse, the entire purport of the psalm is that the Name, or *knowledge*, of God was admirable to David, and the power and kingship of God recognizable to him, through the power and kingship of man, His vicegerent on the earth, as the angels are in heavenly places. And that final purport of the psalm is evermore infallibly true,—namely, that when men rule the earth rightly, and feel the power of their own souls over it, and its creatures, as a beneficent and authoritative one, they recognise the power of higher spirits also ; and the Name of God becomes ' hallowed ' to them, admirable and wonderful ; but if they abuse the earth and its creatures, and become mere contentious brutes upon it, instead of order-commanding kings, the Name of God ceases to be admirable to them, and His power to be felt ; and gradually, license and ignorance prevailing together, even what memories of law or Deity remain to them become intolerable ; and in the exact contrary to David's—" My soul thirsteth for God, for the Living God ; when shall I come and appear before God ? "—you have the consummated desire and conclusive utterance of the modern republican :

" S'il y avait un Dieu, il faudrait le fusiller."

Now, whatever chemical or anatomical facts may appear, to our present scientific intelligences, inconsistent with the Life of God, the historical fact is that no happiness nor power has ever been attained by human creatures unless in that thirst for the presence of a Divine King ; and that nothing but weakness, misery, and death have ever resulted from the desire to destroy their King, and to have thieves and murderers released to them instead Also this fact is historically certain,—that the Life of God is not to be discovered by reasoning, but by obeying ; that on doing what is plainly ordered, the wisdom and presence of the Orderer become manifest ; that only so His way can be known on earth, and His saving health among all nations ; and that on disobedience always follows darkness, the forerunner of death.

And now for corollary on the eighth Psalm, read the first and second of Hebrews, and to the twelfth verse of the third, slowly ; fitting the verse of the psalm—" lunam et stellas quæ tu fundasti," with " Thou, Lord, in the beginning hast laid the foundations of the earth " ; and then noting how the subjection which is merely of the lower creature, in the psalm, becomes the subjection of all things, and at last of death itself, in the victory foretold to those who are faithful to their Captain, made perfect through sufferings ; their Faith, observe, consisting primarily in closer and more constant obedience than the Mosaic law required,—"For if the word spoken by angels was stedfast, and every transgression and disobedience received its just recompense of reward, how shall *we* escape, if we neglect so great salvation ? " The full argument is : "Moses, with but a little salvation, saved you from earthly bondage, and brought you to an earthly land of life ; Christ, with a great salvation, saves you from soul bondage, and brings you to an eternal land of life , but, if he who despised the little salvation, and its lax law, (left lax because of the hardness of your hearts,) died without mercy, how shall we escape, if now, with hearts of flesh, we despise so great salvation, refuse the Eternal Land of Promise, and break the stricter and relaxless law of Christian desert-pilgrimage ? " And if these threatenings and promises still remain obscure to us, it is only because we have resolutely refused to obey the orders which were not obscure, and quenched the Spirit which was already given. How far the world around us may be yet beyond our control, only because a curse has been brought upon it by our sloth and infidelity, none of us can tell , still less may we dare either to praise or accuse our Master, for the state of the creation over which He appointed us kings, and in which we have

chosen to live as swine. One thing we know, or may
know, if we will,—that the heart and conscience of man
are divine ; that in his perception of evil, in his recognition of good, he is himself a God manifest in the
flesh ; that his joy in love, his agony in anger, his
indignation at injustice, his glory in self-sacrifice, are
all eternal, indisputable proofs of his unity with a great
Spiritual Head ; that in these, and not merely in his
more availing form, or manifold instinct, he is king
over the lower animate world ; that, so far as he denies
or forfeits these, he dishonours the Name of his Father,
and makes it unholy and unadmirable in the earth ,
that so far as he confesses, and rules by, these, he
hallows and makes admirable the Name of his Father,
and receives, in his sonship, fulness of power with Him,
whose are the kingdom, the power, and the glory, world
without end.

And now we may go back to our bees' nests, and to
our school-benches, in peace ; able to assure our little
Agnes, and the like of her, that, whatever hornets and
locusts and serpents may have been made for, this at
least is true,—that we may set, and are commanded to
set, an eternal difference between ourselves and them, by
neither carrying daggers at our sides, nor poison in our
mouths : and that the choice for us is stern, between being
kings over all these creatures, by innocence to which they
cannot be exalted, or more weak, miserable and detestable
than they, in resolute guilt to which they cannot fall.

Of their instincts, I believe we have rather held too high than too low estimate, because we have not enough recognized or respected our own We do not differ from the lower creatures by not possessing instinct, but by possessing will and conscience, to order our innate impulses to the best ends

The great lines of Pope on this matter, however often quoted fragmentarily, are I think scarcely ever understood in their conclusion.* Let us, for once, read them to their end :—

" See him, from Nature rising slow to Art,
   To copy instinct then was reason's part
   Thus then to man the voice of Nature spake:
   Go,—from the creatures thy instructions take,
   Learn from the birds what food the thickets yield,
   Learn from the beasts the physic of the field,
   Thy arts of building from the bee receive,
   Learn of the mole to plough, the worm to weave.
   Here too all forms of social union find,
   And hence let reason, late, instruct mankind
   Here subterranean works and cities see,
   There, towns aerial on the waving tree ,
   Learn each small people's genius, policies,
   The ants' republic, and the realm of bees ·

---

* I am sensitive for other writers in this point, my own readers being in the almost universal practice of choosing any bits they may happen to fancy in what I say, without ever considering what it was said for.

How those in common all their wealth bestow,
And anarchy without confusion know ;
And these for ever, though a monarch reign,
Their separate cells and properties maintain.
Mark what unvaried laws preserve each state—
Laws wise as nature, and as fixed as fate ;
In vain thy reason finer webs shall draw,
Entangle justice in her net of law,
And right, too rigid, harden into wrong—
Still for the strong too weak, the weak, too strong.
Yet go, and thus o'er all the creatures sway,
Thus let the wiser make the rest obey,
And for those arts mere instinct could afford
Be crowned as monarchs, or as gods ador'd."

There is a trace, in this last couplet, of the irony, and
chastising enforcement of humiliation, which generally
characterize the 'Essay on Man' ; but, though it takes
this colour, the command thus supposed to be uttered
by the voice of Nature, is intended to be wholly earnest.
"In the arts of which I set you example in the un-
assisted instinct of lower animals, I assist *you* by the
added gifts of will and reason ; be therefore, knowingly,
in the deeds of Justice, kings under the Lord of Justice,
while in the works of your hands, you remain happy
labourers under His guidance

Who taught the nations of the field and wood
To shun their poison, and to choose their food,

Prescient, the tides or tempests to withstand,
Build on the wave, or arch beneath the sand."

Nor has ever any great work been accomplished by
human creatures, in which instinct was not the principal
mental agent, or in which the methods of design could
be defined by rule, or apprehended by reason. It is
therefore that agency through mechanism destroys the
powers of art, and sentiments of religion, together.

And it will be found ultimately by all nations, as it
was found long ago by those who have been leaders in
human force and intellect, that the initial virtue of the race
consists in the acknowledgment of their own lowly nature
and submission to the laws of higher being. " Dust thou
art, and unto dust shalt thou return," is the first truth we
have to learn of ourselves , and to till the earth out of
which we were taken, our first duty : in that labour, and
in the relations which it establishes between us and
the lower animals, are founded the conditions of our
highest faculties and felicities . and without that labour,
neither reason, art, nor peace, are possible to man.

But in that labour, accepting bodily death, appointed
to us in common with the lower creatures, in noble
humility , and kindling day by day the spiritual life,
granted to us beyond that of the lower creatures, in
noble pride, all wisdom, peace, and unselfish hope and love,
may be reached, on earth, as in heaven, and our lives
indeed be but a little lessened from those of the angels.

As I am finishing this Fors, I note in the journals

accounts of new insect-plague on the vine; and the sunshine on my own hills this morning (7th April), still impure, is yet the first which I have seen spread from the daybreak upon them through all the spring; so dark it has been with blight of storm,—so redolent of disease and distress; of which, and its possible causes, my friends seek as the only wise judgment, that of the journals aforesaid. Here, on the other hand, are a few verses* of the traditional wisdom of that king whose political institutions were so total a failure, (according to my supremely sagacious correspondent,) which nevertheless appear to me to reach the roots of these, and of many other hitherto hidden things.

"His heart is ashes, his hope is more vile than earth, and his life of less value than clay.

Forasmuch as he knew not his Maker, and him that inspired into him an active soul, and breathed in him a living spirit.

But they counted our life a pastime, and our time here a market for gain; for, say they, we must be getting every way, though it be by evil means.† Yea, they worshipped those beasts also that are most hateful; (for being compared together, some are worse than others,‡ neither are they beautiful in respect of beasts,)

---

* Collated out of Sapientia xv. and xvi.

† Compare Jeremiah ix. 6; in the Septuagint, τόκος ἐπὶ τόκῳ, καὶ δόλος ἐπὶ δόλῳ: "usury on usury, and trick upon trick."

‡ The instinct for the study of parasites, modes of disease, the lower forms of undeveloped creatures, and the instinctive processes of digestion and

but they went without the praise of God, and his blessing

Therefore by the like were they punished worthily, and by the multitude of beasts tormented.

And in this thou madest thine enemies confess, that it is thou who deliverest them from all evil.

But thy sons not the very teeth of venomous dragons overcame : for thy mercy was ever by them, and healed them.

For thou hast power of life and death : thou leadest to the gates of hell, and bringest up again.

For the ungodly, that denied to know thee, were scourged by the strength of thine arm : with strange rains, hails, and showers, were they persecuted, that they could not avoid, for through fire were they consumed

Instead whereof thou feddest thine own people with angels' food, and didst send them, from heaven, bread prepared without their labour, able to content every man's delight, and agreeing to every taste.

For thy sustenance declared thy sweetness unto thy children, and serving to the appetite of the eater, tempered itself to every man's liking.

For the creature that serveth thee, who art the Maker, increaseth his strength against the unrighteous for their

generation, rather than the varied and noble habit of life,- which shows itself so grotesquely in modern science. is the precise counterpart of the forms of idolatry (as of beetle an l serpent, rather than of clean or innocent creatures,) which were in great part the cause of final corruption in ancient mythology and morals

punishment, and abateth his strength for the benefit of such as put their trust in thee.

Therefore even then was it altered into all fashions, and was obedient to thy grace, that nourisheth all things, according to the desire of them that had need :

That thy children, O Lord, whom thou lovest, might know that it is not the growing of fruits that nourisheth man : but that it is thy word, which preserveth them that put their trust in thee.

For that which was not destroyed of the fire, being warmed with a little sunbeam, soon melted away :

That it might be known, that we must prevent the sun to give thee thanks, and at the dayspring pray unto thee."

NOTES AND CORRESPONDENCE.

"THE PARSONAGE, WERRINGTON, PETERBOROUGH, *April* 7, 1875

"MY DEAR SIR,—Your lady correspondent brings out in her own experience that sound Christian truth, of which the condemnable doctrines of 'substitution' and 'vicarious righteousness' are but the perversions. Her experience shows how true it is that one man may so live and suffer that others shall be morally the better for his life and suffering.

"Such a man's righteousness is 'imputed' because really *imparted* * to those who have faith in him.

"Of Felix Neff I know less than I ought, but if his ministry tended to bring more sweetness and light into your correspondent's life, surely his influence in her mind is moral and healthful.

"I am very faithfully yours,

"EDWARD Z. LYTTEL

"JOHN RUSKIN, Esq"

* If my good correspondent will try practically the difference in the effect on the minds of the next two beggars he meets, between imputing a penny to the one, and imparting it to the other, he will receive a profitable lesson both in religion and English

Of Felix Neff's influence, past and present, I will take other occasion to speak

I transgress the laws of courtesy, in printing, without asking the writer's permission, part of a letter which follows: but my correspondent is not, as far as I know him, a man who shrinks from publicity, or who would write in a private letter anything on general subjects which he would be unwilling openly to maintain, while the letter itself is so monumental as a type of the condition to which the modern average literary mind has been reduced, in its reading of authoritative classical authors, and touches so precisely on points which it happens to be my immediate business to set at rest in the minds of many of my readers, that I cannot but attribute to the Third Fors the direct inspiration of the epistle—and must leave on her hands what blame may be attached to its publication. I had been expressing some surprise to my correspondent (an acquaintance of long standing) at his usually bright and complacent temper; and making some enquiry about his views respecting modern usury, knowing him to have read, at least for literary purposes, large portions of the Old Testament He replies,—

"I am sure I would not be wiser if I were 'more uncomfortable' in my mind; I am perfectly sure, if I can ever do good to any mortal, it will be by calm working, patient thinking, not by running, or raging, or weeping, or wailing But for this humour, which I fancy I caught from Shakespeare and Goethe, the sorrow of the world would drive me mad.

"You ask what I think 'the Psalmist' means by 'usury.' I find from Cruden that usury is mentioned only in the fifteenth Psalm. That is a notable and most beautiful lyric, quite sufficient to demonstrate the superiority, in spirituality and morality, of the Hebrew religion to anything Greek. But the bit about usury is pure nonsense—the only bit of nonsense in the piece. Nonsense, because the singer has no notion whatever of the employment of money for the *common* benefit of lender and borrower. As the Hebrew monarchy was politically a total and disastrous failure, I should not expect any opinion worth listening to from a psalmist, touching directly or indirectly on the organisation of industry. Jesus Christ and Matthew the publican lived in a time of extended intercourse and some commerce; accordingly, in Matthew xxv., verse 27, you have a perfect statement of the truth about usury: 'Thou oughtest to have put my money to the exchangers, and at my coming I should have received mine own with usury.' Ricardo, with all Lombard Street to help him, could not improve upon that. A legitimate, useful, profitable use of money is to accommodate strangers who come with money that will not circulate in the country. The exchanger gives them current money; they pay a consideration for the convenience; and out of this comes the legitimate profit to be divided between lender and borrower. The rule which applies to one fruitful use of money will apply to a thousand, and, between wise lending and honest borrowing, swamp and forest become field and garden, and mountains wave with corn. Some professor or other had written what seemed outrageous rubbish; you confuted or thrust aside, in an early Fors, that rubbish; but against legitimate interest, usury, call it what you like, I have never heard any argument. Mr. Sillar's tracts I have never seen,—he does not advertise, and I have not the second sight.

"My view of the grievous abuses in the publishing and bookselling trades has not altered. But, since writing you first on the subject, I have had careful conversations with publishers, and have constantly pondered the matter; and though I do not see my way to any complete reform, I cannot entertain hope from your methods.

"I am tired, being still very weak. It would only bother you if I went on. Nothing you have ever written has, I think, enabled me to get so near comprehending you as your picture of yourself learning to read and write in last Fors. You can see an individual concrete fact better than any man of the generation; but an invisible fact, an abstraction, an *average*, you have, I fancy, been as incapable of seeing as of seeing through a stone wall. Political Economy is the science of social averages.

" Ever affectionately and faithfully yours.

" P.S. (Sunday morning). Some fancy has been haunting me in the night of its being presumptuous, or your thinking it presumptuous, in me to say that David, or whoever wrote the fifteenth Psalm, spoke, on the subject of interest, pure nonsense. After carefully going over the matter again, I believe that I am accurately correct. Not knowing what lending and borrowing, as a normal industrial transaction, or trading transaction, was, the Psalmist spoke in vague ethical terms, meaning ' you should be friendly to your neighbour'; just as a lady economist of to-day might shriek against the pawn-shop, which, with all its defects, had, in capacity of Poor Man's Bank, saved many a child, or woman, or man, from sheer starvation. Not understanding the matter, the Psalmist could not distinguish between use and abuse, and so talked nonsense. It is exquisitely interesting to me to observe that Christ hits the Psalmist exactly on the point where he goes wrong. Τὸ ἀργύριον αὐτοῦ οὐκ ἔδωκεν ἐπὶ τόκῳ, says the Psalmist; Πονηρὲ δοῦλε . . . ἔδει οὖν σε βαλεῖν τὸ ἀργύριόν μου τοῖς τραπεζίταις, καὶ ἐλθὼν ἐγὼ ἐκομισάμην ἂν τὸ ἐμὸν σὺν τόκῳ, says Christ. The use of the *same word* in the Septuagint (the only Old Testament circulating in Palestine in Christ's time) and in the Gospels of Matthew and Luke, to denote in the one case what no good man would take, in the other, what it was a flagrant dereliction of duty *not* to secure, is most precious as illustrating the simple common sense with which Christ used the old Scriptures, and the infinite falsity of the modern doctrine of infallibility, whether of church, book, or man One of those transcendencies of right-ness which I find in Fors (amid things about Marmontel and Drury Lane, and Darwin and Huxley, worthy only of a Psalmist or pretty economist of fifteen) was your idea of policemen-bishops. I always agree also with what you say about the entirely obsolete and useless bishops at £5000 a-year . .   But what I was going to say is, that you ought to ask your bishop, or the whole bench of them, to find a place, in their cart-loads of sermons, for one on ' usury,' * as condemned by the Psalmist and enjoined by Christ Compare Luke xix , ver. 23.   The only sound basis of banking is the fruitful, industrial use of money I by no means maintain that the present banking system of Europe is safe and sound "

I submitted the proof of this Fors to my correspondent, and think it due to him and to my readers to print, with the above letter, also the following portions of that which he sent in gentle reply. So far as I have misconceived or misrepresented him, he knows me to be sorry. For the rest, our misconceptions of each other are of no moment : the misconception, by either, of the nature of profit by the loan of money, or tools, is of moment to every one over whom we have influence ; we neither of us have any business to be wrong in that matter , and there are few on which it is more immediately every man's business to be right.

" Remonstrance were absurd, where misconception is so total as yours. My infidelity is simply that I worship Christ, thank-ing every one who gives me any glimpse that enables me to get nearer Christ's meaning.   In this light, what you say of a

* See the note at p. 151.

hidden sense or drift in the parables interests me profoundly, but the more I think of the question of interest, the more I feel persuaded that Christ distinguished the use from the abuse. Tradition, almost certainly authentic, imputes to Him the saying γίνεσθε τραπεζῖται δόκιμοι (see M. Arnold's article in March *Contemporary*), and I don't see how there can be honourable bankers,—men living honourably by banking,—if *all* taking of interest is wrong. You speak of my ' supreme confidence ' in my own opinions. I absolutely have confidence only in the resolution to keep my eyes open for light and, if I can help it, not to be to-day exactly where I was yesterday. I have not only read, but lived in, (as a very atmosphere) the works of men whom you say I went to because somebody said it was fine to do so. They have taught me some comprehensiveness, some tolerance, some moderation in judging even the mob. They have taught me to consume my own smoke, and it is this con-sumption of my own smoke which you seem to have mistaken for confidence in my opinions. Which prophet, from Moses to Carlyle, would not *you* confess to have been sometimes in the wrong? I said that I worship Christ. In Him I realize, so far as I can realize, God   Therefore I speak not of Him But the very key-stone of any arch of notions in my mind is that inspiration is one of the mightiest and most blessed of forces, one of the most real of facts, but that infallibility is the error of errors   From no prophet, from no book, do I take what I please and leave what I please, but, applying all the lights I have, I learn from each as wisely as, with my powers and my lights, is possible for me.

" Affectionately yours "

I have received, "with the respects of the author," a pamphlet on the Crystal Palace, which tells me, in its first sentence, that the Crystal Palace is a subject which every cultivated Englishman has at heart; in its second, that the Crystal Palace is a household word, and is the loftiest moral triumph of the world ; and in its third, that the Palace is declining, it is said,—verging towards decay. I have not heard anything for a long time which has more pleased me ; and beg to assure the author of the pamphlet in question that I never get up at Herne Hill after a windy night without looking anxiously towards Norwood in the hope that 'the loftiest moral triumph of the world' may have been blown away.

I find the following lovely little scene translated into French from the Dutch, (M. J. Rigeveld, Amsterdam, C. L. Brinkman, 1875,) in a valuable little periodical for ladies, 'l'Espérance,' of Geneva, in which the entirely good purpose of the editor will, I doubt not, do wide service, in spite of her adoption of the popular error of the desirability of feminine independence.

"A PROPOS D'UNE PAIRE DE GANTS

"'Qu'y a-t-il, Elise?' dit Madame, en se tournant du côté d'une fenêtre ouverte, où elle entend quelque bruit. 'Oh ! moins que rien, maman !' répond sa fille aînée, en train de faire la toilette des cadets, pour la promenade et le concert. 'Ce que c'est, maman?' crie un des petits garçons, 'c'est que Lolotte ne veut pas mettre des gants.' 'Elle dit qu'elle a assez chaud sans cela,' reprend un autre, 'et qu'elle ne trouve pas même joli d'avoir des gants.' Et chacun de rire. Un des rapporteurs continue: 'Elise veut qu'elle le fasse par convenance ; mais Lolotte prétend que la peau humaine est plus convenable qu'une peau de rat.' Cette boutade excite de nouveau l'hilarité de la compagnie. 'Quelle idée, Lolotte,' dit son père d'un ton enjoué : 'montre-toi donc !'

"Apparemment Lolotte n'est pas d'humeur à obéir ; mais les

garçons ne lui laissent pas le choix et la poussent en avant. La voilà donc, notre héroïne   C'est une fillette d'environ quatorze ans, dont les yeux pétillent d'esprit et de vie, on voit qu'elle aime à user largement de la liberté que lui laisse encore son âge, pour dire son opinion sur tout ce qui lui passe par la tête sans conséquence aucune.   Mais bien qu'elle soit forte dans son opinion *anti-gantière,* l'enfant est tant soit peu confuse, et ne paraît pas portée à défendre sa cause en présence d'un étranger.   'Quoi donc,' lui dit son père, en la prenant par la taille, 'tu ne veux pas porter des gants, parce qu'ils sont faits de peaux de rats ! Je ne te croyais pas si folle.   Le rat est mort et oublié depuis longtemps, et sa peau est glacée.'—'Non, papa, ce n'est pas çà '—' Qu'est-ce donc, mon enfant ?   Tu es trop grande fille pour ces manières sans façon.   Ne veux-tu pas être une demoiselle comme il faut ?'   ' Et ces petites mains qui touchent si bien du piano,' reprend le visiteur, désireux de faire oublier la gêne que cause sa présence, par un mot gracieux. 'Ne veux-tu pas plutôt renoncer à la musique, et devenir sarcleuse ?' lui demande son père.—'Non, papa, point du tout. Je ne puis pas dire au juste ma pensée . . . . '   Et elle se dégagea doucement de ses bras ; et en se sauvant, grommela : ' Mort aux gants, et vive la civilisation !'   On rit encore un peu de l'enfant bizarre ; puis on parle d'autres choses, et l'on se prépare pour la promenade.   Lolotte a mis les gants en question, 'pour plaire à maman,' et personne ne s'en occupe plus.

" Mais l'étranger avait saisi au passage sa dernière phrase, qui sans cesse lui revenait à l'esprit.   Se reprochait-il devant cette enfant naïve sa complicité à l'interprétation futile que son hôte avait donnée de *la civilisation ?*   Tant est, que pendant le cours de la soirée, se trouvant un moment en tête-à-tête avec Lolotte, il revint à l'histoire des gants   Il tâcha de réparer sa gaucherie et fit si bien, qu'il gagna la confiance de la petite.   'Sans doute j'en conviens,' dit-il, 'il faut plus pour être civilisé que de porter des gants, mais il faut se soumettre à certaines convenances que les gens comme il faut. . . .' 'C'est ça, Monsieur,' dit-elle, en lui coupant la parole, 'quelle est donc la chance des gens qui voudraient se civiliser, mais qui n'ont pas d'argent pour acheter des gants?' C'était-là sa peine. 'Chère enfant!' dit-il tout bas. Et l'homme, si éloquent d'ordinaire, pressa la petite main sous le gant obligatoire, parce que pour le moment les paroles lui manquaient pour répondre. . . . Est-ce étonnant que malgré lui, plus tard en s'occupant de la question sociale, il pensa souvent à cette jeune fille?

"Et vous, lecteurs, que pensez-vous d'elle et de sa question gantière? Vous paraît-elle un enfantillage, ou bien la considérez-vous tout bonnement comme une exagération? Vous attachez-vous à la surface, ou bien y cherchez-vous un sens plus profond, comme l'ami visiteur? Ne croyez-vous pas aussi que dans ce temps de 'besoins multipliés,' un des plus grands services que les classes supérieures puissent rendre au peuple, serait de faire distinction entre tous ces besoins et de prêcher d'exemple?"

This bit of letter must find room—bearing as it does on last Fors' subject :—

"I was asking a girl this morning if she still took her long walks, and she said she was as fond of them as ever, but that they could only walk in the town now—the field or country walks were not safe for ladies alone. Indeed, I fancy the girls lose all care for, or knowledge of the spring or summer—except as they bring new fashions into the shop windows, not fresh flowers any more here into the fields. It is pitiable to live in a place like this—even worse than in ————. For here the process of spoiling country is going on under one's eyes ;—in ———— it was done long ago. And just now, when the feeling of spring is upon one, it is hard to have the sky darkened, and the air poisoned. But I am wasting time in useless grumbling. Only listen to this :—after all our sacrifices, and with all our money and civilization——I can't tell you now ; it must wait."—[Very well ; but don't keep it waiting longer than you need.]

I have had some good help about bees' tongues from a young correspondent at Merrow Grange, Guildford, and a very clear drawing, to which the subjoined piece of his last letter refers ; but I must not lose myself in microscopic questions just now :—

"The author of ' The Microscope' keeps to the old idea of bees sucking honey and not 'licking it up,' for he says, 'The proboscis, being cylindrical, extracts the juice of the flower in a somewhat similar way to that of the butterfly.' And of the tongue he says, 'If a bee is attentively observed as it settles upon a flower, the activity and promptitude with which it uses the apparatus is truly surprising; it lengthens the tongue, applies it to the bottom of the petals, then shortens it, bending and turning it in all directions, for the purpose of exploring the interior and removing the pollen, which it packs in the pockets in its hind legs, (by, he supposes, the two shorter feelers,) and forms the chief food for the working-bees.' He says that when the waxen walls of the cells are completed, they are strengthened by a varnish collected from the buds of the poplar and other trees, which they smear over the cells by the aid of the wonderful apparatus. That part of the proboscis that looks something like a human head, he says, 'can be considerably enlarged . . . and thus made to contain a larger quantity' of the collected juice of the flowers; at the same time it is in this cavity that the nectar is transformed into pure honey by some peculiar chemical process.' "

⁎ Note on page 145 —My correspondent need not be at a loss for sermons on usury. When the Christian Church was living, there was no lack of such. Here are two specimens of their tenor, furnished me by one of Mr Sillar's pamphlets —

EXTRACT FROM THE EXPOSITION UPON THE FIRST EPISTLE TO THE THESSALONIANS, Ch IV. VER 6. BY BISHOP JEWELL.

" Usury is a kind of lending of money, or corn, or oil, or wine, or of any other thing, wherein, upon covenant and bargain, *we receive again the whole principal* which we delivered, *and somewhat more* for the use and occupying of the same · as, if I lend one hundred pounds, and for it covenant to receive one hundred and five pounds, or any other sum greater than was the sum which I did lend. This is that that we call usury, such a kind of bargaining as no good man, or godly man, ever used , such a kind of bargaining as all men that ever feared God's judgment have always abhorred and condemned. *It is filthy gains, and a work of darkness it is a monster in nature; the overthrow of mighty kingdoms, the destruction of flourishing states; the decay of wealthy cities; the plagues of the world, and the misery of the people It is theft; it is the murdering of our brethren, it is the curse of God, and the curse of the people* This is usury: by these signs and tokens you may know it for wheresoever it reigneth, all those mischiefs ensue. But how, and how many ways, it may be wrought, I will not declare : it were horrible to hear ; and I come now to reprove usury, and not to teach it.

"Tell me, thou wretched wight of the world, thou unkind creature, which art past all sense and feeling of God , which knowest the will of God, and doest the contrary how darest thou come into the church ? It is the church of that God which hath said, 'Thou shalt take no usury', and thou knowest He hath so said. How darest thou read or hear the word of

God? It is the word of that God which condemneth usury; and thou knowest He doth condemn it. How darest thou come into the company of thy brethren? Usury is the plague, and destruction, and undoing of thy brethren; and this thou knowest How darest thou look upon thy children? thou makest the wrath of God fall down from heaven upon them; thy iniquity shall be punished in them to the third and fourth generation this thou knowest How darest thou look up into heaven? thou hast no dwelling there; thou shalt have no place in the tabernacle of the Highest. this thou knowest. Because thou robbest the poor, deceivest the simple, and eatest up the widows' houses therefore shall thy children be naked, and beg their bread; therefore shalt thou and thy riches perish together."

EXTRACT FROM THE FAREWELL SERMON PREACHED IN THE CHURCH OF ST. MARY WOOLNOTH, LOMBARD STREET, BY THE REV. DAVID JONES, WHEN THE PRESENT SYSTEM WAS IN ITS INFANCY.

" And the Pharisees also, who were covetous heard all these things, and they derided Him " - LUKE xvi. 14

"I do openly declare that every minister and every church-warden throughout all England are actually perjured and fore-sworn by the 109th canon of our church, if they suffer any usurer to come to the sacrament till he be reformed, and there is no reformation without restitution.

   .·.   ·:   ·:   *   *

" And that you may know what usury is forbid by the word of God, turn to Ezekiel xviii. 8, 13, and you will find that, whoever giveth upon usury or taketh any increase,—*Mark it,*—he that taketh *any* increase above the principal,—not six in the hundred, but let it be never so little, and never so moderate,—he that taketh *any* increase, is a usurer, and such a one as shall surely die for his usury, and his blood shall be upon his own head This is that word of God by which you shall all be saved or damned at the last day, and all those trifling and shuffling distinctions that covetous usurers ever invented shall never be able to excuse your damnation.

" Heretofore all usurious clergymen were degraded from Holy Orders, and all usurious laymen were excommunicated in their lifetime, and hindered Christian burial after death, till their heirs had made restitution for all they had gotten by usury."

As this sheet is going to press, I receive a very interesting letter from "a poor mother." That no wholesome occupation is at present offered in England to youths of the temper she describes, is precisely the calamity which urged my endeavour to found the St. George's Company. But if she will kindly tell me the boy's age, and whether the want of perseverance she regrets in him has ever been tested by giving him sufficient motive for consistent exertion, I will answer what I can, in next 'Fors.'

FORS CLAVIGERA.

BEFORE going on with my own story to-day, I must fasten down a main principle about doing good work, not yet enough made clear.

It has been a prevalent notion in the minds of well-disposed persons, that if they acted according to their own conscience, they must, therefore, be doing right.

But they assume, in feeling or asserting this, either that there is no Law of God, or that it cannot be known; but only felt, or conjectured.

"I must do what *I* think right." How often is this sentence uttered and acted on—bravely—nobly—innocently; but always—because of its egotism—erringly. You must not do what YOU think right, but, whether you or anybody think, or don't think it, what *is* right.

"I must act according to the dictates of my conscience."

By no means, my conscientious friend, unless you are quite sure that yours is not the conscience of an ass.

" I am doing my best—what can man do more ? "

You might be doing much less, and yet much better —perhaps you are doing your best in producing, or doing, an eternally bad thing.

All these three sayings, and the convictions they express, are wise on.y in the mouths and minds of wise men ; they are deadly, and all the deadlier because bearing an image and superscription of virtue, in the mouths and minds of fools.

" But there is every gradation, surely, between wisdom and folly ? "

No. The fool, whatever his wit, is the man who doesn't know his master—who has said in his heart— there is no God—no Law.

The wise man knows his master. Less or more wise, he perceives lower or higher masters ; but always some creature larger than himself—some law holier than his own A law to be sought—learned, loved—obeyed ; but in order to its discovery, the obedience must be begun first, to the best one knows. Obey *something ,* and you will have a chance some day of finding out what is best to obey. But if you begin by obeying nothing, you will end by obeying Beelzebub and all his seven invited friends.

Which being premised, I venture to continue the history of my own early submissions to external Force.

The Bible readings, described in my last letter, took

place always in the front parlour of the house, which, when I was about five years old, my father found himself able to buy the lease of, at Herne Hill. The piece of road between the Fox tavern and the Herne Hill station, remains, in all essential points of character, unchanged to this day : certain Gothic splendours, lately indulged in by our wealthier neighbours, being the only serious innovations ; and these are so graciously concealed by the fine trees of their grounds, that the passing viator remains unappalled by them ; and I can still walk up and down the piece of road aforesaid, imagining myself seven years old.

Our house was the fourth part of a group which stand accurately on the top or dome of the hill, where the ground is for a small space level, as the snows are (I understand) on the dome of Mont Blanc ; presently falling, however, in what may be, in the London clay formation, considered a precipitous slope, to our valley of Chamouni (or of Dulwich) on the east ; and with a softer descent into Cold Arbour, (nautically aspirated into Harbour)-lane on the west : on the south, no less beautifully declining to the dale of the Effra, (doubtless shortened from Effrena, signifying the " Unbridled " river ; recently, I regret to say, bricked over for the convenience of Mr. Biffin, the chemist, and others) ; while on the north, prolonged indeed with slight depression some half mile or so, and receiving, in the parish of Lambeth, the chivalric title of ' Champion Hill,' it plunges down at last to efface itself in the plains of Peckham, and the rustic solitudes of Goose Green.

The group, of which our house was the quarter, consisted of two precisely similar partner-couples of houses, —gardens and all to match, still the two highest blocks of buildings seen from Norwood on the crest of the ridge, which, even within the time I remember, rose with no stinted beauty of wood and lawn above the Dulwich fields.

The house itself, three-storied, with garrets above, commanded, in those comparatively smokeless days, a very notable view from its upper windows, of the Norwood hills on one side, and the winter sunrise over them, and of the valley of the Thames, with Windsor in the distance, on the other, and the summer sunset over these. It had front and back garden in sufficient proportion to its size; the front, richly set with old evergreens, and well grown lilac and laburnum; the back, seventy yards long by twenty wide, renowned over all the hill for its pears and apples, which had been chosen with extreme care by our predecessor, (shame on me to forget the name of a man to whom I owe so much!)—and possessing also a strong old mulberry tree, a tall white-heart cherry tree, a black Kentish one, and an almost unbroken hedge, all round, of alternate gooseberry and currant bush; decked, in due season, (for the ground was wholly beneficent,) with magical splendour of abundant fruit: fresh green, soft amber, and rough-bristled crimson bending the spinous branches, clustered pearl and pendent ruby joyfully discoverable under the large leaves that looked like vine.

The differences of primal importance which I observed between the nature of this garden, and that of Eden, as I had imagined it, were, that, in this one, *all* the fruit was forbidden; and there were no companionable beasts : in other respects the little domain answered every purpose of Paradise to me; and the climate, in that cycle of our years, allowed me to pass most of my life in it. My mother never gave me more to learn than she knew I could easily get learnt, if I set myself honestly to work, by twelve o'clock. She never allowed anything to disturb me when my task was set; if it was not said rightly by twelve o'clock, I was kept in till I knew it, and in general, even when Latin Grammar came to supplement the Psalms, I was my own master for at least an hour before dinner at half-past one, and for the rest of the afternoon. My mother, herself finding her chief personal pleasure in her flowers, was often planting or pruning beside me,— at least if I chose to stay beside *her.* I never thought of doing anything behind her back which I would not have done before her face; and her presence was therefore no restraint to me; but, also, no particular pleasure; for, from having always been left so much alone, I had generally my own little affairs to see after; and on the whole, by the time I was seven years old, was already getting too independent, mentally, even of my father and mother; and having nobody else to be dependent upon, began to lead a very small, perky, contented, conceited, Cock-Robinson-Crusoe sort of life, in the central point which it appeared to me, (as it must naturally appear to geometrical animals) that I occupied in the universe.

This was partly the fault of my father's modesty; and partly of his pride. He had so much more confidence in my mother's judgment as to such matters than in his own, that he never ventured even to help, much less to cross her, in the conduct of my education; on the other hand, in the fixed purpose of making an ecclesiastical gentleman of me, with the superfinest of manners, and access to the highest circles of fleshly and spiritual society, the visits to Croydon, where I entirely loved my aunt, and young baker-cousins, became rarer and more rare · the society of our neighbours on the hill could not be had without breaking up our regular and sweetly selfish manner of living; and on the whole, I had nothing animate to care for, in a childish way, but myself, some nests of ants, which the gardener would never leave undisturbed for me, and a sociable bird or two; though I never had the sense or perseverance to make one really tame. But that was partly because, if ever I managed to bring one to be the least trustful of me, the cats got it.

Under these favourable circumstances, what powers of imagination I possessed, either fastened themselves on inanimate things—the sky, the leaves, and pebbles, observable within the walls of Eden, or caught at any opportunity of flight into regions of romance, compatible with the objective realities of existence in the nineteenth century, within a mile and a quarter of Camberwell Green.

Herein my father, happily, though with no definite intention other than of pleasing me, when he found he could do so without infringing any of my mother's rules, became my guide. I was particularly fond of watching him shave ; and was always allowed to come into his room in the morning (under the one in which I am now writing), to be the motionless witness of that operation. Over his dressing-table hung one of his own water-colour drawings, made under the teaching of the elder Nasmyth. (I believe, at the High School of Edinburgh.) It was done in the early manner of tinting, which, just about the time when my father was at the High School, Dr. Munro was teaching Turner ; namely, in grey under-tints of Prussian blue and British ink, washed with warm colour afterwards on the lights It represented Conway Castle, with its Frith, and, in the foreground, a cottage a fisherman, and a boat at the water's edge.

When my father had finished shaving, he always told me a story about this picture. The custom began without any initial purpose of his, in consequence of my troublesome curiosity whether the fisherman lived in the cottage, and where he was going to in the boat. It being settled, for peace' sake, that he *did* live in the cottage, and was going in the boat to fish near the castle, the plot of the drama afterwards gradually thickened ; and became, I believe, involved with that of the tragedy of " Douglas," and of the " Castle Spectre," in both of which pieces my father had performed in private theatricals, before my mother, and a select Edinburgh audience, when he was a boy of sixteen, and she, at grave twenty, a model housekeeper, and very scornful and religiously suspicious of theatricals. But she was never weary of telling me, in later years, how beautiful my father looked in his Highland dress, with the high black feathers.

I remember nothing of the story he used to tell me, now ; but I have the picture still, and hope to leave it finally in the Oxford schools, where, if I can complete my series of illustrative work for general reference, it will be of some little use as an example of an old-fashioned method of water-colour drawing not without its advantages ; and, at the same time, of the dangers incidental in it to young students, of making their castles too yellow, and their fishermen too blue.

In the afternoons, when my father returned (always punctually) from his business, he dined, at half-past four, in the front parlour, my mother sitting beside him to hear the events of the day, and give counsel and encouragement with respect to the same;—chiefly the last, for my father was apt to be vexed if orders for sherry fell the least short of their due standard, even for a day or two. I was never present at this time, however, and only avouch what I relate by hearsay and probable conjecture; for between four and six it would have been a grave misdemeanour in me if I so much as approached the parlour door. After that, in summer time, we were all in the garden as long as the day lasted; tea under the white-heart cherry tree; or in winter and rough weather, at six o'clock in the drawing-room,—I having my cup of milk, and slice of bread-and-butter, in a little recess, with a table in front of it, wholly sacred to me; and in which I remained in the evenings as an Idol in a niche, while my mother knitted, and my father read to her,—and to me, so far as I chose to listen.

The series of the Waverley novels, then drawing to-wards its close, was still the chief source of delight in all households caring for literature; and I can no more recollect the time when I did not know them than when I did not know the Bible; but I have still a vivid re-membrance of my father's intense expression of sorrow mixed with scorn, as he threw down 'Count Robert of Paris,' after reading three or four pages; and knew that the life of Scott was ended. the scorn being a very complex and bitter feeling in him,—partly, indeed, of the book itself, but chiefly of the wretches who were tormenting and selling the wrecked intellect, and not a little, deep down, of the subtle dishonesty which had essentially caused the ruin. My father never could forgive Scott his concealment of the Ballantyne partnership.

I permit myself, without check, to enlarge on these trivial circumstances of my early days, partly because I know that there are one or two people in the world who will like to hear of them, but chiefly because I can better assure the general reader of some results of education on after life, by one example in which I know all my facts, than by many, in which every here and there a link might be wanting.

And it is perhaps already time to mark what advantage and mischief, by the changes of life up to seven years old, had been irrevocably determined for me.

I will first count my blessings (as a not unwise friend once recommended me to do, continually ; whereas I have a bad trick of always numbering the thorns in my fingers, and not the bones in them).

And for best and truest beginning of all blessings, I had been taught the perfect meaning of Peace, in thought, act, and word.

I never had heard my father's or mother's voice once raised in any question with each other ; nor seen an angry, or even slightly hurt or offended, glance in the eyes of either. I had never heard a servant scolded, nor even suddenly, passionately, or in any severe manner,

blamed I had never seen a moment's trouble or disorder
in any household matter ; nor anything whatever either
done in a hurry, or undone in due time. I had no
conception of such a feeling as anxiety , my father's
occasional vexation in the afternoons, when he had
only got an order for twelve butts after expecting one
for fifteen, as I have just stated, was never manifested
to *me ;* and itself related only to the question whether
his name would be a step higher or lower in the year's
list of sherry exporters , for he never spent more than
half his income, and therefore found himself little incom-
moded by occasional variations in the total of it. I had
never done any wrong that I knew of—beyond occasionally
delaying the commitment to heart of some improving
sentence, that I might watch a wasp on the window pane,
or a bird in the cherry tree ; and I had never seen any
grief.

Next to this quite priceless gift of Peace, I had received
the perfect understanding of the natures of Obedience
and Faith I obeyed word, or lifted finger, of father or
mother, simply as a ship her helm , not only without
idea of resistance, but receiving the direction as a part
of my own life and force, and helpful law, as necessary
to me in every moral action as the law of gravity in
leaping And my practice in Faith was soon complete :
nothing was ever promised me that was not given ;
nothing ever threatened me that was not inflicted, and
nothing ever told me that was not true.

Peace, obedience, faith ; these three for chief good ; next to these, the habit of fixed attention with both eyes and mind—on which I will not farther enlarge at this moment, this being the main practical faculty of my life, causing Mazzini to say of me, in conversation authentically reported, a year or two before his death, that I had "the most analytic mind in Europe." An opinion in which, so far as I am acquainted with Europe, I am myself entirely disposed to concur.

Lastly, an extreme perfection in palate and all other bodily senses, given by the utter prohibition of cake, wine, comfits, or, except in carefullest restriction, fruit ; and by fine preparation of what food was given me. Such I esteem the main blessings of my childhood ;— next, let me count the equally dominant calamities.

First, that I had nothing to love.

My parents were—in a sort—visible powers of nature to me, no more loved than the sun and the moon : only I should have been annoyed and puzzled if either of them had gone out ; (how much, now, when both are darkened !)—still less did I love God ; not that I had any quarrel with Him, or fear of Him ; but simply found what people told me was His service, disagreeable ; and what people told me was His book, not entertaining. I had no companions to quarrel with, neither, nobody to assist, and nobody to thank. Not a servant was ever allowed to do anything for me, but what it was their duty to do ; and why should I have been grateful to the cook for cooking, or the gardener for gardening,—when the one dared not give me a baked potato without asking leave, and the other would not let my ants' nests alone, because they made the walks untidy? The evil consequence of all this was not, however, what might perhaps have been expected, that I grew up selfish or unaffectionate, but that, when affection did come, it came with violence utterly rampant and unmanageable, at least by me, who never before had anything to manage.

For (second of chief calamities) I had nothing to endure. Danger or pain of any kind I knew not : my strength was never exercised, my patience never tried, and my courage never fortified. Not that I was ever afraid of anything,—either ghosts, thunder, or beasts ; and one of the nearest approaches to insubordination which I was ever tempted into as a child, was in passionate effort to get leave to play with the lion's cubs in Wombwell's menagerie.

Thirdly. I was taught no precision nor etiquette of manners ; it was enough if, in the little society we saw, I remained unobtrusive, and replied to a question without shyness · but the shyness came later, and increased as I grew conscious of the rudeness arising from the want of social discipline, and found it impossible to acquire, in advanced life, dexterity in any bodily exercise, skill in any pleasing accomplishment, or ease and tact in ordinary behaviour.

Lastly, and chief of evils. My judgment of right and wrong, and powers of independent action,* were left entirely undeveloped ; because the bridle and blinkers were never taken off me. Children should have their times of being off duty, like soldiers ; and when once the obedience, if required, is certain, the little creature should be very early put for periods of practice in complete command of itself ; set on the barebacked horse of its own will, and left to break it by its own strength. But the ceaseless authority exercised over my youth left me, when cast out at last into the world, unable for some time to do more than drift with its elements. My present courses of life are indeed not altogether of that compliant nature ; but are, perhaps, more unaccommodating than they need be, in the insolence of reaction ; and the result upon me, of the elements and the courses together, is, in sum, that at my present age of fifty-six, while I have indeed the sincerest admiration for the characters of Phocion, Cincinnatus, and Caractacus, and am minded, so far as I may, to follow the example of those worthy personages, my own private little fancy, in which, for never having indulged me, I am always quarrelling with my Fortune, is still, as it always was, to find Prince Ahmed's arrow, and marry the Fairy Paribanou.

My present verdict, therefore, on the general tenor of my education at that time, must be, that it was at

---

* *Action*, observe, I say here ; in *thought* I was too independent, as I said above.

once too formal and too luxurious ; leaving my character, at the most important moment for its construction, cramped indeed, but not disciplined ; and only by protection innocent, instead of by practice virtuous. My mother saw this herself, and but too clearly, in later years ; and whenever I did anything wrong, stupid, or hard-hearted,—(and I have done many things that were all three),—always said, ' It is because you were too much indulged.'

So strongly do I feel this, as I sip my coffee this morning, (May 24th,) after being made profoundly miserable last night, because I did not think it likely I should be accepted if I made an offer to any one of three beautiful young ladies who were crushing and rending my heart into a mere shamrock leaf, the whole afternoon ; nor had any power to do, what I should have liked better still, send Giafar (without Zobeide's knowing anything about it) to superintend the immediate transport to my palace of all three ;—that I am afraid, if it were left to me at present to institute, without help from kinder counsellors, the education of the younger children on St. George's estate, the methods of the old woman who lived in a shoe would be the first that occurred to me as likely to conduce most directly to their future worth and felicity.

And I chanced, as Fors would have it, to fall, but last week, as I was arranging some books bought two years ago, and forgotten ever since,—on an instance of the use

of extreme severity in education, which cannot but com-
mend itself to the acceptance of every well informed
English gentlewoman.   For all well informed English
gentlewomen and gentle-maidens, have faithful respect
for the memory of Lady Jane Grey.

But I never myself, until the minute when I opened
that book, could at all understand Lady Jane Grey. I have
seen a great deal, thank Heaven, of good, and prudent,
and clever girls ; but not among the very best and wisest
of them did I ever find the slightest inclination to stop
indoors to read Plato, when all their people were in the
Park.   On the contrary, if any approach to such disposition manifested itself, I found it was always, either
because the scholastic young person thought that somebody might possibly call, suppose—myself, the Roger
Ascham of her time,—or suppose somebody else who
would prevent her, that day, from reading " piu avanti,"
or because the author who engaged her attention, so far
from being Plato himself, was, in many essential particulars, anti-Platonic.   And the more I thought of Lady
Jane Grey, the more she puzzled me.

Wherefore, opening, among my unexamined books, Roger
Ascham's Scholemaster, printed by John Daye, dwelling
over Aldersgate, An. 1571, just at the page where he
gives the original account of the thing as it happened,
I stopped in my unpacking to decipher the black letter
of it with attention ; which, by your leave, good reader,
you shall also take the trouble to do yourself, from this,

as far as I can manage to give it you, accurate facsimile
of the old page And trust me that I have a reason for
practising you in these old letters, though I have no
time to tell it you just now.

"And one example, whether Ioue or feare doth woike
more in a childe for bertue and learning, I will gladly report: which may bee heard with some pleasure, ī followed
with more prohte. Before I went into Germanie I came
to Brodegate in Leicestershire, to take my leabe of that noble Lady Jane Grey, to whom I was exceeding much be-
holding. Her parentes, the Duke and the Dutchesse, with
all the householde, Gentlemen and Gentlewemen, were
hunting in the Parke: I found her in her chamber, reading Phædon Platonis in Greeke, ī that with as much de-
lite, as some gentleman would read a mery tale in Bocase.
After salutation, and duetie done, with some other talk, I
asked her, why shee would leese such pastime in the Parke"
Smiling shee answered mee: I wisse, all their sport in the
Parke, is but a shadow to that pleasure ÿ I finde in Plato:
Alas, good folke, they neber felt what true pleasure ment."

Thus far, except in the trouble of reading black letters,
I have given you nothing new, or even freshly old.
All this we have heard of the young lady a hundred
times over. But next to this, comes something which
I fancy will be unexpected by most of my readers. For
the fashion of all literary students, catering for the public,
has hitherto been to pick out of their author whatever
bits they thought likely to be acceptable to Demos,
and to keep everything of suspicious taste out of his

dish of hashed hare. Nay, ' he pares his apple that will cleanly eat,' says honest George Herbert. I am not wholly sure, however, even of that ; if the apple itself be clean off the bough, and the teeth of little Eve and Adam, what teeth should be, it is quite questionable whether the good old fashion of alternate bite be not the method of finest enjoyment of flavour. But the modern frugivorous public will soon have a steam-machine in Covent Garden, to pick the straw out of their straw-berries.

In accordance with which popular principle of natural selection, the historians of Lady Jane's life, finding this first opening of the scene at Brodegate so entirely charm-ing and graceful, and virtuous, and moral, and ducal, and large-landed-estate-ish—without there being the slightest suggestion in it of any principle, to which any-body could possibly object,—pounce upon it as a flawless gem , and clearing from it all the objectional matrix, with delicate skill, set it forth—changed about from one to another of the finest cases of velvet eloquence to be got up for money—in the corner shop—London and Ryder's, of the Bond Street of Vanity Fair.

But I, as an old mineralogist, like to see my gems in the rock ; and always bring away the biggest piece I can break with the heaviest hammer I can carry. Accordingly, I venture to beg of you also, good reader, to decipher farther this piece of kindly Ascham's follow-ing narration :

" And how came you, Madame, quoth I, to this deepe knowledge of pleasure, & what did cheefly allure you unto it, se-
ing not many women, but very fewe men have attayned
thereunto. I will tell you, quoth shee, and tell you a troth,
which perchance ye will marvel at. One of the greatest be-
nefites that ever God gave me, is, that hee sent me so sharpe
and severe parentes, and so gentle a schoolemaster. For whe
I am in presence either of father or mother, whether I
speake, keepe silence, sit, stand, or go, eate, drinke, be mery, or
sad, bee sewing, playing, dancing, or doing anything els, I
must doe it, as it were, in such weight, measure, & number,
even so perfectly, as God made the world, or ells I am so
sharply taunted, so cruelly threatned, yea, presently sometimes, with pinches, nippes, and bobbes, and other wayes
which I will not name for the honor I beare the, so without measure misordered, that I thinke my selfe in hell, till
time come that I must goe to M Elmer who teacheth mee
so gently, so pleasantly, with such faire alluremetes to learning that I thinke all the time nothing, whiles I am with
him. And when I am called fro him, I fall on weeping, because, whatsoever I doe els but learning, is full of greefe,
trouble, feare, and whole misliking unto mee. And thus my
booke hath been so much my pleasure, & bringeth daily to me
more pleasure & more, y in respect of it, all other pleasures,
in very deede, bee but trifles & troubles unto mee.

Lady Jane ceases, Ascham speaks I reme
ber this talke gladly, bothe because it is so worthy of memory & because also it was the last talke that ever I had, and
the last time, that ever I saw that noble & worthy Lady."

Now, for the clear understanding of this passage,
—I adjure you, gentle reader, (if you are such, and

therefore capable of receiving adjuration)—in the name of St. George and all saints,—of Edward III. and all knights,—of Alice of Salisbury and all stainless wives, and of Jeanne of France and all stainless maids, that you put at once out of your mind, under penalty of sharpest Honte Ban, all such thought as would first suggest itself to the modern novel writer, and novel reader, concerning this matter,—namely, that the young girl is in love with her tutor. She loves him rightly, as all good and noble boys and girls necessarily love good masters,—and no otherwise ;—is grateful to him rightly, and no otherwise ;—happy with him and her book— rightly, and no otherwise.

And that her father and mother, with whatever leaven of human selfishness, or impetuous disgrace in the manner and violence of their dealing with her, did, nevertheless, compel their child to do all things that she did,—rightly, and no otherwise, was, verily, though at that age she knew it but in part,—the literally crowning and guiding Mercy of her life,—the plaited thorn upon the brow, and rooted thorn around the feet, which are the tribute of Earth to the Princesses of Heaven.

NOTES AND CORRESPONDENCE.

The minds of many of the friends of Mr. Septimus Hansard appear to have been greatly exercised by my insertion of, and comments on, the newspaper paragraph respecting that gentleman's ministrations to the poor of London.

I thought it unnecessary to take notice of the first communication which I received on the subject, from a fashionable lady, informing me, with much indignation, that Mr. Hansard had caught his fever in the West-End, not in the East; and had been sick in the best society. The following letter is of more importance, and its writer having accepted what he calls "my kind offer" to print it, I have no alternative, though he mistook, or rather misplaced, the real kindness of my private note, which lay in its recommendation to him,* *not* to accept the offer it made.

"135. WATERLOW BUILDINGS, WILMOTT STREET.
"BETHNAL GREEN, E., *May* 14, 1875.

"SIR,—In your 49th Letter you say that we clergy are not priests, and cannot sacrifice. You also say that we are *wholly* responsible for, and the efficient causes of, horrible outrages on women. In your 51st Letter you speak of my friend and chief, Mr. Hansard, as being courageous, impulsive, and generous, but complacent, and living a life "all aglow in vain"; and you compare him, in Bethnal Green, to a moth in candle-grease.

"I know that I, as a priest, am responsible for much wrong-

* At least, I think the terms of my letter might have been easily construed into such recommendation ; I fear they were not as clear as they might have been.

doing; but I must claim you, and all who have failed to be *perfect* stewards of their material and spiritual property, as responsible with me and the rest of the clergy for the ignorance and crime of our fellow-countrymen.

"But I would ask you whether Mr. Hansard's life, even as you know it, (and you don't know half the St. George-like work he has done and is doing,) is not a proof that we *priests can and do sacrifice*,—that we can offer ourselves, our souls and bodies?

"Of course I agree with you and Mr. Lyttel that the preaching of 'Christ's life *instead* of our lives' is false and damnatory; but I am sorry that, instead of backing those who teach the true and salutary Gospel, you condemn us all alike, wholesale. I think you will find that you will want even our help to get the true Gospel taught

"Allow me also to protest pretty strongly against my friends and neighbours here being compared to candle-grease. I fancy that on consideration, you would like to withdraw that parable, perhaps, even, you would like to make some kind of reparation, by helping us, candle-grease-like Bethnal-greeners, to be better and happier.

"I am one of those clergymen spoken of in Letter 49, and 'honestly believe myself impelled to say and do' many things by the Holy Ghost; and for that very reason I am bound to remember that you and other men are inspired also by the same Holy Ghost, and therefore to look out for and take any help which you and others choose to give me.

"It is because I have already received so much help from you that I write this letter.

"I am, yours faithfully,
"STEWART D. HEADLAM,
"Curate of St Matthew's, Bethnal Green.
"To JOHN RUSKIN, Esq., LL.D."

I at first intended to make no comments on this letter, but, as I re-read, find it so modestly fast in its temper, and so perilously loose in its divinity, as to make it my duty, while I congratulate the well-meaning—and, I doubt not, well doing— writer, on his agreement with Mr. Lyttel that the preaching of "Christ's life, instead of our lives," is false and damnatory; also to observe to him that the sacrifice of our own bodies, instead of Christ's body, is an equally heretical, and I can assure him, no less dangerous, reformation of the Doctrine of the Mass. I beg him also to believe that I meant no disrespect to his friends and neighbours in comparing them to candle-grease He is unaccustomed to my simple English, and would surely not have been offended if I had said, instead, " oil for the light"? If our chandlers, now-a-days, never give us any so honest tallow as might fittingly be made the symbol of a Christian congregation, is that my fault?

I feel, however, that I do indeed owe some apology to Mr. Hansard himself, to his many good and well-won friends, and especially to my correspondent, Mr. Lyttel, for reprinting the following article from a Birmingham paper—very imperfectly, I am sure, exemplifying the lustre produced by ecclesiastical labour in polishing what, perhaps, I shall again be held disre-spectful, in likening to the Pewter, instead of the Grease, and Candlestick instead of Candle, of sacredly inflammable Religious Society.

"PROFESSOR RUSKIN ON THE CLERGY.

" Not many years ago one might throw almost any calumny against the Church or her clergy without fear of contradiction or exposure. Happily, for the cause of truth and justice, those days are gone—unhappily, however, for the unfortunate individuals born too late for the safe indulgence of their spleen. Amongst these, we fear, must be reckoned Mr Ruskin, the Oxford Professor of Fine Art. He issues monthly a pamphlet, entitled 'Fors Clavigera,' being ostensibly 'Letters to the Workmen and Labourers of Great Britain,' but the contents of which do not appear likely to edify that class, even if the price (tenpence) were not prohibitory. In the forty-ninth of these letters a furious and wholly unjustifiable attack is made upon the Church. No abuse is deemed too unjust or too coarse to bestow upon the clergy, and they are assailed in a tone of vituperation worthy of the last century. The Professor says that,* 'in general, any man's becoming a clergyman in these days implies that, at best, his sentiment has overpowered his intellect, and that, whatever the feebleness of the latter, the victory of his impertinent piety has been probably owing to its alliance with his conceit, and its promise to him of the gratification of being regarded as an oracle, without the trouble of becoming wise, or the grief of being so.' Much more there is in the same insolent strain, as if the Professor's head had been turned by the height of critical infallibility to which he has elevated himself, and from which he looks down with self-complacent scorn and arrogance upon all fallible humanity, clerical or lay. He concludes by appending 'a specimen of the conduct of the Saints to whom our English clergymen have delivered the Faith.' This specimen is afforded, according to Mr. Ruskin, in two cases of revolting and almost incredible barbarism, tried recently at Liverpool Assizes, in one of which an unoffending man was kicked to death by a gang of street ruffians, in the presence of an admiring crowd, and in the other case, a drunken female tramp, drenched with the rain, was taken into a field and outraged by half-a-dozen youths, after which they left her, and

---

* I permit the waste of type, and, it may well be, of my reader's patience, involved in reprinting (instead of merely referring to) the quoted passages and letter, lest it should be thought that I wished to evade the points, or, by interruption, deaden the eloquence, of the Birmingham article.

she was found there next day dead. We need not enter into the details of these cases, which were given fully enough at the time; suffice it to say that in the records of no age or nation will any tales be found surpassing these two in savagery of mind and body, and in foulness of heart and soul. And what is Mr. Ruskin's reason for resuscitating the memory of these horrors? What is the explanation that he has to give of them? What is the judgment that he has to pass upon them? Let our readers behold it for themselves in his own words :—'The clergy may vainly exclaim against being made responsible for this state of things They, and chiefly their Bishops, are wholly responsible for it; nay, are efficiently the causes of it, preaching a false gospel for hire.' These words have the one merit of being perfectly plain. Mr. Ruskin does not insinuate his vile charge by any indirect hints or roundabout verbiage, but expresses his infamous meaning as unambiguously as possible. The clergy, he says, are 'wholly responsible' for the murders and rapes which horrify us, which, indeed, they 'efficiently cause'; and the chiefs of these incarnate fiends are the Bishops.

"'This very intemperate attack elicited a few temperate remarks from one of the maligned class. The Rev. E. Z. Lyttel, of Werrington, near Peterborough, wrote to Mr. Ruskin thus :—'I have been reading your words to my conscience, but is it my unconscious hypocrisy, my self-conceit, or my sentiment overpowering intellect which hinders me from hearing the word *Guilty?* The Gospel I endeavour with all my might to preach and embody is this—Believe on, be persuaded by, the Lord Jesus Christ; let His life rule your lives, and you shall be safe and sound now and everlastingly. Is this a false Gospel preached for hire? If not, what other Gospel do you refer to?' Mr. Lyttel seems to have thought that the charge brought against himself and his clerical brethren of causing murders and rapes was too gross for notice, or too intoxicated to merit denial. He contented himself with the foregoing very mild reply, which, however, proved adequate to the occasion which called it forth. Mr. Lyttel was recently curate of St Barnabas, in this town, and has also held a curacy in London. His personal experience gives him a claim to be heard when he assures the Professor that he *knows* that the morality of the parishes with which he is best acquainted has been made better, and not worse, by the self-sacrificing efforts of the clergy. It is also pointed out that while Mr. Ruskin has been freely travelling about in the enjoyment of beautiful scenery and fresh air, Mr. Lyttel and other clergymen have been occupied from day to day in stuffy rooms, in crowded parishes, amongst ignorant and immoral people. And whilst this censorious Oxford luminary makes a great fuss about getting paid for ' Fors Clavigera ' and his other writings, Mr. Lyttel hints that surely the clergy should be paid for their teachings too, being quite equally worthy of their hire.

"Our ex-townsman has so effectually disposed of the Professor's charges, that there is no need to endeavour to answer them further We have only noticed them so far in order to show our readers the extent to which hatred of the Church becomes a craze with some persons, otherwise estimable no doubt, whose judgment is for the time swept away by passion. That there is no pleasing such persons is the more apparent from Mr. Ruskin's curious comments upon the well-known story of the Rev. Septimus Hansard, the rector of Bethnal Green, who has caught the small-pox, the typhus fever, and the scarlet fever, on three several occasions* in the discharge

---

* Birmingham accepts, with the child-like confidence due by one able Editor to another, the report of Brighton But all Mr Hansard's friends are furious with me for " spreading it ; " and I beg at once, on their authority, to contradict it in all essential particulars ; and to apologize to Mr. Hansard for ever having suspected him of such things.

of his pastoral duties among the sick poor. When he fell down in his pulpit with the small-pox, he at once said he would go to an hospital, but refused to enter the cab which his friends called, lest he should infect it; and, a hearse happening to pass, he went in it—a fine instance of courage and self-devotion. Mr. Hansard's stipend is five hundred a year, out of which he has to pay two curates. And what has Mr. Ruskin to say to this? Surely this must command his fullest sympathy, admiration, and approval? Far from it. His snarling comment is as follows :—'I am very sure that while he was saving one poor soul in Bethnal he was leaving ten rich souls to be damned at Tyburn, each of which would damn a thousand or two more by their example or neglect.' This peculiar mode of argument has the merit of being available under all circumstances; for, of course, if Mr. Hansard's parish had happened to be Tyburn instead of Bethnal, Mr. Ruskin would have been equally ready with the glib remark that while the rector was saving one rich soul to Tyburn, he was leaving ten poor souls to destruction in Bethnal. Are we to understand that Mr. Ruskin thinks Mr. Hansard ought to be able to be in two places at once, or are we to shrug our shoulders and say that some persons are hard to please? The heroism of self-sacrifice Mr. Ruskin considers to be a waste and a mistake. Mr. Hansard's life has all, says the Professor, 'been but one fit of scarlet fever—and all aglow in vain.' That noble-minded men should devote themselves to the noblest work of the Church for the love of Christ, and of those for whom He died, is apparently beyond Mr. Ruskin's conception. Love of sensation, he says, is the cause of it all. 'Sensation *must* be got out of death, or darkness, or frightfulness. . . . And the culmination of the black business is that the visible misery drags and beguiles to its help all the enthusiastic simplicity of the religious young, and the honest strength of the really noble type of English clergymen, and swallows them, as Charybdis would life-boats.   Courageous and impulsive men, with just sense enough to make them soundly practical, and therefore complacent, in immediate business, but not enough to enable them to see what the whole business comes to when done, are sure to throw themselves desperately into the dirty work, and die like lively moths in candle-grease'   We have read philosophy something like the above extract elsewhere before, and we think the philosopher's name was Harold Skimpole. What the gospel is with which Mr. Ruskin proposes to supplant Christianity and to regenerate the world, we do not know.   A gospel of this tone, however, published in tenpenny instalments, is not likely ever to reach the hands of the workmen and labourers of Great Britain, much less their hearts."

With this interesting ebullition, shall we call it, of Holy Water, or beautiful explosion,—perhaps, more accurately,—of Holy Steam, in one of our great manufacturing centres, a very furnace, it would appear, of heartfelt zeal for the Church, I wish I could at once compare a description of the effects of similar zeal for the—Chapel, given me in a letter just received from Wakefield, for which I sincerely thank my correspondent, and will assume, unless I hear further from him, his permission to print a great part of said letter in next Fors.

My more practical readers may perhaps be growing desperate, at the continued non-announcement of advance in my main scheme But the transference to the St. George's Company of the few acres of land hitherto offered us, cannot be effected without the establishment of the society on a legal basis, which I find the most practised counsel slow in reducing to terms such as the design could be carried out upon.   The form proposed shall, however, without fail, be submitted to the existing members of the Company in my next letter.

FORS CLAVIGERA.

No more letters, at present, reaching me, from clergy-men, I use the breathing-time permitted me, to express more clearly the meaning of my charge,—left in its brevity obscure,—that, as a body, they " teach a false gospel for hire."

It is obscure, because associating two charges quite distinct. The first, that, whether for hire or not, they preach a false gospel. The second, that, whether they preach truth or falsehood, they preach as hirelings.

It will be observed that the three clergymen who have successively corresponded with me—Mr. Tipple, Mr. Lyttel, and Mr. Headlam—have every one, for their own part, eagerly repudiated the doctrine of the Eleventh Article of the Church of England. Nevertheless, the substance of that article assuredly defines the method of salvation commonly announced at this day from British pulpits; and the effect of this supremely pleasant and supremely false gospel, on the British mind, may be best illustrated by the reply, made only the other day, by a dishonest, but sincerely religious, commercial gentleman, to an acquaintance of mine, who had expressed surprise that he should come to church after doing the things he was well known to do : "Ah, my friend, my standard is just the publican's."

In the second place, while it is unquestionably true that many clergymen are doing what Mr. Headlam complacently points out their ability to do,—sacrificing, to wit, themselves, their souls, and bodies, (not that I clearly understand what a clergyman means by sacrificing his soul,) without any thought of temporal reward ; this preaching of Christ has, nevertheless, become an acknowledged Profession, and means of livelihood for gentlemen : and the Simony of to-day differs only from that of apostolic times, in that, while the elder Simon thought the gift of the Holy Ghost worth a considerable offer in ready money, the modern Simon would on the whole refuse to accept the same gift of the Third Person of the Trinity, without a nice little attached income, a pretty church, with a steeple restored by Mr. Scott, and an eligible neighbourhood

These are the two main branches of the charge I meant to gather into my short sentence ; and to these I now further add, that in defence of this Profession, with its pride, privilege, and more or less roseate repose of domestic felicity, extremely beautiful and enviable in country parishes, the clergy, as a body, have, with what energy and power was in them, repelled the advance both of science and scholarship, so far as either interfered with what they had been accustomed to teach, and connived at every abuse in public and private conduct, with which they felt it would be considered uncivil, and feared it might ultimately prove unsafe, to interfere .

And that, therefore, seeing that they were put in charge to preach the Gospel of Christ, and have preached a false gospel instead of it; and seeing that they were put in charge to enforce the Law of Christ, and have permitted license instead of it, they are answerable, as no other men are answerable, for the existing "state of things" in this British nation,—a state now recorded in its courts of justice as productive of crimes respecting which the Birmingham Defender of the Faith himself declares that "in the records of no age or nation will any tales be found surpassing these in savagery of mind and body, and in foulness of heart and soul."

Answerable, as no other men are, I repeat; and entirely disdain my correspondent Mr Headlam's attempt to involve me, or any other layman, in his responsibility. He has taken on himself the office of teacher. Mine is a painter's; and I am plagued to death by having to teach *instead* of him, and his brethren,—silent, they, for fear of their congregations! Which of them, from least to greatest, dares, for instance, so much as to tell the truth to women about their dress? Which of them has forbidden his feminine audience to wear fine bonnets in church? Do they think the dainty garlands are wreathed round the studiously dressed hair, because a woman "should have power on her head because of the angels"? Which of them understands that text?—which of them enforces it? Dares the boldest ritualist order his women-congregation to come all with white napkins over their heads, rich and poor alike, and have done with their bonnets? What, 'You cannot order'? You could say you wouldn't preach if you saw one bonnet in the church, couldn't you? 'But everybody would say you were mad.' Of course they would—and that the devil was in you. "If they have called the Master of the house Beelzebub, how much more them of His household?" but now that 'all men speak well of you,' think you the Son of Man will speak the same?

And you, and especially your wives, (as is likely!) are very angry with me, I hear, on all hands;—and think me hostile to you. As well might a carter asleep on his shafts accuse me of being his enemy for trying to wake him; or his master's enemy, because I would fain not see the cart in the ditch, Nay, this notable paragraph which has given Mr. Hansard's friends so much offence, was credited and printed by me, because I thought it one of the noblest instances I had ever heard of energy and unselfishness ; and though, of all the sects of ecclesiastics, for my own share, I most dislike and distrust the so-called Evangelical, I took the picture of Swiss life, which was meant to stand for a perfect and true one, from the lips of an honest vicar of that persuasion

Which story, seeing that it has both been too long interrupted, and that its entire lesson bears on what I have to say respecting the ministrations of Felix Neff, I will interrupt my too garrulous personal reminiscences by concluding, in this letter, from that of March, 1874.

"The old cart went again as well as ever ; and 'he could never have believed,' said Hansli, 'that a cart could have taken itself up so, and become so extremely changed for the better. That might be an example to many living creatures.'

More than one young girl, however, in her own secret heart reproached Hansli for his choice—saying to herself that she would have done for him quite as well. 'If she had thought he had been in such a hurry, she could have gone well enough, too, to put herself on his road, and prevented him from looking at that rubbishy rag of a girl. She never could have thought Hansli was such a goose,—he, who might easily have married quite differently, if he had had the sense to choose. As sure as the carnival was coming, he would repent before he got to it. All the worse for

him—it's his own fault: as one makes one's bed, one
lies in it.'

But Hansli had not been a goose at all, and never
found anything to repent of.   He had a little wife
who was just the very thing he wanted,—a little,
modest, busy wife, who made him as happy as if he
had married Heaven itself in person.

It is true that she didn't long help Hansli to pull
the cart: he soon found himself obliged to go in the
shafts alone again ; but, aussi, once he saw he had
a mustard,* he consoled himself.   'What a fellow!'
said he, examining him.   'In a wink, he'll be big
enough to help me himself.'   And, thereupon, away
he went with his cart, all alone, without finding any
difference.

It is true that in a very little while his wife wanted
to come again to help him.   'If only we make a
little haste to get back,' said she, 'the little one can
wait well enough—besides that the grandmother can
give him something to drink while we are away.'   But
the mustard himself was not of their mind, and soon
made them walk in his own fashion.   They made all
the haste they could to get home—but before they
were within half a league of their door, the wife cried
out, 'Mercy! what's that?'   'That' was a shrill crying
like a little pig's when it is being killed.   'Mercy on
us, what is it,—what's the matter!' cried she; and

* Moutard—not -arde ; but I can't give better than this English for it.

left the cart, and ran off at full speed : and there, sure enough, was the grandmother, whom the little thing's cries had put into a dreadful fright lest it should have convulsions, and who could think of nothing better than to bring it to meet mamma. The heavy boy, the fright, and the run, had put the old woman so out of breath that it was really high time for somebody to take the child. She was almost beside herself; and it was ever so long before she could say, ' No—I won't have him alone any more : in my life I never saw such a little wretch : I had rather come and draw the cart.'

These worthy people thus learned what it is to have a tyrant in one's house, little one though he be. But all that didn't interrupt their household ways. The little wife found plenty to do staying at home, gardening, and helping to make the brooms. Without ever hurrying anything, she worked without ceasing, and was never tired,—so easily things ran under her hand. Hansli was all surprise to find he got along so well with a wife ; and to find his purse growing fatter so fast. He leased a little field ; and the grandmother saw a goat in it, presently two. He would not hear of a donkey, but arranged with the miller, when he went to the town, to carry some of his brooms for him ; which, it is true, skimmed off a little of the profit, and that vexed Hansli, who could not bear the smallest kreutzer to escape him. But his life soon became quite simple and continuous. The days followed each other like the waves of a river, without much difference between one and another. Every year grew new twigs to make brooms with. Every year, also, without putting herself much about, his wife gave him a new baby. She brought it, and planted it there. Every day it cried a little,—every day it grew a little, and, in a turn of the hand, it was of use for something. The grandmother said that, old as she was, she had never seen anything like it. It was, for all the world, she said, like the little cats, which at six weeks old, catch mice. And all these children were really like so many blessings —the more there came, the more money one made. Very soon—only think of it—the grandmother saw a cow arrive. If she had not with her own eyes seen Hansli pay for it, it would have been almost impossible to make her believe that he had not stolen it. If the poor old woman had lived two years more,* she would even have seen Hansli become himself the owner of the little cottage in which she had lived so long, with forest right which gave him more wood than he wanted; and ground enough to

---

* Fate, and the good novelist, thus dismiss poor grandmamma in a passing sentence—just when we wanted her so much to live a little longer, too! But that is Fors's way, and Gotthelf knows it. A bad novelist would have made her live to exactly the proper moment, and then die in a most instructive manner, and with pathetic incidents and speeches which would have filled a chapter.

keep a cow and two sheep, which are convenient things
enough, when one has children who wear worsted
stockings.

(Upon all that,* Hansli certainly owed a good deal,
but it was well-placed money, and no one would ask
him for it, as long as he paid the interest to the day;
for the rest, 'if God lent him life, these debts did not
trouble him,' said he.) He might then learn that the
first kreutzers are the most difficult to save. There's
always a hole they are running out at, or a mouth
to swallow them. But when once one has got to the
point of having no more debts, and is completely
set on one's legs, then things begin to go!—the very
ground seems to grow under your feet,—everything
profits more and more,—the rivulet becomes a river,
and the gains become always easier and larger . on
one condition, nevertheless, that one shall change
nothing in one's way of life. For it is just then that
new needs spring out of the ground like mushrooms
on a dunghill, if not for the husband, at least for
the wife,—if not for the parents, at least for the
children. A thousand things seem to become necessary of which we had never thought ; and we are
ashamed of ever so many others, which till then had
not given us the smallest concern ; and we exaggerate
the value of what we have, because once we had

* This paragraph implies, of course, the existence of all modern abuses, —
the story dealing only with the world as it is.

nothing, and our own value, because we attribute our success to ourselves,—and,—one changes one's way of life, and expenses increase, and labour lessens, and the haughty spirit goes before the fall.

It was not so with Hansli He continued to live and work just the same, and hardly ever spent anything at the inn ; aussi, he rejoiced all the more to find something hot ready for him when he came home ; and did honour to it Nothing was changed in him, unless that his strength for work became always greater, little by little ; and his wife had the difficult art of making the children serve themselves, each, according to its age,—not with many words neither ; and she herself scarcely knew how.

A pedagogue would never have been able to get the least explanation of it from her. Those children took care of each other, helped their father to make his brooms, and their mother in her work about the house ; none of them had the least idea of the pleasures of doing nothing, nor of dreaming or lounging about ; and yet not one was overworked, or neglected They shot up like willows by a brookside, full of vigour and gaiety. The parents had no time for idling with them, but the children none the less knew their love, and saw how pleased they were when their little ones did their work well. Their parents prayed with them on Sundays the father read them a chapter which he explained afterwards as well

as he could, and on account of that also the children
were full of respect for him, considering him as the
father of the family who talks with God Himself (and
who will tell Him when children disobey*). The degree
of respect felt by children for their parents depends
always on the manner in which the parents bear themselves to God. Why do not all parents reflect more on
this? †

Nor was our Hansli held in small esteem by other
people, any more than by his children. He was so
decided and so sure ; words full of good sense were
plenty with him ; honourable in everything, he never
set himself up for rich, nor complained of being poor ;
so that many a pretty lady would come expressly into
the kitchen, when she heard that the broom-merchant
was there, to inform herself how things went in the
country, and how such and such a matter was turning
out. Nay, in many of the houses he was trusted to
lay in their winter provisions, a business which brought
him many a bright batz. The Syndic's wife at Thun,
herself, often had a chat with him ; it had become, so
to speak, really a pressing need with her to see him at
Thun every Saturday ; and when she was talking to him,
it had happened, not once nor twice, that M. the Syndic

---

* A minute Evangelical fragment dubitable enough

† Primarily, because it is untrue. The respect of a child for its parent
depends on the parent's own personal character ; and not at all, irrespective
of that, on his religious behaviour. Which the practical good sense of the
reverend novelist presently admits.

himself had been obliged to wait for an answer to something he had asked his wife.   After all, a Syndic's wife may surely give herself leave to talk a little according to her own fancy, once a week.

One fine day, however, it was the Saturday at Thun, and there was not in all the town a shadow of the broom-merchant   Thence, aussi, great emotion, and grave faces.   More than one maid was on the doorsteps, with her arms akimbo, leaving quietly upstairs in the kitchen the soup and the meat to agree with each other as best they might   ·

'You haven't seen him then ?—have you heard nothing of him ? '—asked they, one of the other.   More than one lady ran into her kitchen, prepared to dress* her servant well, from head to foot, because she hadn't been told when the broom-merchant was there.   But she found no servant there, and only the broth boiling over   Madame the Syndic herself got disturbed ; and interrogated, first her husband, and then the gendarme.   And as they knew nothing, neither the one nor the other, down she went into the low town herself, in person, to inquire after her broom-merchant. She was quite out of brooms—and the year's housecleaning was to be done next week—and now no broom-merchant—je vous demande ! †   And   truly

---

* We keep the metaphor in the phrase, to 'give a dressing,' but the short verb is better

† Untranslateable

enough, no broom-merchant appeared, and during all the week there was a feeling of want in the town, and an enormous disquietude the next Saturday. Will he come? Won't he come? He came, in effect; and if he had tried to answer all the questions put to him, would not have got away again till the next week. He contented himself with saying to everybody that 'he had been obliged to go to the funeral'

'Whose funeral?' asked Madame the Syndic, from whom he could not escape so easily.

'My sister's,' answered the broom-merchant

'Who was she? and when did they bury her?' Madame continued to ask.

The broom-merchant answered briefly, but frankly : aussi Madame the Syndic cried out all at once,

'Mercy on us!—are you the brother of that servant-girl there's been such a noise about, who turned out at her master's death to have been his wife,—and had all his fortune left to her, and died herself soon afterwards?'

'It is precisely so,' answered Hansli, dryly.*

'But — goodness of Heaven!' cried Madame the Syndic, 'you inherit fifty thousand crowns at least,—

* It was unworthy of Gotthelf to spoil his story by this vulgar theatrical catastrophe ; and his object (namely, to exhibit the character of Hansli in riches as well as poverty,) does not justify him ; for, to be an example to those in his own position, Hansli should have remained in it We will however, take what good we can get ; several of the points for the sake of which I have translated the whole story, are in this part of it.

and behold you still running over the country with your brooms!'

'Why not?' said Hansli; 'I haven't got that money, yet; and I'm not going to let go my sparrow in the hand for a pigeon on the tiles.'

'Pigeon on the tiles, indeed!' said Madame,—'why, we were speaking of it only this morning—I and M. the Syndic; and he said the thing was perfectly sure, and the money came all to the brother.'

'Ah, well, my faith, so much the better,' said Hansli; 'but about what I called to ask,—must you have the brooms in eight days, or fifteen?'

'Ah, bah—you and your brooms!' cried Madame the Syndic; 'come in, will you?—I want to see how wide Monsieur will open his eyes!'

'But, Madame, I am a little hurried to-day; it's a long way home from here, and the days are short.'

'Long or short, come in, always,' said Madame imperatively,—and Hansli had nothing for it but to obey.

She did not take him into the kitchen, but into the dining-room; sent her maid to tell Monsieur that Hansli was there,—ordered up a bottle of wine,—and forced Hansli to sit down, in spite of his continued protesting that he had no time, and that the days were short. But in a wink the Monsieur was there, sat down at the table also, and drank to Hansli's health and happiness; requiring him at the same time to explain how that had all happened.

' Ah, well, I'll tell you in two words,—it is not long. As soon as she had been confirmed, my sister went into the world to look for work She got on from place to place, and was much valued, it seems. As for us at home, she occupied herself little about us : only came to see us twice, in all the time ; and, since my mother died, not at all. I have met her at Berne, it is true ; but she never asked me to come and see where she lived,—only bid me salute the wife and children, and said she would soon come, but she never did It is true she was not long at Berne, but was much out at service in the neighbouring chateaux, and in French Switzerland, from what I hear She had busy blood, and a fanciful head, which never could stay long in the same place but, with that, well-conducted and proof-faithful ; * and one might trust her fearlessly with anything At last there came a report that she had married a rich old gentleman, who did that to punish his relations, with whom he was very angry , but I didn't much believe it, nor much think about it. And then, all of a sudden, I got word that I must go directly to my sister if I wanted to see her alive, and that she lived in the country by Morat. So I set out, and got there in time to see her die , but was not able to say much to her. As soon as she was buried, I came back as fast as I could. I was in a hurry to get home, for since I first set

* " Fidèle a toute épreuve "

up house I had never lost so much time about the world.'

'What's that?—lost so much time, indeed!' cried Madame the Syndic. 'Ah, nonsense;—with your fifty thousand crowns, are you going to keep carrying brooms about the country?'

'But very certainly, Madame the Syndic,' said Hansli, 'I only half trust the thing; it seems to me impossible I should have so much   After all, they say it can't fail; but be it as it will, I shall go on living my own life: so that if there comes any hitch in the business, people shan't be able to say of me, "Ah, he thought himself already a gentleman, did he? Now he's glad to go back to his cart!" But if the money really comes to me, I shall leave my brooms, though not without regret; but it would all the same, then, make the world talk and laugh if I went on; and I will not have that.'

'But that fortune is in safe hands,—it runs no danger?' asked M. the Syndic.

'I think so,' said Hansli. 'I promised some money to the man, if the heritage really came to me; then he got angry, and said, "If it's yours, you'll have it; and if it isn't, money won't get it: for the expenses and taxes, you'll have the account in proper time and place." Then I saw the thing was well placed; and I can wait well enough, till the time's up.'

'But, in truth,' said Madame the Syndic, 'I can't

understand such a sangfroid! One has never seen the like of that in Israel. That would make me leap out of my skin, if I was your wife'

'You had better not,' said Hansli, 'at least until you have found somebody able to put you into it again.'

This sangfroid, and his carrying on his business, reconciled many people to Hansli; who were not the less very envious of him: some indeed thought him a fool, and wanted to buy the succession of him, declaring he would get nothing out of it but law-suits.

'What would you have?' said Hansli. 'In this world, one is sure of nothing. It will be time to think of it if the affair gets into a mess.'

But the affair got into nothing of the sort Legal time expired, he got invitation to Berne, when all difficulties were cleared away.

When his wife saw him come back so rich, she began, first, to cry; and then, to scream

So that Hansli had to ask her, again and again, what was the matter with her, and whether anything had gone wrong

'Ah, now,' said his wife, at last,—(for she cried so seldom, that she had all the more trouble to stop, when once she began),—'Ah, now, you will despise me, because you are so rich, and think that you would like to have another sort of wife than me. I've done what I could, to this day ; but now I'm nothing but an old rag* If only I was already six feet under ground ! '

Thereupon Hansli sat himself down in his arm-chair, and said :

' Wife, listen. Here are now nearly thirty years that we have kept house ; and thou knowest, what one would have, the other would have, too. I've never once beaten thee, and the bad words we may have said to each other would be easily counted. Well, wife, I tell thee, do not begin to be ill-tempered now, or do anything else than you have always done. Everything must remain between us as in the past. This inheritance does not come from me ; nor from thee : but from the good God, for us two, and for our children. And now, I advise thee, and hold it for as sure a thing as if it were written in the Bible, if you speak again of this to me but once, be it with crying, or without, I will give thee a beating with a new rope, such as that they may hear thee cry from here to the Lake of Constance. Behold what is said : now do as thou wilt.'

It was resolute speaking ; much more resolute than the diplomatic notes between Prussia and Austria. The wife knew where she was, and did not recommence her song. Things remained between them as they had been. Before abandoning his brooms, Hansli

* " Patraque,"—machine out of repair, and useless.

gave a turn of his hand to them, and made a present of a dozen to all his customers, carrying them to each in his own person. He has repeated many a time since, and nearly always with tears in his eyes, that it was a day he could never forget, and that he never would have believed people loved him so.

Farming his own land, he kept his activity and simplicity, prayed and worked as he had always done ; but he knew the difference between a farmer and a broom-seller, and did honour to his new position as he had to his old one. He knew well, already, what was befitting in a farmer's house, and did now for others as he had been thankful to have had done for himself.

The good God spared both of them to see their sons-in-law happy in their wives, and their daughters-in-law full of respect and tenderness for their husbands ; and were they yet alive this day, they would see what deep roots their family had struck in their native land, because it has remained faithful to the vital germs of domestic life ; the love of work ; and religion : foundation that cannot be overthrown, unmoved by mocking chance, or wavering winds."

I have no time, this month, to debate any of the debateable matters in this story, though I have translated it that we may together think of them as occasion serves. In the meantime, note that the heads of question are these :—

I. (Already suggested in p. 59 of my letter for March, 1874) What are the relative dignities and felicities of affection, in simple and gentle loves? How far do you think the regard existing between Hansli and his wife may be compared, for nobleness and delight, to Sir Philip Sidney's regard for—his neighbour's wife; or the relations between Hansli and his sister, terminating in the brief 'was not able to say much to her,' comparable to those between Sidney and his sister, terminating in the completion of the brother's Psalter by the sister's indistinguishably perfect song?

II. If there be any difference, and you think the gentle hearts have in anywise the better,—how far do you think this separation between gentle and simple inevitable? Suppose Sir Philip, for instance—among his many accomplishments—had been also taught the art of making brooms,—(as indeed I doubt not but his sister knew how to use them,)—and time had thus been left to the broom-makers of his day for the fashioning of sonnets? or the reading of more literature than a 'chapitre' on the Sunday afternoons? Might such—not 'division' but 'collation'—of labour have bettered both their lives?

III. Or shall we rather be content with the apparent law of nature that there shall be divine Astrophels in the intellectual heaven, and peaceful earthly glowworms on the banks below; or even—on the Evangelical theory of human nature—worms without any glow? And shall we be content to see our broom-makers' children, at the best, growing up as willows by the brook—or in the simplest and innumerablest crowd, as rushes in a marsh ; —so long as they have wholesome pith and sufficing strength to be securely sat upon in rush-bottomed chairs ; while their masters' and lords' children grow as roses on the mount of Sharon, and untoiling lilies in the vales of Lebanon ?

IV. And even if we admit that the lives at Penshurst, and by the woods of Muri, though thus to be kept separate, are yet, each in their manner, good, how far is the good of either of them dependent merely, as our reverend Novelist tells us, on " work " (with lance or willow wand) and " religion," or how far on the particular circumstances and landscape of Kent and Canton Berne,—while, in other parts of England and Switzerland, less favourably conditioned, the ministration of Mr. Septimus Hansard and Mr. Felix Neff will be always required, for the mitigation of the deeper human misery, —meditation on which is to make our sweet English ladies comfortable in nursing their cats ?

Leaving the first two of these questions to the reader's thoughts, I will answer the last two for him , —The extremities of human degradation are not owing to natural causes ; but to the habitual preying upon the labour of the poor by the luxury of the rich ; and they are only encouraged and increased by the local efforts of religious charity. The clergy can neither absolve the rich from their sins, for money—nor release them from their duties, for love. Their business is not to soothe, by their saintly and distant example, the soft moments of cat-nursing ; but sternly to forbid cat-nursing, till no child is left unnursed. And if this true discipline of the Church were carried out, and the larger body of less saintly clerical gentlemen, and *In*felix Neffs, who now dine with the rich and preach to the poor, were accustomed, on the contrary, to dine with the poor and preach to the rich ; though still the various passions and powers of the several orders would remain where the providence of Heaven placed them—and the useful reed and useless rose would still bind the wintry waters with their border, and brighten the May sunshine with their bloom,—for each, their happy being would be fulfilled in peace in the garden of the world ; and the glow, if not of immortal, at least of sacredly bequeathed, life, and endlessly cherished memory, abide even within its chambers of the tomb.

NOTES AND CORRESPONDENCE.

I.—I publish the following legal documents—the first articles for which I have to expend any of St. George's money,—intact : venturing not so much as the profanity of punctuation. The Memorandum is drawn up by one of our leading counsel, from my sketch of what I wanted. The points on which it may need some modification are referred to in my added notes ; and I now invite farther criticism or suggestion from the subscribers to the Fund.

"2, BOYD COURT, WALBROOK, LONDON, E C,
"*June 15th*, 1875.

"ST. GEORGE'S COMPANY.

"Dear Sir,—According to the promise in our Mr. Tarrant's letter of the 11th, we now beg to send you what Mr. Wm. Barber, after reading your sketch, has approved of as the written fundamental laws of the Company,—though we shall be quite prepared to find that some alterations in it are still necessary to express your views correctly.

"We are,
"Dear Sir,
"Yours faithfully,
"TARRANT & MACKRELL.

"Professor Ruskin, Corpus Ch. Coll., Oxford."

MEMORANDUM AND STATUTES OF THE COMPANY OF ST. GEORGE.

The Company is constituted with the object of determining and instituting in practice the wholesome laws of agricultural life and economy and of instructing the agricultural labourer in the science art and literature of good husbandry. (*a*)

With this object it is proposed to acquire by gift purchase or otherwise plots or tracts of land in different parts of the country which will be brought into such state of cultivation or left uncultivated or turned into waste or common land and applied to such purposes as having regard to the nature of the soil and other surrounding circumstances may in each case be thought to be most generally useful.

The members of the Company shall be styled Companions of the Company of St George (*b*) Any person may become a Companion by subscribing not less than £ in money to the funds of the Company or by making a gift to the Company of land not less than £ in value (*c*) and by having his name entered on the Roll of Companions with due solemnity.

The name of every Companion shall be entered on the Roll of Companions either by himself in the presence of two witnesses of full age who shall attest such entry or if the Companion shall so desire by the Master of the Company with the same formalities The Roll of Companions shall be kept in safe custody within the Walls of the College of Corpus Christi in Oxford or at such other safe and commodious place as the Companions shall from time to time direct.

Each Companion shall by virtue of the entry of his name on the Roll be deemed to have bound himself by a solemn vow and promise as strict as if the same had been ratified by oath to be true and loyal to the Company and to the best of his power and might so far as in him lies to forward and advance the objects and interests thereof and faithfully to keep and obey the statutes and rules thereof yet so nevertheless that he shall not be bound in any way to harass annoy injure or inconvenience his neighbour.

Chief among the Companions of the Company shall be the Master thereof who so long as he shall hold office shall have full and absolute power at his will and pleasure to make and repeal laws and byelaws (*d*) and in all respects to rule regulate manage and direct the affairs of the Company and receive apply and administer funds and subscriptions in aid of its objects and to purchase acquire cultivate manage lease sell or otherwise dispose of the estates and properties of the Company and generally direct and control the operations thereof.

The Master shall be elected and may from time to time and at any time be deposed by the votes of a majority in number of the Companions in General Meeting assembled but except in the event of his resignation or deposition shall hold office for life The first Master of the Company shall be John Ruskin who shall however (subject to re-election) only hold office until the first General Meeting of the Companions.

The Master shall render to each Companion and shall be at liberty if he shall so think fit to print for public circulation a monthly report and account of the operations and financial position of the Company.

No Master or other Companion of the Company shall either directly or indirectly receive any pay profit emolument or advantage whatsoever from out of by or by means of his office or position as a member of the Company

The practical supervision and management of the estates and properties of the Company shall subject to the direction and control of the Master be entrusted to and carried out by land agents tenants and labourers who shall be styled Retainers of the Company.

The name of each Retainer in the permanent employ of the Company shall be entered in a Register to be called the Roll of Retainers and to be kept at the same place as the Roll of Companions Such entry shall be made either by the Retainer himself in the presence of one witness of full age who shall attest the entry or if the Retainer shall so desire by the Master with the same formalities

No pecuniary liability shall attach to any Retainer of the Company by virtue of his position as such but each Retainer shall by virtue of the entry of his name on the Roll be deemed to have bound himself by a solemn vow and promise as strict as if the same had been ratified by oath to be true and loyal to the Company and faithfully to keep and obey the statutes and rules thereof and the orders and commands of the officers of the Company who from time to time may be set over him

Each land agent and labourer being a Retainer of the Company shall receive and be paid a fixed salary in return for his services and shall not by perquisites commissions or any other means whatever either directly or indirectly receive or acquire any pay profit emolument or advantages whatever other than such fixed salary from out of or by means of his office or position as a Retainer of the Company.

The rents and profits to be derived from the estates and properties of the Company shall be applied in the first instance in the development of the land (*e*) and the physical intellectual moral social and religious improvement of the residents thereon in such manner as the Master shall from time to time direct or approve and the surplus rents and profits if any shall be applied in reduction of the amount paid by the tenants in proportion to their respective skill and industry either by a gradual remission of rent towards the close of the tenancy or in such other way as may be thought best but in no case shall the Companions personally derive any rents or profits from the property of the Company.

All land and hereditaments for the time being belonging to the Company shall be conveyed to and vested in any two or more of the Companions whom the Master may from time to time select for the office as Trustees of the Company and shall be dealt with by them according to the directions of the Master. (*f*)

The property of the Company shall belong to the Companions in the shares and proportions in which they shall have respectively contributed or by succession or accruer become entitled to the same.

Each Companion shall be entitled by writing under his hand during his lifetime or by will or codicil to appoint one person as his successor in the Company and such person shall on entry of his name on the Roll of Companions in compliance with the formalities hereinbefore prescribed become a Companion of the Company and become entitled to the share of his apponitor in the property of the Company. (*g*)

Each Companion shall at any time be entitled to resign his position by giving to the Master a Notice under his hand of his desire and intention so to do.

If any Companion shall resign his position or die without having appointed a successor or if the person so appointed shall for   calendar months after the date when notice of such resignation shall have been received by the Master or after the date of such death as the case may be fail to have his name entered on the Roll of Companions in compliance with the formalities hereinbefore prescribed his share in the property of the Company shall forthwith become forfeited and shall accrue to the other Companions in the shares and proportions in which they shall *inter se* be for the time being entitled to the property of the Company. (*h*)

The Company may at any time be dissolved by the Votes of three-fourths of the Companions in General Meeting assembled and in the event of the Company being so dissolved or being dissolved by any other means not hereinbefore specially provided for the property of the Company shall subject to the debts liabilities and engagements thereof become divisible among the Companions for the time being in the shares and proportions in which they shall for the time being be entitled thereto yet so nevertheless that all leases agreements for leases and other tenancies for the time being subsisting on the property of the Company shall bind the persons among whom the property comprised therein shall so become divisible and shall continue as valid and effectual to all intents and purposes as if the Company had not been dissolved

NOTES ON THE ABOVE MEMORANDUM.

(*a*) This sentence must be changed into: "such science art and literature as are properly connected with husbandry."

(*b*) In my sketch, I wrote Companions of St. George. But as the existence of St George cannot be legally proved or assumed, the tautologically legal phrase must be permitted.

(*c*) This clause cannot stand. The admission into the Company must not be purchaseable; also many persons capable of giving enthusiastic and wise help as Companions, may be unable to subscribe money. Nothing can be required as a condition of entrance, except the consent of the Master, and signature promising obedience to the laws.

(*d*) This clause needs much development. For though the Master must be entirely unrestrained in action within the limits of the Laws of the Company, he must not change or add to them without some manner of consultation with the Companions. Even in now founding the Society, I do not venture to write a constitution for it without inviting the help of its existing members; and when once its main laws are agreed upon, they must be inabrogable without the same concurrence of the members which would be necessary to dissolve the Society altogether.

(*e*) To the development, and enlargement, of the Society's operations, also.

(*f*) I do not think the Master should have the power of choosing the Trustees I was obliged to do so, before any Society was in existence; but the Trustees have to verify the Master's accounts, and otherwise act as a check upon him. They must not, therefore, be chosen by him.

(*g*) A questionable clause, which I have not at present time to discuss.

(*h*) Partly the corollary of (*g*) The word 'forfeited' is morally, if not legally, objectionable. No idea of forfeiture ought to attach to the resolved surrender of transferable claim , or to the accidental inability to discover a fitting successor.

Reserving, therefore, the above clauses for future modification, the rest of the Memorandum fully expresses what seems to me desirable for the first basis of our constitution; and I shall be glad to hear whether any of the present subscribers to St George's Fund will join me on these conditions.

II.—I should willingly have printed the letter from which the following extracts are taken, (with comments,) as a 'Fors' by itself, but having other matters pressing, must content myself to leave it in the smaller print. The more interesting half of it is still reserved for next month.

"What long years have passed since my eyes first saw the calm sweet scene beyond Wakefield Bridge ! I was but a small creature then, and had never been far from my mother's door It was a memorable day for me when I toddled a full mile from the shady up-town street where we lived, past strange windows, over unfamiliar flags, to see the big weir and the chapel on the Bridge. Standing on tiptoe, I could just see over the parapet and look down-stream.

" That was my first peep into fair, green England, and destined never to be forgotten. The gray old chapel, the shining water below, the far-winding green banks spangled with buttercups, the grove-clad hills of Heath and Kirkthorpe,—all seemed to pass into my heart for ever.

"There was no railway then, only the Doncaster coach careering over the Bridge with a brave sound of horn; fields and farmsteads stood where the Kirkgate station is, where the twenty black throats of the foundry belch out flame and soot, there were only strawberry grounds and blossoming pear-orchards, among which the throstles and blackbirds were shouting for gladness.

"The chapel lay neglected in a nest of wild willows, and a peaceful cobbler dwelt in it. As I looked at it, Duke Richard and King Edward became living realities to me; the dry bones of Pinnock's Catechism started suddenly into life. That was the real old chapel of the fifteenth century. Some years after, they ousted the cobbler, pulled down the old stones, restored it, and opened it for ritualistic worship; but the cheap stonework has crumbled away again, and it now looks as ancient as in days of yore. Only, as I remember it, it had a white hoariness: the foundry smoke has made it black at the present day.

"Some of my companions had been farther out in the world than myself. They pointed out the dusky shape of Heath Hall, seen through the thinly-clad elm-trees, and told me how old Lady ——'s ghost still walked there on stormy nights. Beyond was Kirkthorpe, where the forlorn shapes of the exiled Spanish nuns had been seen flitting about their graves in the churchyard.

"There on the right was the tree-crowned mound of Sandal Castle, which Cromwell had blown down; the dry ditch was full of primroses, they told me; those woods bounded Crofton, famous for its cowslip fields; and in Heath wood you would see the ground white with snowdrops in March.

"I do not think that it is the partiality of a native that makes me think you could hardly find a fairer inland pastoral scene than the one I beheld from Wakefield Bridge the first time I stood there. On the chapel side there was the soft green English landscape, with woods and spires and halls, and the brown sails of boats silently moving among the flowery banks ; on the town side there were picturesque traffic and life ; the thundering weir, the wide still water beyond, the big dark-red granaries, with balconies and archways to the water, and the lofty white mills grinding out their cheering music.

"But there were no worse shapes than honest, dusty millers' men, and browned boatmen, decent people ; no open vileness and foul language were rampant in our quiet clean town in those days I can remember how clean the pavement used to look there, and at Doncaster. Both towns are incredibly dirty now. I cannot bear to look at the filthy beslavered causeway, in places where I remember to have never seen anything worse than the big round thunder-drops I used to watch with gleeful interest.

"In those days we were proud of the cleanness and sweet air and gentility of Wakefield. Leeds was then considered rather vulgar, as a factory town, and Bradford was obscure, rough and wild ; but Wakefield prided itself in refined living on moderate means, and cultured people of small income were fond of settling there.

"Market day used to be a great event for us all.

"I wish that you could have seen the handsome farmers' wives ranged round the church wal's, with their baskets of apricots and cream cheese, before reform came, and they swept away my dear old school-house of the seventeenth century, to make an ugly barren desert of a market ground. You might have seen, too, the pretty cottagers' daughters, with their bunches of lavender and baskets of fruit, or heaps of cowslips and primroses for the wine and vinegar Wakefield housewives prided themselves upon. On certain days they stood to be hired as maid-servants, and were prized in the country round as neat, clean, modest-spoken girls.

"I do not know where they are gone to now,—I suppose to the factories. Anyhow, Wakefield ladies cry out that they must get servants from London, and Stafford, and Wales. So class gets parted from class.

"Things were different then. Well-to-do ladies prided themselves on doing their marketing in person, and kindly feeling and acquaintanceship sprang up between town and country folk. My Wakefield friends nowadays laugh at the idea of going to market. They order everything through the cook, and hardly know their own tradespeople by sight. We used to get delicious butter at tenpence a pound, and such curds and cream-cheese as I never taste now. 'Cook' brings in indifferent butter mostly, at near two shillings.

"As for the farmers' wives, they would not like to be seen with a butter-basket. They mostly send the dairy produce off by rail to people whom they never see, and thus class is more sundered from class every day, even by the very facilities that railways afford. I can remember that the townspeople had simple merry-makings and neighbourly ways that this generation would scorn. Many a pleasant walk we had to the farms and halls that belted the old town, and boating parties on the Calder, and tea-drinkings and dances—mostly extempore,—in the easy fashion of Vicar Primrose's days.

"But pleasure must be sought farther off now. Our young folks go to London or Paris for their recreation. People seem to have no leisure for being neighbourly, or to get settled in their houses. They seem to be all expecting to make a heap of money, and to be much grander presently, and finally to live in halls and villas, and look down on their early friends.

"But I am sorry for the young people. They run through everything so soon, and have nothing left to hope for or dream of in a few years. They are better dressed than we were, and have more accomplishments; but I cannot help thinking that we young folks were happier in the old times, though shillings were not half so plentiful, and we had only two frocks a year.

"Tradespeople were different, too, in old Wakefield.

"They expected to live with us all their lives; they had high notions of honour as tradesmen, and they and their customers respected each other.

"They prided themselves on the 'wear' of their goods. If they had passed upon the housewives a piece of sized calico or shoddy flannel, they would have heard of it for years after.

"Now the richer ladies go to Leeds or Manchester to make purchases, the town tradesmen are soured and jealous. They put up big plate-glass fronts, and send out flaming bills; but one does not know where to get a piece of sound calico or stout linen, well spun and well woven.

"Give me back our dingy old shops where everything was genuine, instead of these glass palaces where we often get pins without points, needles without eyes, and sewing thread sixty yards to the hundred—which I actually heard a young Quaker defend the other day as an allowable trade practice."

III.—I venture to print the following sentences from "a poor mother's" letter, that my reply may be more generally intelligible. I wish I could say, useful; but the want of an art-grammar is every day becoming more felt:—

"I am rather ashamed to tell you how young he is (not quite eleven), fearing you will say I have troubled you idly; but I was sincerely anxious to know your views on the training of a boy for some definite sort of art-work, and I have always fancied such training ought to begin very early,—[yes, assuredly,]—also, there are reasons why we must decide early in what direction we shall look out for employment for him."

(I never would advise any parents to look for employment in art as a means of their children's support. It is only when the natural bias is quite uncontrollable, that future eminence, and comfort of material circumstances, can be looked for. And when it is uncontrollable, it ceases to be a question whether we should control it. We have only to guide it.)

"But I seem to dread the results of letting him run idle until he is fourteen or fifteen years old—[most wisely]—and a poor and busy mother like me has not time to superintend the employment of a boy as a richer one might. This makes me long to put him to work under a master early. As he does so little at book-learning, would the practical learning of stone cutting under the village stonemason (a good man) be likely to lead to anything further?"

I do not know, but it would be of the greatest service to the boy meanwhile. Let him learn good joiners' work also, and to plough, with time allowed him for drawing. I feel more and more the need of a useful grammar of art for young people, and simple elementary teaching in public schools. I have always hoped to remedy this want, but have been hindered hitherto

FORS CLAVIGERA.

LETTER THE 56th.

TIME-HONOURED LANCASTER.

I BELIEVE my readers will scarcely thank me for printing, this month, instead of the continuation of the letter
from Wakefield, a theological essay by Mr. Lyttel. But
it is my first business, in Fors, to be just,—and only
my second or third to be entertaining; so that any
person who conceives himself to have been misrepresented must always have my types at his command.
On the other side, I must point out, before entering
further into controversy of any kind, the constant
habit in my antagonists of misrepresenting *me*. For
instance ; in an article forwarded to me from a local
paper, urging what it can in defence of the arrangements noticed by me as offensive, at Kirby Lonsdale
and Clapham, I find this sentence :

" The squire's house does not escape, though one can
see no reason for the remark unless it be that Mr.
Ruskin dislikes lords, squires, and clergymen."

Now I have good reason for supposing this article

to have been written by a gentleman ;—and even an amiable gentleman,—who, feeling himself hurt, and not at all wishing to hurt anybody, very naturally cries out : and thinks it monstrous in me to hurt *him ;* or his own pet lord, or squire But he never thinks what wrong there may be in printing his own momentary impression of the character of a man who has been thirty years before the public, without taking the smallest pains to ascertain whether his notion be true or false.

It happens, by Fors' appointment, that the piece of my early life which I have already written for this month's letter, sufficiently answers the imputation of my dislike to lords and squires. But I will preface it, in order to illustrate my dislike of clergymen, by a later bit of biography ; which, at the rate of my present progress in giving account of myself, I should otherwise, as nearly as I can calculate, reach only about the year 1975.

Last summer, in Rome, I lodged at the Hotel de Russie ; and, in the archway of the courtyard of that mansion, waited usually, in the mornings, a Capuchin friar, begging for his monastery.

Now, though I greatly object to any clergyman's coming and taking me by the throat, and saying ' Pay me that thou owest,' I never pass a begging friar without giving him sixpence, or the equivalent fivepence of foreign coin ;—extending the charity even occasionally as far as tenpence, if no fivepenny-bit chance to be in my purse. And this particular begging friar having a

gentle face, and a long white beard, and a beautiful
cloak, like a blanket, and being altogether the plea-
santest sight, next to Sandro Botticelli's Zipporah, I
was like to see in Rome in the course of the day, I
always gave him the extra fivepence for looking so
nice, which generosity so worked on his mind,—(the
more usual English religious sentiment in Rome ex-
pending itself rather in buying poetical pictures of
monks than in filling their bellies)—that, after some
six or seven doles of tenpences, he must needs take
my hand one day, and try to kiss it. Which being
only just able to prevent, I took him round the neck
and kissed his lips instead : and this, it seems, was
more to him than the tenpences, for, next day, he
brought me a little reliquary, with a certificated fibre
in it of St Francis' cloak, (the hair one, now pre-
served at Assisi), and when afterwards I showed my
friend Fra Antonio, the Assisi sacristan, what I had
got, it was a pleasure to see him open his eyes, wider
than Monsieur the Syndic at Hansli's fifty thousand
crowns. He thought I must have come by it dis-
honestly, but not I, a whit,—for I most carefully
explained to the Capuchin, when he brought it me,
that I was more a Turk than a Catholic ;—but he said
I might keep the reliquary, for all that.

Contenting myself, for the moment, with this illustration of my present dislike of clergymen, I return to
earlier days.

But for the reader's better understanding of such further progress of my poor little life as I may trespass on his patience in describing, it is now needful that I give some account of my father's mercantile position in London.

The firm of which he was head partner may be yet remembered by some of the older city houses, as carrying on their business in a small counting-house on the first floor of narrow premises, in as narrow a thoroughfare of East London,—Billiter Street, the principal traverse from Leadenhall Street into Fenchurch Street.

The names of the three partners were given in full on their brass plate under the counting-house bell,— Ruskin, Telford, and Domecq.

Mr. Domecq's name should have been the first, by rights, for my father and Mr. Telford were only his agents. He was the sole proprietor of the estate which was the main capital of the firm,—the vineyard of Macharnudo, the most precious hillside, for growth of white wine, in the Spanish peninsula. The quality of the Macharnudo vintage essentially fixed the standard of Xeres 'sack,' or 'dry'—secco— sherris, or sherry, from the days of Henry the Fifth to our own ;—the unalterable and unrivalled chalk-marl of it putting a strength into the grape which age can only enrich and darken,—never impair.

Mr. Peter Domecq was, I believe, Spanish born ; and partly French, partly English bred : a man of strictest honour, and kindly disposition ; how descended, I do not know ; how he became possessor of his vineyard, I do not know , what position he held, when young, in the firm of Gordon, Murphy, and Company, I do not know , but in their house he watched their head-clerk, my father, during his nine years of duty, and when the house broke up, asked him to be his own agent in England. My father saw that he could fully trust Mr Domecq's honour, and feeling ;—but not so fully either his sense, or his industry. and insisted, though taking only his agent's commission, on being both nominally, and practically, the head-partner of the firm.

Mr. Domecq lived chiefly in Paris ; rarely visiting his Spanish estate, but having perfect knowledge of the proper process of its cultivation, and authority over its labourers almost like a chief's over his clan. He kept the wines at the highest possible standard , and allowed my father to manage all matters concerning their sale, as he thought best. The second partner, Mr Henry Telford, brought into the business what capital was necessary for its London branch. The premises in Billiter Street belonged to him , and he had a pleasant country home at Widmore, near Bromley , a quite far-away Kentish village in those days.

He was a perfect type of an English country gentle-man of moderate fortune ,—unmarried, living with three unmarried sisters—who, in the refinement of their highly educated, unpretending, benevolent, and felicitous lives, remain in my memory more like the figures in a beautiful story than realities.   Neither in story, nor in reality, have I ever again heard of, or seen, anything like Mr. Henry Telford ;—so gentle, so humble, so affectionate, so clear in common sense, so fond of horses,—and so entirely incapable of doing, thinking, or saying, anything that had the slightest taint in it of the racecourse or the stable.

Yet I believe he never missed any great race ; passed the greater part of his life on horseback ; and hunted during the whole Leicestershire season ;—but never made a bet, never had a serious fall, and never hurt a horse.   Between him and my father there was absolute confidence, and the utmost friendship that could exist without community of pursuit.   My father was greatly proud of Mr. Telford's standing among the country gentlemen ; and Mr. Telford was affectionately respectful to my father's steady industry and infallible commercial instinct.   Mr. Telford's actual part in the conduct of the business was limited to attendance in the counting-house during two months at Midsummer, when my father took his holiday, and sometimes for a month at the beginning of the year, when he travelled for orders.   At these times Mr. Telford rode into London daily from Widmore, signed what letters and bills needed signature, read the papers, and rode home again : any matters needing deliberation were referred to my father, or awaited his return. All the family at Widmore would have been limitlessly kind to my mother and me, if they had been permitted any opportunity ; but my mother always felt, in cultivated society,—and was too proud to feel with patience,—the defects of her own early education, and therefore (which was the true and fatal sign of such defect) never familiarly visited any one whom she did not feel to be, in some sort, her inferior.

·Nevertheless, Mr. Telford had a singularly important influence in my education. By, I believe, his sister's advice, he gave me, as soon as it was published, the illustrated edition of Rogers' ' Italy.' This book was the first means I had of looking carefully at Turner's work : and I might, not without some appearance of reason, attribute to the gift the entire direction of my life's energies. But it is the great error of thoughtless bio-graphers to attribute to the accident which introduces some new phase of character, all the circumstances of character which gave the accident importance. The essential point to be noted, and accounted for, was that I could understand Turner's work when I saw it ; not by what chance or in what year it was first seen.

Poor Mr. Telford, nevertheless, was always held by papa and mamma primarily responsible for my Turner insanities.

In a more direct, though less intended way, his help to me was important. For, before my father thought it right to hire a carriage for the above mentioned

Midsummer holiday, Mr. Telford always lent us his own travelling chariot.

Now the old English chariot is the most luxurious of travelling carriages, for two persons, or even for two persons and so much of third personage as I possessed at three years old. The one in question was hung high, so that we could see well over stone dykes and average hedges out of it ; such elevation being attained by the old-fashioned folding-steps, with a lovely padded cushion fitting into the recess of the door,—steps which it was one of my chief travelling delights to see the hostlers fold up and down ; though my delight was painfully alloyed by envious ambition to be allowed to do it myself .—but I never was,—lest I should pinch my fingers.

The 'dickey,'—(to think that I should never till this moment have asked myself the derivation of that word, and now be unable to get at it !)—being, typically, that commanding seat in her Majesty's mail, occupied by the Guard ; and classical, even in modern literature, as the scene of Mr Bob Sawyer's arrangements with Sam,—was thrown far back in Mr. Telford's chariot, so as to give perfectly comfortable 100m for the legs (if one chose to travel outside on fine days), and to afford beneath it spacious area to the boot, a storehouse of rearward miscellaneous luggage. Over which—with all the rest of forward and superficial luggage—my nurse Anne presided, both as guard and packer; unrivalled, she, in the flatness and precision of her in-laying of dresses, as in turning of pancakes; the fine precision, observe, meaning also the easy wit and invention of her art; for, no more in packing a trunk than commanding a campaign, is precision possible without foresight.

Posting, in those days, being universal, so that at the leading inns in every country town, the cry " Horses out !" down the yard, as one drove up, was answered, often instantly, always within five minutes, by the merry trot through the archway of the booted and bright-jacketed rider, with his caparisoned pair,—there was no driver's seat in front: and the four large, admirably fitting and sliding windows, admitting no drop of rain when they were up, and never sticking as they were let down, formed one large moving oriel, out of which one saw the country round, to the full half of the horizon. My own prospect was more extended still, for my seat was the little box containing my clothes, strongly made, with a cushion on one end of it; set upright in front (and well forward), between my father and mother. I was thus not the least in their way, and my horizon of sight the widest possible. When no object of particular interest presented itself, I trotted, keeping time with the postboy—on my trunk cushion for a saddle, and whipped my father's legs for horses; at first theoretically only, with dexterous motion of wrist; but ultimately in a quite practical and efficient manner, my father having presented me with a silver-mounted postillion's whip.

The Midsummer holiday, for better enjoyment of which Mr. Telford provided us with these luxuries, began usually on the fifteenth of May, or thereabouts; —my father's birthday was the tenth; on that day I was always allowed to gather the gooseberries for his first gooseberry pie of the year, from the tree between the buttresses on the north wall of the Herne Hill garden; so that we could not leave before that *festa*. The holiday itself consisted in a tour for orders through half the English counties; and a visit (if the counties lay northward) to my aunt in Scotland.

The mode of journeying was as fixed as that of our home life. We went from forty to fifty miles a day, starting always early enough in the morning to arrive comfortably to four-o'clock dinner. Generally, therefore, getting off at six o'clock, a stage or two were done before breakfast, with the dew on the grass, and first scent from the hawthorns: if in the course of the mid-day drive there were any gentleman's house to be seen, —or, better still, a lord's—or best of all, a duke's,—my father baited the horses, and took my mother and me reverently through the state rooms; always speaking a little under our breath to the housekeeper, major domo, or other authority in charge; and gleaning worship-fully what fragmentary illustrations of the history and domestic ways of the family might fall from their lips.

My father had a quite infallible natural judgment in painting ; and though it had never been cultivated so as to enable him to understand the Italian schools, his sense of the power of the nobler masters in northern work was as true and passionate as the most accomplished artist's. He never, when I was old enough to care for what he himself delighted in, allowed me to look for an instant at a bad picture ; and if there were a Reynolds, Velasquez, Vandyck, or Rembrandt in the rooms, he would pay the surliest housekeepers into patience until we had seen it to heart's content ; if none of these, I was allowed to look at Guido, Carlo Dolce—or the more skilful masters of the Dutch school —Cuyp, Teniers, Hobbima, Wouvermans ; but never at any second-rate or doubtful examples.

I wonder how many of the lower middle class are now capable of going through a nobleman's house, with judgment of this kind ; and yet with entirely unenvious and reverent delight in the splendour of the abode of the supreme and beneficent being who allows them thus to enter his paradise ?

If there were no nobleman's house to be seen, there was certainly, in the course of the day's journey, some ruined castle or abbey ; some celebrated village church, or stately cathedral. We had always unstinted time for these ; and if I was at disadvantage because neither my father nor mother could tell me enough history to make the buildings authoritatively interesting, I had at least leisure and liberty to animate them with romance in my own fashion.

I am speaking, however, now, of matters relating to a more advanced age than that to which I have yet brought myself :—age in which all these sights were only a pleasant amazement to me, and panoramic apocalypse of a lovely world.

Up to that age, at least, I cannot but hope that my readers will agree with me in thinking the tenour of my life happy, and the modes of my education, on the whole, salutary.

Admitting them to have been so, I would now question farther ; and, I imagine, such question cannot but occur to my readers' minds, also,—how far education, and felicities, of the same kind, may be attainable for young people in general.

Let us consider, then, how many conditions must meet ; and how much labour must have been gone through, both by servile and noble persons, before this little jaunty figure, seated on its box of clothes, can trot through its peaceful day of mental development.

I. A certain number of labourers in Spain, living on dry bread and onions, must have pruned and trodden grapes ;—cask-makers, cellarmen, and other functionaries attending on them.

II. Rough sailors must have brought the wine into the London Docks.

III. My father and his clerks must have done a great

deal of arithmetical and epistolary work, before my father could have profit enough from the wine to pay for our horses, and our dinner.

IV. The tailor must have given his life to the dull business of making clothes—the wheelwright and carriage-maker to their woodwork—the smith to his buckles and springs—the postillion to his riding—the horse-breeder and breaker to the cattle in his field and stable,—before I could make progress in this pleasant manner, even for a single stage.

V. Sundry English Kings and Barons must have passed their lives in military exercises, and gone to their deaths in military practices, to provide me with my forenoons' entertainments in ruined castles ; or founded the great families whose servants were to be my hosts.

VI. Vandyck and Velasquez, and many a painter before them, must have spent their lives in learning and practising their laborious businesses.

VII. Various monks and abbots must have passed their lives in pain, with fasting and prayer ; and a large company of stonemasons occupied themselves in their continual service, in order to provide me, in defect of castles and noblemen's seats, with amusement in the way of abbeys and cathedrals.

How far, then, it remains to be asked, supposing my education in any wise exemplary, can all these advantages be supplied by the modern school board, to every little boy born in the prosperous England of this day? And much more in that glorious England of the future; in which there will be no abbeys, (all having been shaken down, as my own sweet Furness is fast being, by the luggage trains); no castles, except such as may have been spared to be turned into gaols, like that of "time-honoured Lancaster," also in my own neighbourhood; no parks, because Lord Derby's patent steam agriculture will have cut down all the trees; no lords, nor dukes, because modern civilization won't be Lorded over, nor Led anywhere; no gentlemen's seats, except in the Kirby Lonsdale style; and no roads anywhere, except trams and rails?

Before, however, entering into debate as to the methods of education to be adopted in these coming times, let me examine a little, in next letter, with help from my readers of aristocratic tendencies, what the real product of this olden method of education was intended to be; and whether it was worth the cost.

For the impression on the aristocratic mind of the day was always (especially supposing I had been a squire's or a lord's son, instead of a merchant's) that such little jaunty figure, trotting in its easy chariot, was, as it were, a living diamond, without which the watch of the world could not possibly go; or even, that the diminutive darling was a kind of Almighty Providence in its first breeches, by whose tiny hands and infant fiat the blessings of food and raiment were continually provided for God's Spanish labourers in His' literal vineyard; for God's English sailors, seeing His wonders in the deep , for God's tailors' men, sitting in attitude of Chinese Josh for ever; for the divinely appointed wheelwrights, carpenters, horses and riders, hostlers and Gaius-mine-hosts, necessary to my triumphal progress ; and for my nurse behind in the dickey. And it never once entered the head of any aristocratic person,—nor would ever have entered mine, I suppose, unless I had " the most analytical mind in Europe," —that in verity it was not I who fed my nurse, but my nurse me ; and that a great part of the world had been literally put behind me as a dickey,— and all the aforesaid inhabitants of it, somehow, appointed to be nothing but my nurses ; the beautiful product intended, by papa and mamma, being—a Bishop, who should graciously overlook these tribes of inferior beings, and instruct their ignorance in the way of their souls' salvation.

As the master of the St. George's Company, I request their permission to convey their thanks to Mr Plimsoll, for his Christian, knightly, and valiant stand, made against the recreant English Commons, on Thursday, 22nd July, 1875.

NOTES AND CORRESPONDENCE.

I have thankfully received this month, from the first donor of land to the St. George's Company, Mrs. Talbot, £11 os. 4d, rent of cottages on said land, at Barmouth, North Wales, and I have become responsible, as the Master of the Company, for rent or purchase of a room at Sheffield, in which I propose to place some books and minerals, as the germ of a museum arranged first for workers in iron, and extended into illustration of the natural history of the neighbourhood of Sheffield, and more especially of the geology and flora of Derbyshire The following letter respecting the neighbouring town of Leeds will be found interesting in connection with this first opening of St. George's work :—

"LEEDS, *June* 21*st*, 1875

"DEAR SIR,—Being more or less intimately mixed up with the young of the working classes, in night schools and similar works, I am anxious to know what I can do to counteract two or three growths, which seem likely to be productive of very disastrous results, in the young men from seventeen to twenty-five, who are many of them earning from 20s. to 35s. per week,—the almost morbid craving for drink, and the excitement which is to be found in modern French dramas of very questionable morality, concert halls and singing rooms, where appeal is principally made to their animal passions and lusts— whose chief notion of enjoyment seems to be in getting drunk 'I hen the young men of similar ages, and earning from 14s. to

20s., who are in a chronic state of unrest, ever eager for novelty and sensationalism, though not quite so much given to drink as the men, yet treading a similar course. They have no pleasure in going to the country, to see flowers, birds, and fish, or to the seaside to see the sea ; if there be no fireworks, no prize band, no dancing on the green, or something of the sort, they will not attempt to go. Now, where is all this to end ? Nature has no charms for them ; music little attraction, except in the form of *dance,* pictures nothing : what remains ? And yet something should, and must be done, and that speedily, —otherwise what will become of the poor things ?

"Then, in your 'Elements of Drawing,' you lay down certain books to be studied, etc.

"Now, suppose a woman or man has been brought up to have a kind of contempt for 'Grimm's Goblins,' 'Arabian Nights,' etc , as childish and frivolous,—and on account of the Calvinistic tendency of relatives, has been precluded from reading *books*,—how should a healthy tendency be brought about? For the mind is not a blank, to receive impressions like a child, but has all sorts of preconceived notions and prejudices in the way,—Shakspeare looked upon as immoral, or childish, and the rest treated in an equally cavalier manner by people who probably never looked inside the books."

I should like to answer the above letter at some length ; but have, to-day, no time. The sum of answer is—Nothing *can* be done, but what I am trying to form this St George's Company to do.

For the sake of my female, and theological, readers, I print the next following letter :—

"THE PARSONAGE, WERRINGTON, PETERBOROUGH, *July* 7, 1875

"MY DEAR SIR,—In your comment on a former letter of mine you acknowledged (*a*) that the Gospel which I endeavour to preach—Be persuaded by the Lord Jesus Christ, let His life rule your lives—is eternally true and salutary, but, because I have joined with you in condemning a doctrine opposed to this, you have rather hastily assumed (*b*) that I have 'eagerly repudiated the doctrine of the Eleventh Article of the Church of England,' to which Article I have given, and not withdrawn, my public assent.

" You have of course taken for granted (*c*) that the Eleventh Article teaches the 'pleasant and supremely false gospel'—Let His life be instead of your lives ; you may be saved by faith without righteousness. But does it ?

" The Article says ·

" ' *We are accounted righteous before God, only for the merit of our Lord and Saviour Jesus Christ, by Faith, and not for our own works or deservings . Wherefore, that we are justified by Faith only is a most wholesome doctrine, and very full of comfort, as more largely is expressed in the Homily of Justification* '

" This teaches, in simple English enough, that there is but one righteousness in God's sight—the righteousness of Christ, and that this righteousness becomes ours by faith . so that faith alone sets us right with God.

" Before the court of public opinion (*d*) men may be accounted righteous for 'works and deservings' of their own, like those which were so eminently satisfactory to the Pharisee who went up to the Temple to pray ; but before God, whose judgments are true, the only merit for which any man is accounted righteous is the merit of Jesus Christ. The Publican 'went down to his house justified' because of that faith in God which led him to hunger and thirst after a righteousness higher than his own, and in due time to be filled with it.

" A man is 'justified by faith only' because by faith only he accepts the righteousness of Christ, not instead of, but *for*, (*e*) his own. He is therefore accounted righteous before God because, in His sight, who sees the end from the beginning, he *is* righteous.

"But, while the righteousness is verily his own, he confesses that, in the deepest sense, it is not his own, for the source and efficient cause of it is Christ—the merit is His.

"From all this it will appear that what I repudiate is not the Eleventh Article, but the eternally false and damnatory doctrine which has seemed to you to be set forth therein.

"I cannot think that the Article was intended to teach that a man can be accounted righteous before God without righteousness—that faith will serve as a substitute for it, since I read in the Homily in which the doctrine of the Article is 'more largely expressed' such words as the following :

"'*This true Christian faith neither any devil hath, nor yet any man who, in the outward profession of his mouth, and his outward receiving of the Sacraments, in coming to the Church, and in all other outward appearances, seemeth to be a Christian man, and yet in his living and deeds sheweth the contrary.*'

"I am, my dear Sir,

"Very faithfully yours,

"JOHN RUSKIN, Esq.   "EDWARD Z. LYTTEL."

(*a*) My correspondent cannot quit himself of the idea that I am his antagonist. If he preaches what is true, I say so—if what is false, I say so. I congratulate him in the one case, and am sorry for him in the other; but have nothing to 'acknowledge' in either case.

(*b*) and (*c*) "You have rather hastily assumed." "You have of course taken for granted." Compare Mr. Headlam's "I fancy that, on consideration, you would like to withdraw," p. 176. These clerical gentlemen, who habitually and necessarily write *without* consideration, and as habitually and necessarily 'take for granted' the entire grounds of their profession, are quaintly unable to enter into the mind of a man who for twenty years has not written a word without testing it syllable by syllable ; nor taken for granted one principle or fact, in art, science, or history,—having somewhat wide work in all three. ¶

In the present case, I am very sorry to have to tell my correspondent that the last thing I should 'take for granted' would be the completeness and accuracy of his own account of himself. What his words actually mean, my twenty years' study of English enables me to tell him with authority ;—but what he means by them *he* only knows !

(*d*) Who is talking of public opinion ? Does my correspondent suppose that in any—even among the rudest or most ignorant— debates on this subject, 'righteousness' was ever supposed to mean worldly credit ? The question is, was, and will be—simply how men escape being damned—if they do.

(*e*) It is no part of my duty in Fors to occupy myself in exposing the verbal, or probing the mental, sophistries by which the aerial ingenuity of divines may guide itself in gossamer over the inconveniently furrowed ground of religious dogma. There are briefly two, and two only, forms of possible Christian, Pagan, or any other gospel, or 'good message'. one, that men are saved by themselves doing what is right, and the other that they are saved by believing that somebody else did right instead of them. The first of these Gospels is eternally true, and holy, the other eternally false, damnable, and damning. Which of them Mr Lyttel preaches, matters much to himself and his parishioners ; but, to the world, considerably less than he seems to suppose. That the Eleventh Article of the Church of England teaches the second, "in very simple English," is as certain as Johnson's dictionary can make it : and that it (the said sweet message) is currently preached with unction, and received with gladness, over the whole of England, and of Protestant France, Switzerland, and Italy, by the most active and influential members of the Protestant church, I take upon me to assert, on the grounds of an experience gained, (while Mr. Lyttel was, by his own account, "occupied from day to day in stuffy rooms among ignorant and immoral people") by the carefullest study of the best Protestant divines, and the hearing of sermons by the most eloquent pastors, in every important city of evangelical Europe.   Finally, I must beg Mr. Lyttel to observe that I only printed his first letter because it expressed some degree of doubt, and discomfort, which I hoped to relieve. His succeeding letters show him, on the contrary, to be supremely confident and comfortable,—in which enviable state I must here take leave of him.   For my challenge (as yet unanswered) was to his Bishop, and not to the clergy of the diocese; nor, if it had been, has Mr. Lyttel offered any evidence that he is their accredited champion.

I think I do Mr. Lyttel more justice by printing his kind and graceful last words on my impatient comments, than I should by disarranging my types and altering my letter; which, indeed, I have no time to do.

"My dear Sir,—It is both my fault and misfortune that you have taken parts of my letters 'clean from the purpose of the words themselves;' and I write at once in hope that you may be able to erase two unserviceable paragraphs, which my want of simple English, or some other misdirection, has produced.

"1. If you will allow me to substitute the word 'said' for 'acknowledged' in my letter, it will save paragraph (*a*).

"2. Then I should like to assure you that the feeling which called forth my first letter also produced the rest, and no one who knows me well would think of attributing to me 'supreme confidence and comfort.' Moreover, I have throughout spoken for myself alone, and have not for one moment pretended to be the 'accredited champion' of any one. So that if you can spare the latter part of paragraph (*e*), beginning with 'Finally,' I think neither you nor I would lose anything by the omission.

"Other parts of your comment I am sorry for, but I have not the same reason to object to them as I have to those I have specified.

"I am most faithfully yours,

"EDWARD Z. LYTTEL."

Some slips of newspaper have been forwarded to me, containing an abstract of a sermon by the Bishop of Manchester, in which some reference was made to 'Fors'. but of course I cannot take any notice of expressions thus accidentally conveyed to me, and probably reported with inaccuracy. The postscript to the following interesting letter of Mr. Sillar's may perhaps receive from the Bishop of Manchester more honourable attention —

"KINGSWOOD LODGE, LEE GREEN, S E., 13*th* *January*, 1875.

"MY DEAR MR. RUSKIN,—I have great sympathy with your lady correspondent, and, for the life of me, I cannot tell what you would have me to do I am not a landed proprietor, nor a country gentleman, though I am the son of one, a retired physician, and brought up in the blessed green fields, and among streams that were as clear as crystal, and full of trout; but coal-pits appeared on the horizon, and gradually drove us out. I well remember the first vile red shaft that appeared within about a mile of our windows, and how the beastly smoke reconciled my mother to leave one of the loveliest country seats in Lancashire, which she had adorned with roses and laurels, I was going to say with her own hands, and I am not sure that it would be wrong to say so, for she saw every one (and the grounds were seven or eight acres in extent) planted with her own eyes, and superintended the doing of it.

"Living there in the country, and under a tutor, my education has not been that of an ordinary country gentle-man; I early learned to work with my hands as well as with my head, and though I must confess that personally I never had much taste for gardening, I had plenty of work to do in the open air. You tell me our education has to begin—yours as well as mine; and expect me to say that I cannot make a brick or a tile, or build a rude dwelling. Singularly enough, I helped to do so when a boy, and it will be long before any of us forget the miniature cottage we built, and thatched, complete, with window, door, and fireplace, and with a cellar moreover, with wine of our own making, and beer of our own brewing made from treacle; for we did everything ourselves, even to grooming our own ponies.

"In later life, my lot was cast in Liverpool, and after six or seven years spent in China, where I have seen the horrors of war, and where a cannon shot came through our roof, as we sat at tiffin, I found myself in London.

"My old business of a merchant I cannot carry on; though I have capital sufficient for fair trade, I cannot carry it on in the face of the fierce competition by unprincipled men on borrowed money:

'Where man competes with man like foe with foe,
   Till death that thins them scarce seem public woe'—

my business as a banker and bullion broker is sealed to me as iniquitous.

"At present, therefore, I am free to act; I fret because I

am in a state of inactivity I feel that I have health and strength, and that in a thousand ways I could be useful, but wherever I turn I am stopped. I am a good rough joiner ; I can do small work in iron and brass ; and I am a good practical chemist my laboratory was recommended as an example of how a laboratory should be kept, by the editor of the 'Chemical News' and an F R S.

"Now allow me to ask you seriously, would you have me to go out alone into the wilderness, and live like a Robinson Crusoe till I see an opening? The point is, the opening might come directly, or it might not come for years, and meantime I am standing in the market-place, such as it is (why is there not a real one?) It is this uncertainty that distresses me, for I must work for my living, and my substance is gradually melting away.

" Believe me, my dear Mr. Ruskin, ever yours affectionately,
" ROB. G. SILLAR.

" P.S — I am glad to see you have challenged Dr. Fraser I had a correspondence with him some years ago. I saw in one of Carlyle's works, that I might do some good, if I had two fingers and a pen , so, after getting no answer from my own clergyman, and the secretary of the Society for Promoting Christian Knowledge, relative to the leaving out of a verse in the fifteenth Psalm in our collection, I appealed to the bishop. He was very polite, and corresponded with me till he felt it dangerous to go on, and then informed me that he really had no time to examine into the lawfulness of interest

" I confess I don't like an officer who has no time to read and examine his standing orders, but who yet retains the command of the regiment ; so as you told me in 'Sheepfolds'

* I am reprinting this pamphlet word for word as it was first issued from the press Mr Allen will have it ready for distribution by the first of September

that in our army the King was beside every one of us to appeal to in case of doubt, I ended by telling his lordship, as he had no time to hear me, I must leave it in other hands, *videat Altissimus,* and our correspondence closed."

FORS CLAVIGERA.

[*I am honoured in the charge given me, without dissent, by the present members of the St. George's Company, to convey their thanks to* MR. SAMUEL PLIMSOLL, *in the terms stated at the close of my last letter.*]

LETTER THE 57th.

MICHAL'S SCORN.

I HAVE received, from the author, M. Emile de Lavelaye, his pamphlet,—" Protestantism and Catholicism in their bearing upon the Liberty and Prosperity of Nations, with an introductory Letter by Mr. Gladstone." I do not know why M. de Lavelaye sent me this pamphlet. I thank him for the courtesy; but he has evidently read none of my books, or must have been aware that he could not have written anything more contrary to the positions which I am politically maintaining. On the other hand, I have read none of *his* books, and I gather from passages in his pamphlet that there may be much in them to which I should be able to express entire adhesion.

But of the pamphlet in question, and its preface, he

will, I trust, pardon my speaking in the same frank terms which I should have used had it accidentally come under my notice, instead of by the author's gift. The pamphlet is especially displeasing to me, because it speaks of 'Liberty' under the common assumption of its desirableness ; whereas my own teaching has been, and is, that Liberty, whether in the body, soul, or political estate of men, is only another word for Death, and the final issue of Death, putrefaction · the body, spirit, and political estate being alike healthy only by their bonds and laws ; and by Liberty being instantly disengaged into mephitic vapour.

But the matter of this pamphlet, no less than the assumption it is based on, is hateful to me ; reviving, as it does, the miserable question of the schism between Catholic and Protestant, which is entirely ridiculous and immaterial ; and taking no note whatever of the true and eternal schism, cloven by the very sword of Michael, between him that serveth God, and him that serveth Him not.

*   *   *   *   *

(The passage now and henceforward omitted in this place, contained an attack on Mr. Gladstone written under a complete misconception of his character. See, for explanation of it, the beginning of the third letter in the second series of Fors. The blank space is left partly in order not to confuse the Index references, partly in due memorial of rash judgment.)

*　　*　　*　　*　　*

The fact being that I am, at this central time of my life's work, at pause because I cannot set down any form of religious creed so simple, but that the requirement of its faithful signature by persons desiring to become Companions of St. George, would exclude some of the noblest champions of justice and charity now labouring for men ; while, on the other hand, I cannot set down the first principles of children's noble education without finding myself in collision with an almost resistless infidel mob, which is incapable of conceiving—how much less of obeying—the first laws of human decency, order, and honour. So that indeed I am fain to ask, with my Leeds correspondent, in last Fors, page 234, what is to be done for young folks to whom "music has little attraction, except in the form of dance, and pictures are nothing" ?

With her pardon, pictures are much to this class of young people. The woodcuts of halfpenny novels representing scenes of fashionable life,—those representing men murdering their wives, in the 'Police News,'— and, finally, those which are to be bought only in the back-shop,—have enormous educational influence on the

young British public : which its clergymen, alike ignorant
of human nature and human art, think to counteract
—by decorating their own churches, forsooth,—and by
coloured prints of the story of Joseph ; while the lower
tribes of them—Moodys and Sankeys—think to turn
modern musical taste to account by fitting negro
melodies to hymns.

And yet, my correspondent may be thankful that
some remnant of delight *is* still taken in dance-music.
It is the last protest of the human spirit, in the poor
fallen creatures, against the reign of the absolute Devil,
Pandemonium with Mammon on the throne, instead of
Lucifer,—the Son of the Earth, Lord of Hell, instead
of the Son of the Morning.

Let her stand in the midst of the main railroad
station at Birmingham ; and think—what music, or
dancing, or other entertainment fit for prodigal sons
could be possible in that pious and little prodigal
locality.* Let her read the account of our modern
pastoral music, at page 15 of my fifth letter,—of
modern Venetian "Barcarolle," page 14 of Letter XIX.
and 12 of Letter XX,—and of our modern Campanile,
and Muezzin call to prayer, at page 262 of this Fors.

"Work is prayer"—thinks your Wakefield Maho-
metan ;—his vociferous minaret, in the name, and by
the name, of the Devil, shall summon English votaries

---

* Compare my Birmingham correspondent's opinion of David s "twangling
on the harp, page 10, Letter VI.

to such worship for five miles round; that is to say, over one hundred square miles of English land, the Pandemoniacal voice of the Archangel-trumpet thus arouses men out of their sleep; and Wakefield becomes Wakeful-field, over that blessed space of acreage.

Yes; my correspondent may be thankful that still some feeble lust for dancing on the green,—still some dim acknowledgment, by besotted and stupefied brains, of the laws of tune and time known to their fathers and mothers—remains possible to the poor wretches discharged by the excursion trains for a gasp of breath, and a gleam of light, amidst what is left to them, and us, of English earth and heaven. Waltzing, drunk, in the country roads by our villages; yet innocently drunk, and sleepy at sunset; not like their born masters and teachers, dancing, wilfully, the cancan of hell, with harlots, at seven in the morning.*

Music and dancing! They are quite the two primal instruments of education. Make them licentious, let Mr. John Stuart Mill have the dis-ordering of them, so that—(see page 18 of Letter XII.)—"no one shall be guided, or governed, or directed in the way they should go,"—and they sink to lower and lower depth—till the dance becomes Death's; and the music—a shriek of death by strychnine. But let Miriam and David, and the Virgins of Israel, have the ordering of them, and

---

* 'Sesame and Lilies.' (page 53 of "The Revised Series of Entire Works," and page 80 of the small edition).

the music becomes at last the Eternal choir; and the Dance, the Karol-dance of Christmas, evermore.[*]

Virgins of Israel, or of England, richly clad by your kings, and "rejoicing in the dance," how is it you do not divide this sacred,—*if* sacred,—joy of yours with the poor? If it can ever be said of you, as birds of God,

> "Oh beauteous birds, methinks ye measure
> Your movements to some heavenly tune,"

can you not show wherein the heavenliness of it consists, to—suppose—your Sunday-school classes? At present, you keep the dancing to yourselves, and graciously teach *them* the catechism. Suppose you were to try for a little while, learning the catechism yourselves; and teaching *them*—to dance?

Howbeit, in St. George's schools, this, the most 'decorous,' rightly taught, of all exercises, shall not fail of its due discipline to any class whatsoever:— reading, writing, and accounts may all be spared where pupils show no turn to any of those scholarships, but music and dancing, never.[†] Generally, however, it will be the best singers and dancers who ask for teaching also in literature and art; for all, there shall at least

---

[*] Compare Letter XXIV., page 20; and Dante, Paradiso, xxiv. 16:

> " Cosi, quelle carole differente—
> Mente danzando, della sua ricchezza
> Mi si facean stimar, veloci e lente."

[†] Compare Letter VIII., p 16; and Letter IX., p. 17.

be the way open to these ; and for none, danger or corruption possible in these. For in their libraries there shall be none but noble books, and in their sight none but noble art.

There is no real difficulty or occasion for dispute in choosing these. Admit the principle of selection, and the practice is easy enough ; only, like all practical matters, the work must be done by one man, suffi- ciently qualified for it, and not by a council. If he err, the error may be represented by any one cognizant of it, and by council corrected. But the main work must be done single-handed.

Thus, for the use of the St. George's Company, I shall myself, if my life is spared, write out a list of books which without any question will be found service- able in their libraries, *—a system of art instruction which will be secure so far as it reaches ; and a list of purchaseable works of art, which it will be desirable to place in the national schools and museums of the company. With this list of purchaseable works, I shall name, as I have time, those in the museums of Europe which ought to be studied, to the exclusion of those on which time would be wasted.

I have no doubt that this work, though done at first for the St. George's Company, will be found gene- rally useful, and especially that the system of drawing

---

* This will be added to by future Masters of the Company, with the farther means of specification indicated in pages 4 and 5 of Letter XXI.

arranged for them will in many respects.supersede that
of Kensington. I had intended to write it separately
for the use of schools; but after repeated endeavours
to arrange it in a popular form, find that it will not
so shape itself availably, but must consist of such
broad statements of principle as my now enlarged experience enables me to make; with references to the
parts of my other books in which they are defended
or illustrated : and of directions for practice given as
I can get illustrations of them prepared ; leaving the
systematization of them to be made by the master of
each drawing school, according to the requirements of
his scholars. (See page 19 of Letter IX.)

For example of the impossibility of publishing on a
system It happens to be now fine weather here in
Lancashire ;—I am able, therefore, to draw out of
doors; and am painting a piece of foreground vege-
tation, which I don't want to be used by students
till after at least fifty other exercises have been gone
through But I must do this one while light and life
serve; and not wait till I am sixty, to do work which
my eyes are not good enough for at fifty-five.

And if the readers of Fors think my letters too
desultory, let them consider what this chief work, specified in page 20 of Letter IX., involves. No one has
the least notion of the quantity of manual labour I
have to go through, to discharge my duty as a teacher
of Art Look at the frontispiece to Letter XX., which

is photographed from one of my architectural sketches ; and if you can draw, copy a bit of it ;—try merely the bead moulding with its dentils, in the flat arch over the three small ones, lowest on the left. Then examine those three small ones themselves. You think I have drawn them distorted, carelessly, I suppose. No. That distortion is essential to the Gothic of the Pisan school ; and I measured every one of the curves of those cusps on the spot, to the tenth of an inch ; and I ought to be engraving and publishing those drawings, by rights ; but, meantime, your Pisan Republicans dash the chapel down, for a job in rebuilding it ,— and the French Emperor dashes every cathedral in France to pieces, to find his masons work,—and gets for result, Reuter's telegram, (page 21 of Letter VI.) ; and I, with my eyes full of dust and driven smoke, am obliged to leave my own work, and write Fors, more and more necessarily becoming principal, as I find all my other work rendered vain.

Nevertheless, in the course of Fors itself, I shall try to give, as aforesaid, art instruction enough for all need, if any one cares to obey it. How little any one is likely to care, the closing paragraphs of the letter from Wakefield show so clearly that I think it desirable to print them here consecutively, as part of the text of Fors itself.

"Yet people tell me that those were very benighted Tory days I am regretting. Wakefield was always held to be a Tory place, given up hand and foot to the magnates who owned the great estate round. I know how when a small thing in frilled slops, but with my bosom full of patriotic pride in our town, I used to feel bitterly depressed at hearing a rising Radical Leeds clothier, who came to see us, sometimes denounce Wakefield as a 'one-eyed hoil,' his emphatic way of indicating our want of sweep of vision. I remember he generally capped his arguments by demanding, in sonorous tones, if any men worthy of the name of Britons would put up with that 'obsolete monopoly' of the soke mills.

"To tell truth, I am afraid that we felt a good deal of mean-spirited admiration for the neighbouring squires and lords on the occasions when they showed themselves and their handsome carriages in our streets: but at least the Wentworths and Pilkingtons and Squire Waterton were gentlemen and scholars; our new magnates have nothing to boast but their money. It seems to me better that people should boast of the old oaks of Walton, and the old pictures of —— Priory, than tell how many thousands an iron lord made by the last rise in iron : and that is what they talk of now. And if the iron kings have supplanted the landlords, they are not any more free. The old farmers might vote blindly out of blind respect for the old landlords, but is it not better than the newly-enfranchised puddlers and strikers selling votes openly for the price of a

gallon of whisky ? We have lost a good deal, although
we are long rid of the soke monopoly, which used
to be a standing reproach to us. I think that the
town bought off the soke just after the Corn Law
agitation, when the great railways began to enclose
the wide meadows about the town with their ugly
ramparts and arches, where the trains keep up a continual scream.

"But the wool and corn magnates of the place held
to their old traditions long after that ; and when Titus
Salt asked for a footing in the town that he might
build there his great alpaca factories, he was rejected.
I had gone abroad then, but my heart was in the
old place, and I caught up eagerly all concerning it.
Sometimes I heard doleful accounts of its decadence
—how the big houses were empty altogether, how the
inns were closed, the coaches stopped, the river traffic
diminished, and the great corn warehouses by the bridge
falling to ruin. There was no trace left of the gaieties
that once gave the town the name of 'Merrie Wakefield.' All the smart young men were leaving it to
push their way in Leeds or Manchester, and the girls
left behind were growing up into a population of old
maids.

"So the doleful story went on for many a year.
But insensibly the key changed. Mills were springing
up, and shops ; and the houses had gone up in rent.
The sleepy streets were thronged with workers , in

short the town seemed new-born altogether. And the
————s,—I knew the ————s,—nobody would have thought
it, such a simple kind of man as old ———— seemed ;
yet the tale ran that he could buy up all Wakefield,
and young Bill was going to live in ———— Hall ! ! Young
Bill in ———— Hall ! one of the most sacred spots my
memory cherished.

"I remembered him well,—an audacious boy, with
a gift for wry faces, and always up to some street
prank I remember the well-worn jacket and battered
cap that his father's thrift imposed on him. And he
was to be one of new rulers of the bright new time !
and lord it in those venerable oaken chambers sacred
to Lady ————'s ghost ! It seemed incredible ; but
twenty years had changed everything Old ————, the
father—a man of the true old English grain, had, in
my young days, a foundry at the lower end of the
town, and was said even then to be worth a 'mint
of money.' Worthy folks were he and his ; but still
people of whom the loftier town's-folk took no cogni-
zance socially, for was not the wife's father old Robin
the Pedlar ? A good old soul he was, who peddled
to frugal farm wives the best thread and needles that
could be got,—and took no alms from his kinsfolk,
and lived and died in blameless humble honesty. And
his grandson now rules in the hall where old Robin,
perchance, took a humble bit and sup at the back
door He has a Scotch estate besides, and only failed

of Parliament last year because he bribed his way a little too openly. My enlightened friends look upon his rise as one of the grandest signs of the grand new time, but I cannot rejoice with them. When I see how he and his like are doing their worst to foul the air and blacken the fields about the town, I cannot help wishing the squires back in —— Hall.

"Men say, too, that he is a stronger Tory than the bluest of the old squires. He has forgotten old Robin of the bobbins, and rules the people from whom he sprang, with an iron hand, as such often do. Naturally, his success has attracted others, and the town will soon be surrounded with forges. On the once green Calder bank, where I used to see garlands of brown pears ripening in the sweet sunshine, there is a desert of dross and ashes, and twenty black throats vomiting fire and fumes into the summer sky; and under the big sheds you see hundreds of the liberated Britons of these improved days, toiling, half-naked, in sweltering heat and din, from morning to evening. This, however, is 'the activity and spread of the iron trade,' which our local paper tells us 'are the most satisfactory pledge of the future progress and prosperity of our town.'

"I wish that I could believe it; but it vexes me beyond comfort to see the first landscape I knew and loved blighted by the smoke of the forges, and to find one sweet association after another swept away.

"Even Sunday brings no respite to the eye. The forges are fired up shortly after noonday, and many of the long chimneys follow suit. And in the town the noise is so constant, you can scarcely hear the church chimes unless you are close to the tower.

"Did you ever hear Wakefield chimes? We were very proud of them in the old time. They had a round of pleasant sleepy tunes, that never failed us through summer suns and winter frost; and came to be bound up indelibly with the early memories of us children. How I loved to hear them as I bounded, full of morning gladness, across the green Vicar's Croft to school; or at night when lying an unwilling prisoner in bed, before the warm summer evening was ended. To my childish fancy there was a strange wizardry bound up with that dark church steeple, frosted and crumbling with age, which would break out overhead into mysterious music when I was far afield, but expecting it.

"Years after, when poor and lonely in a great foreign city, I came, one bitter winter's day, upon an obscure cloister church standing by a frozen river. It was a city without bells, and I had often longed for the familiar sound. I was dreadfully homesick that day, and stood upon the bridge, hapless, and listless; looking at the strange spire, the strange houses and frozen-up boats, in a kind of dream. Suddenly the cloister tower struck the hour,—four o'clock of a dark December day, and presently it broke into a chime.

"It was a very simple ditty ; but what a passion of longing it wakened for England and the old chimes of that little English town ! I felt as if my heart could bear no more. I *must* go home ; I *must* see the old places again, cost what it might. But morning brought fresh counsels, and many a year passed before I re-visited the old place.

"At last I was there again, after many disappoint-ments, and laid my head to rest once more beneath the shadow of the old steeple.

"I woke with an expectant heart. It was a bright May day, such as I remembered twenty years before. The big church bell tolled nine : then came a pause, and my thirsty ears were strained to catch the first sounds of the dear old chimes 'Ding' went a treble bell high in the air, the first note of 'Tara's Halls,' and then !—a hideous sound I cannot describe, a pro-longed malignant yell, broke from the sky and seemed to fill the earth. I stopped my ears and ran indoors, but the sound followed to the innermost chambers. It gathered strength and malignancy every moment, and seemed to blast all within its reach. It lasted near two minutes, and ended with a kind of spasm and howl that made every nerve shudder. I do not exaggerate. I cannot adequately describe the hideous sound. When I had recovered my wits, I asked the meaning of this horrible noise. My informant, a rising young townsman of the new stamp, told me that it was the new steam-whistle at the foundry, commonly called the ' American Devil ; ' that it was the most powerful in the West Riding, and could be heard five miles off.

" It was only at half-power then, calling the workmen from breakfast ; but at six in the morning I could hear it in double force. I asked if it was possible that people would quietly put up with such a hideous disturbance. He owned that the old inhabitants did not like it ; but then, he said, they were a sleepy set, and wanted stirring up.

"Indeed, I actually found that the town was infected by four other similar whistles, profaning dawn and eve with their heaven-defying screech

" The nuisance has been abolished since, I hear. They say it actually killed one old lady by starting her up just at the only moment when it was possible for her weary nerves to get sleep. She happened to have a relation in the town council : a stir was made about it, and the whistles were suppressed.

" But the peaceful, half town, half rural life of Wakefield is gone for ever, I fear.

" Silk-mills and dye-works are encroaching on the corn-fields and pastures ; rows of jerry-built cottages are creeping up Pinder's Fields, where I used to pull orchises ; greasy mill-girls elbow ladies in the Westgate, and laugh and jeer at passing young men in a way that would have horrified the old inhabitants. And everywhere there is an indescribable smokiness and dirtiness more demoralizing than any tongue can tell, or mind conceive.

" Well, it is the ' march of the times.' It will go on, I suppose, as in other quiet pleasant English towns, until all the sweet Calder valley is swallowed up in the smoke of Tophet. They will cut the snowdrop wood down, and cover Heath Common with cheap villas, and make the old hall into an 'institution.' You know how it will be. A river black with filth and stagnant with foulness, a wilderness of toiling suburbs such as you saw at Brad-ford ; and where the cowslips and the corn grew, the earth will be thick with 'institutions.' There will be a Blind Institution, and an Eye and Ear Institution, an Orthopædic Institution, and a Magdalen Institution, and Mechanics' Institutions ; and we shall hear a great deal of the liberality and beneficence of the cotton and iron kings of the place. But will all this compensate one little child for robbing it of its God-given birthright of earth and sky ?

" I cannot believe it

" Poor little martyrs ! There will be no ' swallow twit-tering from the straw-built shed ' for them,—only the American Devil calling father to his hot, hard day's labour. What can they make of it all ? What kind of outlook will *they* have in coming years from the bridge of my early recollections ? What I saw on the Medlock yesterday—such a hideous sight '—yet my husband re-members catching fish there. The gases would kill a fish like a lightning-stroke, now.

" And the poor children ! It makes me so sad, having

some of my own, to think of those who will be born there, with hearts as hungry for nature and truth as mine was ; who will never see God's heaven, save through grimy panes and smoke ; who will have no sweet cowslip-fields to walk in,—only the defiled pavement ; who will grow hard and sour before childhood is over, with the riddle of their joyless lives.

"How I have drifted on.

" Your allusion to Wakefield Bridge in the Fors of February (?) unloosed a flood of long-buried recollections.

"This is what you draw on yourself by opening your heart to others. Pray forgive the trespass on your time.

"Yours gratefully,

"E. L."

NOTES AND CORRESPONDENCE.

The following two paragraphs have been sent me by correspondents, from country papers. I do not answer for the facts stated in them , but however mythic either may be, they form part of the current history of the day, and are worth preserving ; the latter especially in illustration of what I meant by the phrase " roseate repose of domestic felicity," in the Fors of July, this year, p. 184. One of the pamphlets written by John Hopper will become a subject of inquiry in a future Fors.

JOHN HOPPER.—On Tuesday, July 6, passed away from our midst the pioneer of Co-operation in Sunderland, John Hopper, shipwright, aged forty-seven on the 22nd April last, after a lingering illness of six weeks' duration, of paralysis of the right side, and the breaking of a blood-vessel in the brain. This was caused by his constant and unremitting study and writing on all questions relating to the progress of his fellow-workmen. More especially had he devoted his time and money to publishing several pamphlets on Co-operation. He also ably advocated the cause of Working Men's Unions and Trade Arbitration Councils instead of strikes. He looked forward to Co-operation for the solution of all the great questions in dispute between the employer and employed. and lived to see some portion of his ideas carried out with great success in the organization of a co-operative store in our own town, which now possesses two branch establishments, and does a very large, extensive, and profitable business, and possesses also two libraries. The organization and successful carrying out of this store was largely due to his own exertions. As its first secretary he gave his arduous labours free to it for several years. Though frequently offered superior situations in his own trade as a shipwright, he conscientiously refused all such offers, preferring to cast his lot amongst the working classes, and with them finish his days, toiling on side by side with them, as an example of honesty, toil, and love of his trade, before all other things; for *work* indeed to him was only *worship*. He scorned to earn his bread by any other means than by his own trade. He often lamented over men of superior talent who deserted their class for wealth and gain, and did not stay by their fellow-men, and by so doing try to elevate them by their example. He had been ailing some fifteen months, but kept at his work until quite exhausted, some six weeks before he died. He worked in the yard of Mr. Oswald, of Pallion, for many years, and also at Mr. J. Laing's, at Deptford. With the latter gentleman he served his apprenticeship as a shipwright. He leaves a widow and seven children unprovided for. The eldest is now serving his apprenticeship to his father's trade with Mr. Oswald. Simple and retired he lived, despite all their praise—content to live and die a working man. Often after a hard day's toil he was too ill to walk all the way home, and had to lay himself down to rest by the roadside for awhile. The following is a list of his pamphlets, eight in number :—Causes of Distress ; History of the Sunderland Co-operative Store ; Organization of Labour ; Co-operative Store System , The Commercial Reformer's Bookkeeper ; The Workman's Path to Independence , The Rights of Working Men ; and, Elections, Trades Unions, and the Irish Church.

MARRIAGE OF MISS VENABLES, FORMERLY OF LEICESTER — From the Yarmouth papers, we learn that on Wednesday week Miss Eveline Mary Venables, the only daughter of the Rev.

George Venables, vicar of Great Yarmouth, and formerly vicar of St. Matthew's, Leicester, was married at the parish church, Great Yarmouth, in the presence of 4,000 spectators, to the Rev. E. Manners Sanderson, M A, vicar of Weston St Mary's, Lincolnshire. The bridegroom was formerly curate of Great Yarmouth. Very extensive preparations, we are told, were made for the wedding festivities, both in the church and at the vicarage. A number of lady friends of the bride undertook to decorate the nave and chancel of the fine old church, and for several days they worked assiduously at this labour of love Nearly the whole length of the chancel was tastefully decorated with a choice assortment of flowers, plants, mosses, and ferns, the gas standards being also similarly clothed, while along the communion rails were placed leaves of ferns, intermingled with roses and water-lilies Within the communion rails were displays of cut flowers and plants, which gave a most pleasing effect to that portion of the church. The reredos was beautifully dressed in wreaths and flowers, and above the communion table were the words in white letters on a scarlet ground, " Jesus was called to the marriage." The effect of all these magnificent decorations was beautiful, and presented such a picture as our grand old church probably never before exhibited The nave and chancel were converted into an avenue of flowers, and as the richly dressed bridal procession wended its way from the south porch the scene was one of the most imposing and affecting nature. It was understood that the marriage would take place immediately after the usual morning service, and long before that service commenced (eleven o'clock), several hundreds of people had congregated in front of the church gates, and when they were thrown open, they flocked into the church, and soon every available space in the church was filled with thousands of people. A number of seats near and in the chancel were set apart for the bridal party and friends, and these were kept vacant until the arrival of the ladies and gentlemen for whom they were reserved, and who were admitted for the most part by ticket at the east door. The morning service concluded about half-past eleven, and the clergymen who were to take part in the ceremony, and who had been waiting in the vestry, then walked in procession down the chancel, taking up their position under the tower, where they awaited the arrival of the bridal party. Their names were as follows, besides the Vicar : Rev. E. Venables (canon of Lincoln), Rev. Dr. J. J. Raven (master of the Grammar School), Rev. Bowyer Vaux (minister of St. Peter's church,) Rev. A. J. Spencer, Rev. F. G. Wilson (vicar of Rudham), Rev. G. Merriman, Rev. A. B. M. Ley, Rev. R. H. Irvine, Rev. F. C. Villiers, and Rev. R. J. Tacon (Rollesby). The first to arrive was the bridegroom, accompanied by his bestman, the Rev. R. V. Barker, who were shortly after-wards followed by the bridesmaids and other ladies and gentlemen constituting the bridal party, who entered by the south door and awaited the arrival of the bride. The bridesmaids were most elegantly attired in bleu de ciel silk dresses, with long trains, trimmed en tablier, with Mousseline d'Indienne, pink briar roses and white heath, wreaths to match, and long tulle veils. Their names were as follows : Miss Rose Venables, Miss Sanderson, Miss L. Sanderson, Miss M. Sanderson, Miss Wilson, Miss Ruth Venables, and Miss Mander. Each bridesmaid carried a bouquet of white roses, pink geraniums, and forget-me-nots, the gift of the bestman, the Rev. R. V. Barker. The last to arrive was the bride, who wore a dress of superb white satin, with a very long train, garnie en tulle et fleurs d'orange, the corsage correspond-ing. The veil tulle de Bruxelles, brodé en soie, the trailing wreath clematis, myrtle, and orange blossoms; and a necklet of sprays of silver ivy leaves (the gift of Mr. Percy Sanderson). Her magnificent bouquet was composed of orange flowers, stephanotis, Cape jasmine, white roses, and ferns, and was the gift of the bridegroom. The bride was supported by her brother, Mr. E. Venables, and was received at the south porch of the church by her bridesmaids, who accompanied her up the nave to the chancel, where they were received by the vicar and clergymen. The choir were stationed in the triforium, and Mr. H. Stonex presided at the organ, which was used on this the first occasion since its removal, although the repairs are not yet complete. While the bridal party were entering the church, Mr. Stonex performed "The Wedding March" composed by Sir George Elvey on the occasion of the marriage of Princess Louise (Marchioness of Lorne) The bridal party took their places under the tower, and the marriage service began, the Vicar being assisted in his office by Canon Venables, and the bride being given away by her elder brother Mr Gilbert Venables. After singing the hymn, "The voice that breathed o'er Eden," to the tune St. Alphege, Canon Venables read the first address of the Marriage Service The Vicar has just printed this service with a few explanatory remarks, and about a thousand copies were distributed on the occasion After that portion of the Marriage Service ordered to be performed in the body of the church was completed, the clergy, bride and bridegroom, and bridesmaids proceeded up the choir to the chancel, the singers and congregation chanting the 128th Psalm. The clergy having taken their positions, the bride and bridegroom, with the bridesmaids and the Rev. R V. Barker, knelt at the communion rails ; the service was continued, and a short sermon read by the Vicar, from the text, "Heirs together of the grace of life ; that your prayers be not hindered" The service concluded with the benediction, and as the party left the church, Mr Stonex performed Mendelssohn's "Wedding March," in a very skilful manner The bride's trousseau was entirely supplied from Yarmouth, and the wedding cake, which weighed 100 lb , was manufactured by Mr. Wright, of King Street, Yarmouth. After the marriage, the bridal party assembled at the Vicarage, where the register was signed, and then sat down to a récherché breakfast, the management of which was placed in the hands of Mr. and Mrs. Franklin, of the Crown and Anchor Hotel. The following is a list of those who were present at the wedding breakfast: the Vicar and Mrs Venables, the Honourable and Mrs. Sanderson, T. H. Sanderson, Esq., Lord Hastings, Chas Venables, Esq (Taplow, Bucks), and Mrs. C Venables, Miss Sanderson, Miss Lucy Sanderson, Miss Maud Sanderson, Canon Venables (Lincoln) and Mrs. Venables, Miss Ruth Venables (Lincoln), Miss Rose Venables (London), Gilbert Venables, Esq., B.A. (Lower Norwood), and Mrs Gilbert Venables, Rev F. G. Wilson (Vicar of Rudham) and Mrs. and Miss Wilson, Rev J. J. Raven, D D. (Yarmouth), and Mrs Raven, Rev. R. V Barker, M A. (Yarmouth), Edward Venables, Esq (Emmanuel College, Cambridge), and Mrs Edward Venables, Rev. Bowyer Vaux, M.A., and Mrs. Vaux, Rev R. H. Irvine and Mrs Irvine, Mrs. Palgrave (Yarmouth), Mrs. Woollnough, Rev F C. Villiers, M A., and the Misses Villiers, E. Villiers, Esq (Galway), Rev. A. B. M. Ley, M.A (Yarmouth), Rev. G. Merriman, M.A, Rev. A J Spencer, B A., Miss Mander (Tettenhall Wood), Mrs. Palmer, Rev. R. J. Tacon, M A (rector of Rollesby), Mr. Stonex The presents to the bride were very numerous, and among the donors we find the names of Mr. and Mrs. T. North, of Leicester, a bread platter and knife; and Mr. and Mrs. Burbidge Hambly, of Mountsorrel, a dessert service. The honeymoon is being spent at Sans Souci, Dorsetshire.

FORS CLAVIGERA.

LETTER THE 58th.

THE CATHOLIC PRAYER

"Deus, a quo sancta desideria, recta consilia, et justa sunt opera, da servis tuis illam quam mundus dare non potest pacem, ut et corda nostra mandatis tuis, et, hostium sublata formidine, tempora, sint tuâ protectione tranquilla."

"God, from whom are all holy desires, right counsels, and just works, give to Thy servants that peace which the world cannot, that both our hearts, in Thy commandments, and our times, the fear of enemies being taken away, may be calm under Thy guard."

THE adulteration of this great Catholic prayer in our English church-service, (as needless as it was senseless, since the pure form of it contains nothing but absolutely Christian prayer, and is as fit for the most stammering Protestant lips as for Dante's), destroyed all the definite meaning of it,[*] and left merely the vague expression of desire for peace, on quite unregarded terms For

---

[*] Missing, in the phrase 'that our hearts may be set to obey' the entire sense of the balanced clause in the original,—namely, that the Law of God is *given* to be the shield and comfort of the soul against spiritual enemies, as the merciful angels encamp round us against earthly ones.

of the millions of people who utter the prayer at least weekly, there is not one in a thousand who is ever taught, or can for themselves find out, either what a holy desire means, or a right counsel means, or a just work means,—or what the world is, or what the peace is which it cannot give. And half an hour after they have insulted God by praying to Him in this deadest of all dead languages, not understanded of the people, they leave the church, themselves pacified in their perennial determination to put no check on their natural covetousness ; to act on their own opinions, be they right or wrong ; to do whatever they can make money by, be it just or unjust ; and to thrust themselves, with the utmost of their soul and strength, to the highest, by them attainable, pinnacle of the most bedrummed and betrumpeted booth in the Fair of the World.

The prayer, in its pure text, is essentially, indeed, a monastic one ; but it is written for the great Monastery of the Servants of God, whom the world hates. It cannot be uttered with honesty but by these ; nor can it ever be answered but with the peace bequeathed to these, ' not as the world giveth '

Of which peace, the nature is not to be without war, but undisturbed in the midst of war ; and not without enemies, but without fear of them. It is a peace without pain, because desiring only what is holy; without anxiety, because it thinks only what is right ; without disappointment, because a just work is always successful ; without

sorrow, because 'great peace have they which love Thy
Law, and nothing shall offend them ,' and without terror,
because the God of all battles is its Guard

So far as any living souls in the England of this day
can use, understandingly, the words of this collect, they
are already, consciously or not, companions of all good
labourers in the vineyard of God. For those who use it
reverently, yet have never set themselves to find out what
the commandments of God are, nor how loveable they
are, nor how far, instead of those commandments, the
laws of the world are the only code they care for,
nor how far they still think their own thoughts and
speak their own words, it is assuredly time to search
out these things And I believe that, after having
searched them out, no sincerely good and religious
person would find, whatever his own particular form
of belief might be, anything which he could reasonably
refuse, or which he ought in anywise to fear to profess
before all men, in the following statement of creed and
resolution, which must be written with their own hand,
and signed, with the solemnity of a vow, by every
person received into the St. George's Company.

I. I trust in the Living God, Father Almighty, Maker of
heaven and earth, and of all things and creatures
visible and invisible

I trust in the kindness of His law, and the
goodness of His work

And I will strive to love Him, and keep His law, and see His work, while I live.

II. I trust in the nobleness of human nature, in the majesty of its faculties, the fulness of its mercy, and the joy of its love.

And I will strive to love my neighbour as myself, and, even when I cannot, will act as if I did.

III. I will labour, with such strength and opportunity as God gives me, for my own daily bread ; and all that my hand finds to do, I will do with my might.

IV. I will not deceive, or cause to be deceived, any human being for my gain or pleasure ; nor hurt, or cause to be hurt, any human being for my gain or pleasure ; nor rob, or cause to be robbed, any human being for my gain or pleasure.

V. I will not kill nor hurt any living creature needlessly, nor destroy any beautiful thing, but will strive to save and comfort all gentle life, and guard and perfect all natural beauty, upon the earth.

VI. I will strive to raise my own body and soul daily into higher powers of duty and happiness ; not in rivalship or contention with others, but for the help, delight, and honour of others, and for the joy and peace of my own life.

VII. I will obey all the laws of my country faithfully ; and the orders of its monarch, and of all persons appointed to be in authority under its monarch, so

far as such laws or commands are consistent with
what I suppose to be the law of God ; and when
they are not, or seem in anywise to need change, I
will oppose them loyally and deliberately, not with
malicious, concealed, or disorderly violence.

VIII And with the same faithfulness, and under the
limits of the same obedience, which I render to the
laws of my country, and the commands of its rulers,
I will obey the laws of the Society called of St.
George, into which I am this day received ; and
the orders of its masters, and of all persons appointed to be in authority under its masters, so
long as I remain a Companion, called of St.
George.

I will not enter in the present letter on any notice of
the terms of this creed and vow ; nor of the grounds
which many persons whose help I sincerely desire, may
perceive for hesitation in signing it. Further definitions
of its meaning will be given as occasion comes ; nor
shall I ever ask any one to sign it whom I do not know
to be capable of understanding and holding it in the
sense in which it is meant. I proceed at once to define
more explicitly those laws of the Company of St. George
to which it refers, and which must, at least in their
power, be known before they can be vowed fealty to.

The object of the Society, it has been stated again
and again, is to buy land in England ; and thereon to

train into the healthiest and most refined life possible, as many Englishmen, Englishwomen, and English children, as the land we possess can maintain in comfort ; to establish, for them and their descendants, a national store of continually augmenting wealth ; and to organize the government of the persons, and administration of the properties, under laws which shall be just to all, and secure in their inviolable foundation on the Law of God.

" To buy land," I repeat, or beg it ; but by no means to steal it, or trespass on it, as I perceive the present holders of the most part of it are too ready to do, finding any bits of road or common which they can pilfer unobserved. Are they quite mad, then ; and do they think the monster mob, gaining every day in force and knowledge, will let their park walls stand much longer, on those dishonest terms ? Doubtful enough their standing is, even on any terms !

But our St. George's walls will be more securely founded, on this wise. The rents of our lands, though they will be required from the tenantry as strictly as those of any other estates, will differ from common rents primarily in being lowered, instead of raised, in proportion to every improvement made by the tenant ; secondly, in that they will be entirely used for the benefit of the tenantry themselves, or better culture of the estates, no money being ever taken by the landlords unless they earn it by their own personal labour.

For the benefit of the tenantry, I say ; but by no

means, always, for benefit of which they can be immediately conscious. The rents of any particular farmer will seldom be returned to him in work on his own fields, or investment in undertakings which promote his interest. The rents of a rich estate in one shire of England may be spent on a poor one in another, or in the purchase of wild ground, anywhere, on which years of labour must be sunk before it can yield return, or in minerals, or Greek vases, for the parish school. Therefore with the use made of the rents paid, the tenantry will have no practical concern whatever; they will only recognise gradually that the use has been wise, in finding the prices of all serviceable articles diminishing, and all the terms and circumstances of their lives indicative of increased abundance. They will have no more right, or disposition, to ask their landlord what he is doing with the rents, than they have now to ask him how many race-horses he keeps—or how much he has lost on them. But the difference between landlords who live in Piccadilly, and spend their rents at Epsom and Ascot, and landlords who live on the ground they are lords of, and spend their rents in bettering it, will not be long in manifesting itself to the simplest minded tenantry, nor, I believe, to the outside and antagonist world.

Sundry questions lately asked me by intelligent correspondents as to the intended relations of the tenantry to the Society, may best be answered by saying simply what I shall do, if ever the collected wealth of the Company enables me to buy an estate for it as large as I could have bought for myself, if I had been a railroad contractor

Of course I could not touch the terms of the existing leases The only immediate difference would be, the definitely serviceable application of all the rents, as above stated. But as the leases fell in, I should offer renewal of them to the farmers I liked, on the single condition of their complying with the great vital law of the St. George's Company,—"no use of steam power, —nor of any machines where arms will serve"; allowing such reduction of rent as should fully compensate them for any disadvantage or loss which they could prove they incurred under these conditions. I should give strict orders for the preservation of the existing timber ; see that the streams were not wantonly polluted, and interfere in nothing else

Such farms as were thrown up by their tenants, rather than submit to these conditions, I should be in no haste to re-let ; but put land agents on them to cultivate them for the Society in the best manner, and sell their produce ;—as soon as any well recommended tenant offered for them, submitting to our laws, he should have them for fixed rent Thus I should give room for development of whatever personal faculty and energy I could find, and set, if successful, more easily followed example. Meantime my schools and museums, always small and instantly serviceable, would be multi-plying among the villages,—youth after youth being instructed in the proper laws of justice, patriotism, and domestic happiness ;—those of the Companions who could reside on the lands would, each on their own farm, establish entirely strict obedience to the ultimate laws determined upon as necessary :—if these laws are indeed, as I do not doubt but that sincere care can make them, pleasantly tenable by honest humanity,* they will be gradually accepted voluntarily by the free tenants , and the system is as certain to extend itself, on all sides, once seen to be right, as the branches of an oak sapling.

While, therefore, I am perfectly content, for a be-ginning, with our acre of rocky land given us by Mrs. Talbot, and am so little impatient for any increase that I have been quietly drawing ragged-robin leaves in Malham cove, instead of going to see another twenty acres promised in Worcestershire,—I am yet thinking out my system on a scale which shall be fit for wide European work. Of course the single Master of the Company cannot manage all its concerns as it extends He must have, for his help, men holding the same relation to him which the Marshals of an army do to its General ,—bearing, that is to say, his own authority

---

* Most of these will be merely old English laws revived , and the rest, Florentine or Roman None will be instituted but such as have already been in force among great nations.

where he is not present ; and I believe no better name than 'Marshal' can be found for these Beneath whom, there will again be the landlords, resident each in his own district; under these, the land agents, tenantry, tradesmen, and hired labourers, some of whom will be Companions, others Retainers, and others free tenants : and outside all this there will be of course an irregular cavalry, so to speak, of more or less helpful friends, who, without sharing in the work, will be glad to further it more or less, as they would any other benevolent institution.

The law that a Companion shall derive no profit from his companionship does not touch the results of his own work. A Companion farmer will have the produce of his farm as much as a free tenant; but he will pay no dividends to the Companions who are *not* farmers

The landlords will in general be men of independent fortune, who, having gifts and ingenuity, choose to devote such gifts to the service of the Society ; the first condition of their appointment to a lordship will be that they can work as much better than their labourers at all rural labour as a good knight was wont to be a better workman than his soldiers in war. There is no rule of supremacy that can ever supersede this eternal, natural, and divine one Higher by the head, broader in the shoulders, and heartier in the will, the lord of lands and lives must for ever be, than those he rules ; and must work daily at their head, as Richard at the trenches of Acre.

And what am I, myself then, infirm and old, who take, or claim, leadership even of these lords? God forbid that I should claim it ; it is thrust and compelled on me—utterly against my will, utterly to my distress, utterly, in many things, to my shame. But I have found no other man in England, none in Europe, ready to receive it,—or even desiring to make himself capable of receiving it. Such as I am, to my own amazement, I stand—so far as I can discern—alone in conviction, in hope, and in resolution, in the wilderness of this modern world. Bred in luxury, which I perceive to have been unjust to others, and destructive to myself ; vacillating, foolish, and miserably failing in all my own conduct in life—and blown about hopelessly by storms of passion—I, a man clothed in soft raiment,—I, a reed shaken with the wind, have yet this Message to all men again entrusted to me : " Behold, the axe is laid to the root of the trees. Whatsoever tree therefore · bringeth not forth good fruit, shall be hewn down and cast into the fire."

This message, yet once more ; and, more than message, the beginning of the acts that must fulfil it. For, long since, I have said all that needs to be said,—all that it was my proper charge and duty to say. In the one volume of ' Sesame and Lilies '—nay, in the last forty pages of its central address to Englishwomen —everything is told that I know of vital truth, everything urged that I see to be needful of vital act ,—but no creature answers me with any faith or any deed. They read the words, and say they are pretty, and go on in their own ways. And the day has come for me therefore to cease speaking, and begin doing, as best I may ; though I know not whether shall prosper, either this or that.

And truly to all wholesome deed here in England, the chances of prosperity are few, and the distinctness of adversity only conquerable by fixed imagination and exhaustless patience—'Adversis rerum immersabilis undis.' The wisest men join with the fools, and the best men with the villains, to prevent, if they may, any good thing being done permanently—nay, to provoke and applaud the doing of consistently evil things permanently. To establish a National debt, and in the most legal terms— how easy ! To establish a National store, under any legal or moral conditions of perpetuity—how difficult ! Every one calls me mad for so much as hoping to do so. 'This looks like a charity, this educating of peasants,' said the good lawyer, who drew up the already published conditional form of association. 'You must not establish a fund for charity , it is sure to lead to all sorts of abuses, and get into wrong hands.'

Well, yes—it in merely human probability may. I do verily perceive and admit, in convinced sorrow, that I live in the midst of a nation of thieves and murderers ;*

* See first note in the Correspondence.

that everybody round me is trying to rob everybody
else, and that, not bravely and strongly, but in the
most cowardly and loathsome ways of lying trade ; that
' Englishman ' is now merely another word for black-
leg and swindler, and English honour and courtesy
changed to the sneaking and the smiles of a whipped
pedlar, an inarticulate Autolycus, with a steam hurdy-
gurdy instead of a voice Be this all so, be it so to
the heart's content—or liver and gall's content—of
every modern economist and philosopher I yet do
verily trust that out of this festering mass of scum of
the earth, and miserable coagulation of frog-spawn
soaked in ditch-water, I can here and there pluck up
some drowned honour by the locks, and leave written
orders for wholesome deed, and collected moneys for
the doing thereof, which will be obeyed and guarded
after I am gone, and will by no means fall into the
power of the mendicant tribe who, too cowardly and
heartless to beg from the face of the living, steal the
alms of the dead, and unite the apparently inconsistent
characters of beggar and thief, seasoning the compound
with sacrilege.

Little by little, if my life is spared to me, therefore
(and if I die, there will I doubt not be raised up some
one else in my room)—little by little, I or they, will
get moneys and lands together, handful gleaned after,
handful, field joined to field, and landmarks set which
no man shall dare hereafter remove. And over those

fields of ours the winds of Heaven shall be pure ; and upon them, the work of men shall be done in honour and truth

In such vague promise, I have for the most part hitherto spoken, not because my own plans were unfixed, but because I knew they would only be mocked at, until by some years of persistence the scheme had run the course of the public talk, and until I had publicly challenged the denial of its principles in their abstract statement, long enough to show them to be invincible. Of these abstract principles, the fifteenth, sixteenth, twentieth, twenty-second and twenty-third letters in Time and Tide, express all that is needful ; only, in the years that have passed since they were written, the 'difficulties' stated in the seventeenth chapter have been under constant review by me, and of the ways in which I mean to deal with them it is now time to speak

Let us understand then, in the outset, the moral difference between a national debt and a national store.

A national debt, like any other, may be honestly incurred in case of need, and honestly paid in due time. But if a man should be ashamed to borrow, much more should a people : and if a father holds it his honour to provide for his children, and would be ashamed to borrow from them, and leave, with his blessing, his note of hand, for his grandchildren to pay, much more should a nation be ashamed to borrow, in any case, or in any manner ; and if it borrow at all, it is at least in honour bound to borrow from living men, and not indebt itself to its own unborn brats. If it can't provide for them, at least let it not send their cradles to the pawnbroker, and pick the pockets of their first breeches.

A national debt, then, is a foul disgrace, at the best. But it is, as now constituted, also a foul crime. National debts paying interest are simply the purchase, by the rich, of power to tax the poor. Read carefully the analysis given of them above, Letter VIII., p. 7.

The financial·operations of the St George's Company will be the direct reverse of these hitherto approved arrangements. They will consist in the accumulation of national wealth and store, and therefore in distribution to the poor, instead of taxation of them ; and the fathers will provide for, and nobly endow, not steal from, their children, and children's children.

My readers, however, will even yet, I am well aware, however often I have reiterated the statement to them, be unable to grasp the idea of a National Store, as an existing possession. They can conceive nothing but a debt,— nay, there are many of them who have a confused notion that a debt *is* a store !

The store of the St. George's Company, then, is to be primarily of food ; next of materials for clothing and covert , next of books and works of art,—food, clothes, books, and works of art being all good, and every poi-

sonous condition of any of them destroyed The food
will not be purveyed by the Borgia, nor the clothing dyed
by Deianira, nor the scriptures written under dictation of
the Devil instead of God

The most simply measurable part of the store of food
and clothing will be the basis of the currency, which will
be thus constituted

The standard of value will be a given weight or
measure of grain, wine, wool, silk, flax, wood, and
marble ; all answered for by the government as of
fine and pure quality, variable only within narrow
limits.   .

The grain will be either wheat, oats, barley, rice, or
maize ; the wine of pure vintage, and not less than ten
years old ; * the wool, silk, and flax of such standard as
can be secured in constancy ; the wood, seasoned oak
and pine ; and for fuel in log and faggot, with finest wood
and marble for sculpture The penny's worth, florin's
worth, ducat's worth, and hundred ducats' worth of each
of these articles will be a given weight or measure of
them, (the penny roll of our present breakfast table
furnishing some notion of what, practically, the grain
standard will become). Into the question of equivalent
value I do not enter here ; it will be at once determined practically as soon as the system is in work
Of these articles the government will always have in its

---

* Thus excluding all inferior kinds wine which will keep ten years will
keep fifty

possession as much as may meet the entire demand of its
currency in circulation. That is to say, when it has a
million in circulation, the million's worth of solid property
must be in its storehouses: as much more as it can
gather, of course; but never less. So that, not only, for his
penny, florin, ducat, or hundred-ducat note, a man may
always be certain of having his pound, or ton, or pint, or
cask, of the thing he chooses to ask for, from the government storehouses, but if the holders of the million of
currency came in one day to ask for their money's worth,
it would be found ready for them in one or other form of
those substantial articles. Consequently, the sum of the
circulating currency being known, the minimum quantity
of store will be known. The sum of the entire currency,
in and out of circulation, will be given annually on every
note issued (no issues of currency being made but on the
first day of the year), and in each district, every morning,
the quantities of the currency in and out of circulation
in that district will be placarded at the doors of the
government district bank.

The metallic currency will be of absolutely pure gold
and silver, and of those metals only ; the ducat and half-
ducat in gold, the florin, penny, halfpenny, and one-fifth
of penny in silver ; the smaller coins being beat thin
and pierced, the halfpenny with two, the one-fifth of
penny with five, apertures* I believe this double-

---

* I shall use this delicate coinage as a means of education in fineness of
touch, and care of small things, and for practical lessons in arithmetic. to the

centime will be as fine a divisor as I shall need. The florin will be worth tenpence ; the ducat, twenty florins

The weight of the ducat will be a little greater than that of the standard English sovereign, and, being in absolutely pure gold, it will be worth at least five-and-twenty shillings of our present coinage. On one of its sides it will bear the figure of the archangel Michael , on the reverse, a branch of Alpine rose · above the rose-branch, the words ' Sit splendor ',* above the Michael, ' Fiat voluntas' ; under the rose-branch, ' sicut in cœlo ' ; under the Michael, ' et in terrâ,' with the year of the coinage . and round the edge of the coin, ' Domini.'

The half-ducat will bear the same stamp, except that while on the ducat the St. Michael will be represented standing on the dragon, on the half-ducat he will be simply armed, and bearing St George's shield.

On the florin, the St George's shield only , the Alpine rose on all three.

On the penny, St. George's shield on one side and the English daisy on the other, without inscription The pierced fractional coins will only bear a chased wreathen fillet, with the required apertures in its interstices.

younger children, in whose hands it will principally be. It will never be wanted for alms ; and for small purchases, as no wares will be offered at eleven-pence three-farthings for a shilling, or ninepence four-fifths for a florin. there will be no unreasonable trouble The children shall buy their own toys, and have none till they are able to do so

* The beginning of the last verse of the prayer of Moses, Psalm xc.

There will be a considerable loss by wear on a coinage of this pure metal ; but nothing is so materially conducive to the honour of a state in all financial function as the purity of its coinage , and the loss will never, on the whole currency, equal annually the tenth part of the value of the gunpowder spent at present in salutes or fireworks , and, if a nation can afford to pay for loyal noise, and fancies in fire, it may also, and much more rationally, for loyal truth and beauty in its circulating signs of wealth Nor do I doubt that a currency thus constituted will gradually enter into European commerce, and become everywhere recognised and exemplary.

Supposing any Continental extension of the Company itself took place, its coinage would remain the same for the ducat, but the shield of the State or Province would be substituted for St George's on the minor coins.

There will be no ultimate difficulty in obtaining the bullion necessary for this coinage, for the State will have no use for the precious metals, except for its currency or its art. An Englishman, as he is at present educated, takes pride in eating out of a silver plate, and in helping, out of a silver tureen, the richest swindlers he can ask to dinner. The companions of St George may drink out of pewter, and eat off delft, but they will have no knaves for guests, though often beggars , and they will be always perfectly well able to afford to buy five or ten pounds' worth of gold and silver for their pocket

change ; and even think it no overwhelming fiscal calamity if as much even as ten shillings should be actually
lost in the year, by the wear of it ; seeing that the wear
of their dinner napkins will be considerably greater in
the same time.   I suppose that ten pounds' worth of
bullion for the head of each family will amply supply
the necessary quantity for circulation ; but if it should
be found convenient to have fifteen—twenty—or fifty
pounds in such form, the national store will assuredly
in time accumulate to such desirable level.   But it will
always be a matter of absolute financial indifference,
what part of the currency is in gold and what in
paper ; its power being simply that of a government
receipt for goods received, giving claim to their return
on demand   The holder of the receipt may have it, if
he likes, written on gold instead of paper, provided he
bring the gold for it to be written on ; but he may
no more have a bar of gold made into money than a
roll of foolscap, unless he brings the goods for which
the currency is the receipt.   And it will therefore, by
St. George's law, be as much forgery to imitate the
national coin in gold, as in paper.

Next to this store, which is the basis of its currency,
the government will attend to the increase of store of
animal food—not mummy food, in tins, but living, on
land and sea ; keeping under strictest overseership its
breeders of cattle, and fishermen, and having always at
its command such supply of animal food as may enable

it to secure absolute consistency of price in the main markets. In cases when, by any disease or accident, the supply of any given animal food becomes difficult, its price will not be raised, but its sale stopped. There can be no evasion of such prohibition, because every tradesman in food will be merely the salaried servant of the company, and there will be no temptation to it, because his salary will be the same, whether he sells or not. Of all articles of general consumption, the government will furnish its own priced standard ; any man will be allowed to sell what he can produce above that standard, at what price he can get for it, but all goods below the government standard will be marked and priced as of such inferior quality ;—and all bad food, cloth, or other article of service, destroyed. And the supervision will be rendered simple by the fewness of the articles permitted to be sold at all, for the dress being in all classes as determined as the heraldry of coronets, and for the most part also rigorously simple ; and all luxurious living disgraceful, the entire means of domestic life will be within easy definition.

Of course the idea of regulating dress generally will be looked upon by the existing British public as ridiculous. But it has become ridiculous because masters and mistresses attempt it solely for their own pride. Even with that entirely selfish end, the natural instinct of human creatures for obedience, when in any wholesome relations with their superiors, has enabled the masters to powder their coachmen's wigs, and polish their footmen's legs with silk stockings; and the mistresses to limit their lady's maids, when in attendance, to certain styles of cap.

Now as the dress regulations of the St George's Company will be quite as much for the pride of the maid as the mistress, and of the man as the master, I have no fear but they will be found acceptable, and require no strictness of enforcement The children of peasants, though able to maintain their own families, will be required to be as clean as if they were charity-boys or girls, nobody will be allowed to wear the cast clothes of other people, to sell or pawn their own, or to appear on duty, agricultural or whatever other it may be, in rags, any more than the Horse Guards or the Queen's dairymaids are now; also on certain occasions, and within such limits as are needful for good fellow-ship, they will be urged to as much various splendour as they can contrive. The wealth of the peasant women will be chiefly in hereditary golden ornaments of the finest workmanship; and in jewellery of uncut gems,—agates only, or other stones of magnitude, being allowed to be cut, and gems of large size, which are worth the pains, for their beauty; but these will be chiefly used in decorative architecture or furniture, not in dress The dress of the officers of the company will be on all occasions plainer than that of its peasants; but hereditary nobles will retain all the insignia of their rank, the one only condition of change required on their entering the St George's Company being the use of uncut jewels, and therefore—seldom of diamonds.*

The next main staple of the Company's store will be its literature.

A chosen series of classical books will be placed in every village library, in number of copies enough to supply all readers ; these classics will be perfectly printed and perfectly bound, and all in one size of volume, unless where engravings need larger space : besides these village libraries, there will be a museum in every district, containing all good ancient books obtainable : gradually, as the design expands itself, and as time passes on, absorbing, by gift, or purchase, the contents of private libraries, and connecting themselves with similarly expanding museums of natural history. In all schools, the books necessary for their work will be given to the pupils ; and one of their earliest lessons will be the keeping of them clean and orderly

By ordering of Fors, I went only this last month to see the school in which Wordsworth was educated. It remains, as it was then, a school for peasant lads only ; and the doors of its little library, therefore, hang loose on their decayed hinges ; and one side of the schoolroom is utterly dark—the window on that side

* I never saw a rough diamond worth setting until the Bishop of Natal gave me a sharply crystallized one from the African fields. Perhaps a star or two of cut ones may be permitted to the house-mistresses on great occasions.

having been long ago walled up, either 'because of the window-tax, or perhaps it had got broken,' suggested the guardian of the place.

Now it is true that this state of things cannot last long ; but the cure will be worse than the disease. A fit of reactionary vanity and folly is sure to seize the village authorities ; that old schoolroom, with its sacred associations, will be swept from the hillside, and a grand piece of Birmingham Gothic put up, with a master from Kensington, and enforced weekly competitive examination in Sanscrit, and the Binomial Theorem.

All that the school wants is, hinges to its library doors as good as every shop in the street has to its shutters , the window knocked through again where it was originally ; the books whose bindings are worn out, rebound, and a few given (in addition to those on the subjects of arithmetic and grammar), which the boys may rather ask leave to read, than take opportunity to throw into corners.

But the ten or twenty pounds needed for this simple reformation could, I suppose, at present, by no persuasion nor argument be extracted from the united pockets of the gentlemen of the neighbourhood. Meantime, while the library doors flap useless on their hinges, the old country churchyard is grim with parallelograms of iron palisade, enforced partly to get some sacred market for the wares of the rich ironmongers who are buying up the country ; and partly to protect their valuable carcases in their putrefying pride. Of such iron stores the men of St George's Company, dead, will need none, and living, permit none But they will strictly enforce the proper complement of hinges to their school-library doors.

The resuscitation of the, at present extinct, art of writing being insisted upon in the school exercises of the higher classes, the libraries will be gradually enriched· with manuscripts of extreme preciousness. A well-written book is as much pleasanter and more beautiful than a printed one as a picture is than an engraving ; and there are many forms of the art of illumination which were only in their infancy at the time when the wooden blocks of Germany abolished the art of scripture, and of which the revival will be a necessary result of a proper study of natural history

In next Fors, I shall occupy myself wholly with the subject of our Art education and property , and in that for December, I hope to publish the legal form of our constitution revised and complete The terminal clauses respecting the Companions' right of possession in the lands will be found modified, or in great part omitted, in the recast deed ; but I am neither careful nor fearful respecting the terms of this instrument, which is to be regarded merely as a mechanical means of presently getting to work and having land legally secured to us The ultimate success or failure of the design will not in the least depend on the terms of our constitution, but on the quantity of living honesty and pity which can be found, to be constituted. If there is not material enough out of which to choose Companions, or energy enough in the Companions chosen to fill the chain-mail of all terms and forms with living power, the scheme will be choked by its first practical difficulties ; and it matters little what becomes of the very small property its promoters are ever likely to handle. If, on the contrary, as I believe, there be yet honesty and sense enough left in England to nourish the effort, from its narrow source there will soon develop itself a vast Policy, of which neither I nor any one else can foresee the issue, far less verbally or legally limit it ; but in which, broadly, by the carrying out of the primally accepted laws of Obedience and Economy, the Master and Marshals will become the Ministry of the State, answerable for the employment of its revenues, for its relations with external powers, and for such change of its laws as from time to time may be found needful : the Landlords will be the resident administrators of its lands, and immediate directors of all labour,—its captains in war, and magistrates in peace : the tenants will constitute its agricultural and military force, having such domestic and acquisitive independence as may be consistent with patriotic and kindly fellowship : and the artists, schoolmen, tradesmen, and inferior labourers, will form a body of honourably paid retainers, undisturbed in their duty by any chance or care relating to their means of subsistence.

NOTES AND CORRESPONDENCE.

———————◆———————

Mem. for Professor Ruskin.

The following is taken from the 'Edinburgh Courant' of 2nd inst. —

'The "Nautical Magazine" leads off with a bold and original article, the second of a series, on the somewhat startling subject of "The Commercial Value of Human Life," in which it states that human life has its commercial value, and that "those who bring forward its sacredness as a plea for protective legislation of any and every kind are assuming not only a false position, but a position that is likely to work a serious injury upon the country at large." An elaborate discussion of "The Plimsoll Protest," and a description of the "Inman Line" of steamers, with the usual technical matter, make up an unusually interesting number.'

What can this mean? Does it point to something still more brutal than the 'carnivorous teeth' theory?*

Submitted, with much respect, to Mr. Ruskin, for the *Notes and Correspondence* in 'Fors'—if deemed admissible.

J. M.

4th September 1875

* Yes, certainly It points to teeth which shall have no meat to eat, but only the lead of coffins, and to tongues which shall have no water to drink, but only the burnt sulphur of hell. See, for example, succeeding article

A peculiarly sad instance of death from lead-poisoning was investigated this week before Dr Hardwicke, at an inquest held in London. The deceased, Mary Ann Wilson, only three weeks ago went to work at a white-lead factory. After being there two or three days she felt the effects of lead-poisoning, which turned her lips blue. Subsequently the neighbours found her lying on the floor in convulsions, and in a dying state, and the next day she died from congestion of the brain, and disease of the chest organs, consequent on the evil effects of her employment. The coroner recommended that persons who follow this employment should drink diluted sulphuric acid, to counteract the action of the poison —*Birmingham Daily Post*, Sept 2, 1875.

FORS CLAVIGERA.

HERNE HILL, *3rd October*, 1875.

THE day before yesterday I went with a young English girl to see her nurse ; who was sick of a lingering illness during which, with kindliest intent, and sufficient success, (as she told me,) in pleasing her, books had been chosen for her from the circulating library, by those of her pious friends whose age and experience qualified them for such task.

One of these volumes chancing to lie on the table near me, I looked into it, and found it to be ' Stepping Heavenward ;'—as far as I could make out, a somewhat long, but not unintelligent, sermon on the text of Wordsworth's ' Stepping Westward.' In the five minutes during which I strayed between the leaves of it, and left the talk of my friend with her nurse to its own liberty, I found that the first chapters described the conversion of an idle and careless young lady of sixteen to a solemn view of her duties in life, which she thus expresses at the end of an advanced chapter:

" I am resolved never to read worldly books any more ; and my music and drawing I have laid aside for ever."*

The spiritually walled cloister to which this charming child of modern enlightenment thus expresses her determination to retire, differs, it would appear, from the materially walled monastic shades of the Dark Ages, first, by the breadth and magnanimity of an Index Expurgatorius rising to interdiction of all uninspired books whatever, except Baxter's ' Saint's Rest,' and other classics of evangelical theology ; and, secondly, by its holy abhorrence of the arts of picture and song, which waste so much precious time, and give so much disagreeable trouble to learn , and which also, when learned, are too likely to be used in the service of idols ; while the skills which our modern gospel substitutes for both, of steam-whistle, namely, and photograph, supply, with all that they need of terrestrial pleasure, the ears which God has redeemed from spiritual deafness, and the eyes which He has turned from darkness to light.

My readers are already, I hope, well enough acquainted with the Institutes of the St. George's Company to fear no monastic restrictions of enjoyment, nor imperative choice of their books, carried to this celestially Utopian

---

* I quote from memory, and may be out in a word or two ; not in the sense : but I don't know if the young lady is really approved by the author, and held up as an example to others ; or meant, as I have taken her, for a warning The method of error, at all events, is accurately and clearly shown.

strictness. And yet, understanding the terms of the sentence with true and scholarly accuracy, I must, in educational legislation, insist on the daughters of my Companions fulfilling this resolution to the letter : " I am resolved never to read worldly books any more, and *my* music and drawing I have laid aside for ever."

" Worldly books " ? Yes ; very certainly, when you know which they are ; for I will have you to abjure, with World, Flesh, and Devil, the literature of all the three .— and *your* music and drawing,—that is to say, all music and drawing which you have learned only for your own glory or amusement, and respecting which you have no idea that it may ever become, in a far truer sense, other people's music and drawing.

For all the arts of mankind, and womankind, are only rightly learned, or practised, when they are so with the definite purpose of pleasing or teaching others. A child dancing for its own delight,—a lamb leaping, —or a fawn at play, are happy and holy creatures ; but they are not artists. An artist is—and recollect this definition, (put in capitals for quick reference,)— A PERSON WHO HAS SUBMITTED TO A LAW WHICH IT WAS PAINFUL TO OBEY, THAT HE MAY BESTOW A DELIGHT WHICH IT IS GRACIOUS TO BESTOW.*

* To make the definition by itself complete, the words ' in his work ' should be added after ' submitted ' and ' by his work ' after ' bestow ' ; but it is easier to learn, without these phrases, which are of course to be understood.

"A painful law," I say ; yet full of pain, not in the sense of torture, but of stringency, or constraint ; and labour, increasing, it may be, sometimes into aching of limbs, and panting of breasts : but these stronger yet, for every ache, and broader for every pant ; and farther and farther strengthened from danger of rheumatic ache, and consumptive pant.

This, so far as the Arts are concerned, is 'entering in at the Strait gate,' of which entrance, and its porter's lodge, you will find farther account given in my fourth morning in Florence, which I should like you to read, as a preparation for the work more explicitly now to be directed under St George. The immediate gist of it, for those who do not care to read of Florence, I must be irksome enough again to give here ; namely, that the word Strait, applied to the entrance into Life, and the word Narrow, applied to the road of Life, do not mean that the road is so fenced that few can travel it, however much they wish, (like the entrance to the pit of a theatre,)* but that, for each person, it is at first so stringent, so difficult, and so dull, being between close hedges, that few *will* enter it, though all *may.* In a second sense, and an equally vital one, it is not merely a Strait, or narrow, but a straight, or right road ; only, in this rightness of it, not at all traced by hedges, wall, or telegraph wire, or even marked by posts higher

---

* The 'few there be that find it' is added, as an actual fact ; a fact consequent not on the way's being narrow, but on its being disagreeable.

than winter's snow ; but, on the contrary, often difficult
to trace among morasses and mounds of desert, even by
skilful sight ; and by blind persons, entirely untenable
unless by help of a guide, director, rector, or rex :
which you may conjecture to be the reason why, when
St. Paul's eyes were to be opened, out of the darkness
which meant only the consciousness of utter mistake,
to seeing what way he should go, his director was
ordered to come to him in the " street which is called
Straight."

Now, bringing these universal and eternal facts down
to this narrow, straight, and present piece of business
we have in hand, the first thing we have to learn to
draw is an extremely narrow, and an extremely direct,
line. Only, observe, true and vital direction does
not mean that, without any deflection or warp by
antagonist force, we can fly, or walk, or creep at
once to our mark ; but that, whatever the antagonist
force may be, we so know and mean our mark, that we
shall at last precisely arrive at it, just as surely, and
it may be in some cases more quickly, than if we had
been unaffected by lateral or opposing force. And this
higher order of contending and victorious rightness, which
in our present business is best represented by the track
of an arrow, or rifle-shot, affected in its course both by
gravity and the wind, is the more beautiful rightness
or directness of the two, and the one which all fine
art sets itself principally to achieve. But its quite first

step must nevertheless be in the simple production of the mathematical Right line, as far as the hand can draw it, joining two points, that is to say, with a straight visible track, which shall as nearly as possible fulfil the mathematical definition of a line, "length without breadth"

And the two points had better at first be placed at the small distance of an inch from each other, both because it is easy to draw so short a line, and because it is well for us to know, early in life, the look of the length of an inch. And when we have learned the look of our own English inch, we will proceed to learn the look of that which will probably be our currency measure of length, the French inch, for that is a better standard than ours, for European acceptance.

Here, I had made arrangements for the production of a plate, and woodcut, to illustrate the first steps of elementary design; but the black-plague of cloud already more than once spoken of (as connected probably with the diminution of snow on the Alps), has rendered it impossible for my assistants to finish their work in time. This disappointment I accept thankfully as the ordinance of my careful and prudent mistress, Atropos,—the third Fors; and am indeed quickly enough apprehensive of her lesson in it. She wishes me, I doubt not, to recognize that I was foolish in designing the intrusion of technical advice into my political letters ; and to understand that the giving of clear and separate directions for elementary art-practice is now an imperative duty for me, and that these art-lessons must be in companionship with my other school books on the Earth and its Flowers.

I must needs do her bidding ; and as I gather my past work on rocks and plants together, so I must, day by day, gather what I now know to be right of my past work on art together ; and, not in sudden thought, but in the resumption of purpose which I humbly and sincerely entreat my mistress to pardon me for having abandoned under pressure of extreme fatigue, I will publish, in the same form as the geology and botany, what I desire to ratify, and fasten with nails in a sure place, with instant applicability to school and university exercises, of my former writings on art.*

But this, I beg my readers to observe, will be the seventh large book I have actually at this time passing through the press ; † besides having written and published four volumes of university lectures ‡ in the

---

* Namely, Modern Painters, Stones of Venice, Seven Lamps, and Elements of Drawing I cut these books to pieces, because in the three first all the religious notions are narrow, and many false , and in the fourth, there is a vital mistake about outline, doing great damage to all the rest

† Fors, Ariadne, Love's Meinie, Proserpina, Deucalion, Mornings in Florence —and this : and four of these require the careful preparation of drawings for them by my own hand, and one of these drawings alone, for Proserpina, this last June, took me a good ten days' work, and that hard.

‡ Inaugural Lectures, Aratra Pentelici, Val d'Arno, and Eagle's Nest;

last six years ; every word of them weighed with care. This is what I observe the 'Daily Telegraph' calls giving 'utterances few and far between.' But it is as much certainly as I am able at present to manage ; and I must beg my correspondents, therefore, to have generally patience with me when I don't answer their letters by return of post ; and above all things, to write them clear, and in a round hand, with all the *m*s and *n*s well distinguished from *u*s.

The woodcut, indeed, prepared for this Fors was to have been a lesson in writing ; but that must wait till next year, now ; meantime you may best prepare yourself for that, and all other lessons to be given in my new edition of the Elements of Drawing, by beginning to form your own cherished and orderly treasures of beautiful art. For although the greatest treasury in that kind, belonging to St. George's Company, will be as often aforesaid public property, in our museums, every householder of any standing whatever among us will also have his own domestic treasury, becoming hereditary as accumulative ; and accurately catalogued, so that others may know what peculiar or separate good things are to be found in his house, and have graciously permitted use of them if true necessity be.

The basis, however, of such domestic treasury will of course be common to all ; every household having its

besides a course on Florentine Sculpture, given last year, and not yet printed, the substance of it being in re-modification for *Mornings in Florence.*

proper books for religious and economic service, and its classic authors, and engravings.

With the last we must at present class, and largely use, the more perishable treasure of good photographs, these, however, I do not doubt but that modern science will succeed, (if it has not already done so,) in rendering permanent, and, at all events, permanent copies of many may soon be placed in all our schools. Of such domestic treasure we will begin with a photograph of the picture by Fra Filippo Lippi, representing the Madonna; which picture last year had its place over the door of the inner room of the Uffizii of Florence, beyond the Tribune. This photograph can of course eventually be procured in any numbers, and, assuming that my readers will get one, I shall endeavour in this and future numbers of Fors, to make it useful to them and therefore a treasure *

The first thing you are to observe in it is that the figures are represented as projecting in front of a frame or window-sill. The picture belongs, therefore, to the class meant to be, as far as possible, deceptively like reality; and is in this respect entirely companionable with one long known in our picture-shops, and greatly popular with the British innkeeper, of a smuggler on the look-out, with his hand and pistol projecting

* Mr W Ward, 2, Church Terrace, Richmond, Surrey, will give any necessary information about this or other photographs referred to in Fors; and generally have them on sale, but see terminal Note

over the window-sill. The only differences in purpose
between the painter of this Anglican subject and the
Florentine's, are, first, that the Florentine wishes to
give the impression, not of a smuggler's being in
the same room with you, but of the Virgin and
Child's being so ; and, secondly, that in this repre-
sentation he wishes not *merely* to attain deceptive
reality , but to concentrate all the skill and thought .
that his hand and mind possess, in making that
reality noble.

Next, you are to observe that with this unusually
positive realism of representation, there is also an unusually mystic spiritualism of conception. Nearly all
the Madonnas, even of the most strictly devotional
schools, themselves support the child, either on their
knees or in their arms.   But here, the Christ is
miraculously borne by angels ;—the Madonna, though
seated on her throne, worships with both hands lifted.

Thirdly, you will at first be pained by the decision
of line, and, in the children at least, uncomeliness of
feature, which are characteristic, the first, of purely-
descended Etruscan work ; the second, of the Florentine
school headed afterwards by Donatello. But it is absolutely necessary, for right progress in knowledge, that
you begin by observing and tracing decisive lines ; and
that you consider dignity and simplicity of expression
more than beauty of feature   Remember also that a
photograph necessarily loses the most subtle beauty

of all things, because it cannot represent blue or grey colours,* and darkens red ones ; so that all glowing and warm shadows become too dark Be assured, nevertheless, that you have in this photograph, imperfect as it is, a most precious shadow and image of one of the greatest works ever produced by hand of man : and begin the study of it piece by piece If you fancy yourself able to draw at all, you may begin by practice over and over again the little angular band on the forehead, with its studs, and the connected chain of pearls. There are seven pearls and fourteen studs , the fifteenth, a little larger, at the angle of the transparent cap ; and four more, retiring. They are to be drawn with a fine brush and sepia, measuring the exact length of the band first , then marking its double curve, depressed in the centre, and rising over the hair, and then the studs and pearls in their various magnitudes. If you can't manage these, try the spiral of the chair ; if not that, buy a penny's worth of marbles and draw them in a row, and pick up a snail shell, and meditate upon it, if you have any time for meditation. And in my Christmas Fors I will tell you something about marbles, and beads, and coral, and pearls, and shells , and in time—it is quite possible—you may be able to draw a boy's marble and a snail's shell ; and a sea urchin , and a Doric capital , and an Ionic capital ; and a Parthenon, and a Virgin in

* The transparent part of the veil which descends from the point of the cap is entirely lost, for instance, in the Madonna.

it ; and a Solomon's Temple, and a Spirit of Wisdom in it ; and a Nehemiah's Temple, and a Madonna in it.

This photograph, then, is to be our first domestic possession in works of art ; if any difficulty or improper cost occur in attaining it, I will name another to answer its purpose ; but this will be No. 1 in our household catalogue of reference : which will never be altered, so that the pieces may always be referred to merely by their numbers.

Of public, or museum property in art, I have this month laid also the minute foundation, by the purchase, for our schools, of the engravings named in the annexed printseller's account *

And respecting the general operation of these schools and of the museums connected with them, the conclusion, which I am happy to announce, of the purchase of a piece of ground for the first of them, for six hundred pounds, requires some small special commentary.

Of such science, art, and literature as are properly connected with husbandry, (see Note *a*, p 210 of this volume,) St. George primarily acknowledges the art which provides him with a ploughshare,—and if need still be for those more savage instruments,—with spear, sword, and armour.

Therefore, it is fitting that of his schools " for the workmen and labourers of England," the first should be placed in Sheffield : (I suppose, originally Sheaf-field ;

* Last but one article in the Notes.

but do not at all rest on that etymology, having had no time to inquire into it.)

Besides this merely systematic and poetical fitness, there is the farther practical reason for our first action being among this order of craftsmen in England ; that in cutler's ironwork, we have, at this actual epoch of our history, the best in its kind done by English hands, unsurpassable, I presume, when the workman chooses to do all he knows, by that of any living nation.

For these two principal reasons, (and not without further direction from Fors of a very distinct nature,) I expressed, some time since, my purpose to place the first museum of the St. George's Company at Sheffield.

Whereupon, I received a letter, very well and kindly meant, from Mr. Bragge, offering me space in the existing Sheffield museum for whatever I chose to put there : Mr. Bragge very naturally supposing that this would be the simplest mode of operation for me ; and the most immediately advantageous to the town. To that (as I supposed private) communication I replied, in what I meant to be a private letter ; which letter Mr. Bragge, without asking my permission, read at a public dinner, with public comment on what he imagined to be the state of my health.

Now, I never wrote a letter in my life which all the world are not welcome to read, if they will : and as Fors would have it so, I am glad this letter *was* read aloud, and widely circulated : only, I beg Mr. Bragge and the other gentlemen who have kindly interested themselves in the existing Sheffield museum to understand that, had I intended the letter for publicity, it would have been couched in more courteous terms, and extended into clearer explanation of my singular and apparently perverse conduct in what I observe the Sheffield press, since it has had possession of the letter in question, characterizes as "setting up an opposition museum at Walkley."

I am glad to find the Sheffield branch of English journalism reprobating, in one instance at least, the— I had imagined now by all acclamation, divine— principle of Competition. But surely, the very retirement to the solitude of Walkley of which the same journalist complains, might have vindicated St. George's first quiet effort in his own work, from this unexpected accusation,—especially since, in so far as I can assert or understand the objects of either of the supposedly antagonist showmen, neither Mr. Bragge nor St. George intend taking shillings at the doors.

Nevertheless, the impression on the mind of the Sheffield journalist that museums are to be opened as lively places of entertainment, rivals for public patronage, and that their most proper position is therefore in a public thoroughfare, deserves on St. George's part some careful answer. A museum is, be it first observed, primarily, not at all a place of entertainment, but a place of Education. And a museum is, be it secondly observed, not a place for elementary education, but for that of already far-advanced scholars. And it is by no means the same thing as a parish school, or a Sunday school, or a day school, or even—the Brighton Aquarium.

Be it observed, in the third place, that the word 'School' means 'Leisure,' and that the word 'Museum' means 'Belonging to the Muses,' and that all schools and museums whatsoever, can only be, what they claim to be, and ought to be, places of noble instruction, when the persons who have a mind to use them can obtain so much relief from the work, or exert so much absti-nence from the dissipation, of the outside world, as may enable them to devote a certain portion of secluded laborious and reverent life to the attainment of the Divine Wisdom, which the Greeks supposed to be the gift of Apollo, or of the Sun ; and which the Christian knows to be the gift of Christ. Now, I hear it con-tinually alleged against me, when I advocate the raising of working men's wages, that already many of them have wages so high that they work only three days a week, and spend the other three days in drinking. And I have not the least doubt that under St. George's rule, when none but useful work is done, and when all classes are compelled to share in it, wages may indeed be so high, or, which amounts to the same thing as far as our present object is concerned, time so short, that at least two, if not three days out of every week, (or an

equivalent portion of time taken out of each day,) may
be devoted by some British workmen—no more to the
alehouse, but to, what British clergymen ought to mean,
if they don't, by the 'concerns of their immortal souls,'
that is to say, to the contemplation and study of the
works of God, and the learning that complete code of
natural history which, beginning with the life and death
of the Hyssop on the wall, rises to the knowledge of
the life and death of the recorded generations of mankind, and of the visible starry Dynasties of Heaven.

The workmen who have leisure to enter on this
course of study will also, I believe, have leisure to walk
to Walkley. The museum has been set there, not by
me, but by the second Fors, (Lachesis,) on the top of a
high and steep hill,—with only my most admiring concurrence in her apparent intention that the approach to
it may be at once symbolically instructive, and practically
sanitary.

NOTES AND CORRESPONDENCE.

I. The following communication was sent to me on a post-card, without the writer's name ; but it is worth notice —

" 'Ut et corda nostra mandatis tuis *dedita*.' If some manu-script Breviary has omitted ' dedita,' it must be by a slip of the pen. The sense surely is this that while there is either war or only an evil and deceitful peace within, self-surrender to the Divine commandments above and freedom from terror of foes around are alike impossible.

" In the English Prayer-book ' set' has the same meaning as in Psalm lxxviii. ver. 9 (*sic* the writer means ver 8), and the context shows the ' rest and quietness ' desired, to be rest and quietness of spirit "

The ' context' cannot show anything of the sort, for the sentence is an entirely independent one : and the MS. I use is not a Breviary, but the most perfect Psalter and full service, including all the hymns quoted by Dante, that I have seen in English thirteenth-century writing The omission of the word ' dedita ' makes not the smallest difference to the point at issue—which is not the mistranslation of a word, but the breaking of a clause The mistranslation nevertheless exists also ; precisely *because*, in the English Prayer-book, ' set' *has* the same meaning as in Psalm lxxviii. ; where the Latin word is ' direxit,' not ' dedit '; and where discipline is meant, not surrender.

I must reserve my comments on the two most important letters next following, for large type and more leisure.

II. " I hope that you will live to see Fors and everything printed without steam : it's the very curse and unmaking of us. I can see it dreadfully in every workman that I come across. Since I have been so happily mixed up with you these eighteen years, great changes have taken place in workmen. It was beginning fearfully when I last worked as a journeyman. One instance among many :—The head foreman came to me at Messrs. Bakers', and threatened discharge if he caught me using a hand bow-saw to cut a little circular disc, which I could have done in ten minutes. I then had to go and wait my turn at the endless steam saw—or, as commonly called, a band saw. I had to wait an hour and a half to take my turn : the steam saw did it in perhaps three minutes ; but the head foreman said, ' We've gone to great expense for steam machinery, and what is the use if we don't employ it ? ' This little occurrence was by no means uncommon. What workpeople have been brought to is beyond conception, in tone of feeling and character. Here, as I have told you, we do all we can ourselves, indoors and out ; have no servant, but make the children do : and because we are living in a tidy-sized house, and a good piece of ground, the labouring people make a dead set against us because we are not dependent upon them, and have even combined to defeat us in getting a charwoman now and then. We ought, I suppose, to employ two servants, whether we can pay for them or not, or even obtain them (which we couldn't). They have been picking hops here next our hedge : this is done by people in the neighbourhood, not imported pickers ; and their children called over the hedge to ours, and said, ' Your mother is not a lady ; she don't keep a servant, but does the work herself ' I name this little incident because it seems so deep."

III. " My dear Mr. Ruskin,—I write to ask leave to come and enter my name on the Roll of Companions of the Company of

St. George.* I have seen enough and read enough of the pace at which we are going, more especially in business matters, to make me long to see some effort made to win back some of the honesty and simplicity of our fathers And although I am afraid I can be but of very little use to the Company, I would gladly do anything that lay within my power, and it would be a great help to feel oneself associated with others, however feebly, in a *practical* work.

"I am trying to carry out what you have taught me in business, where I *can* do it. Our trade is dressing and buying and selling leather, etc, and making leather belting, hose, and boots I am trying to the utmost to make everything as good as it can be made, then to ask a fair price for it, and resist all attempts to cheapen or depreciate it in any way First, because the best thing is, as far as I know, invariably the 'best value', secondly, because shoe manufacturing, as now carried on, is, through the division of labour, a largely mechanical work, (though far less so than many trades),—and I believe the surest way of diminishing, as it is surely our duty to do, the amount of all such work, is to spend no labour, nor allow of its being spent, on any but the *best thing for wear* that can be made, and thirdly, because workmen employed even somewhat mechanically are, I think, far less degraded by their employment when their work and materials are good enough to become the subjects of honest pride You will understand that, being only in the position of manager of the business, I can only carry out these ideas to a certain point Still I have been able to reduce the amount of what is called 'fancy stitching' on parts of boots, on the stated ground of the injury the work ultimately causes to the operator's eyesight And in the dressing of some descriptions of leather, where we used to print by machinery an artificial grain on the skin or hide, we have

* The writer is now an accepted Companion.

dispensed with the process, and work up the natural grain by hand-power.

"And this brings me to the point I want to put to you about the permitted use of the sewing machine (see Fors XXXIV., p. 30).* It may seem unreasonable, when our firm employs so many. But it seems to me that the *admission* of machinery at all is unwise in principle. Machinery, especially the sewing machine, has demoralised the shoe trade,—the same I think you would find in all other trades,—notably in piece-goods for ladies' dresses—which, owing to the cheapness with which they can be made up, are far more in number than they *could* have been if no sewing machine had been used. And a manufacturer told me, only the other day, that common piece-goods, both woollen and others. take *as much* and generally *more* labour in making than the best. If all work required to supply clothing to the race were to be done by *hand*, it would be worth no one's while to make rubbish of any kind,—the work would be done by fewer people, and all raw material would be cheapened

" In your advice to a young lady, printed at page 29, Letter XXXIV., in the third volume of Fors Clavigera, you give her permission to use a sewing machine. I hope that, on fuller consideration of the subject, you will advise all who set the weal of their country above their own convenience, to discontinue its use wherever it can possibly be dispensed with.

* I am only too happy to be justified in withdrawing it. But my errors will, I trust, always be found rather in the relaxation than the unnecessary enforcement, even of favourite principles ; and I did not see what line I could draw between the spinning-wheel, which I knew to be necessary, and the sewing machine, which I suspected to be mischievous, and gave therefore *permission* only to use, while I shall earnestly urge the use of the spinning-wheel. I will give the reason for distinction, (so far as my correspondent's most interesting letter leaves me anything more to say,) in a future letter.

" For the effect of the sewing machine upon the great industries connected with clothing has been most disastrous

"Given a certain quantity of cloth, or calico, or leather; and, before it can be made available as clothing, it must be joined or stitched together in certain shapes.

"Now so long as this stitching was, of necessity, all done by hand, it was never worth while, supposing the labour to be paid for at a just rate, to use any but good materials. A print dress at three-halfpence per yard, which might wear a week, would cost as much to make as a dress that would wear a year, and, except for the rich and luxurious, all extravagance of trimming, and all sewing useless for wear, were unattainable.

" But with the introduction of the sewing machine a great change took place. It would be impossible within the limits of a letter to follow it out in every trade which has felt its influence. But briefly,—when it was found that the stitching process could be got through, though less solidly, at a very much reduced cost, it became possible for all classes to have dresses, clothes, and shoes in far greater number, and to embody in all kinds of clothing a larger amount of useless and elaborate work.

" And then arose among manufacturers generally a vigorous competition,—each one striving, not to make the most enduring and sound fabric (*the best value*), but that which, retaining some appearance of goodness, should be saleable at the lowest price and at the largest apparent profit

" The Statutes of the old Trade Guilds of England constantly provide for the purity of their several manufactures, as did Richard Cœur de Lion, in his law for the cloth makers, (Fors, Letter III., p 15,)—on this thoroughly wise and just ground: namely, that the best cloth, leather, etc., producible, being accurately the cheapest to the consumer,—the man who used his knowledge of his trade to make other than the best, was guilty of fraud Compare this view of the duty of a manufacturer with modern practice !

"It may be said that the customer is not cheated; since he knows, when he buys what is called a cheap thing, that it is not the best. I reply that the consumer never knows to the full what bad value, or unvalue, the common article is. And whose fault is it that he buys any but the best value?

"The answer involves a consideration of the duty and position of the retailer or middleman, and must be given, if at all, hereafter.

"One might multiply instances to show how this kind of competition has lowered the standard of our manufactures; but here most readers will be able to fall back upon their own experience.

"Then these common fabrics require for their production always a larger amount of labour in proportion to their value, —often actually as much, and sometimes more, than would suffice to make an equal quantity of material of the best value. So that, roughly, when we demand two common coats where one good one would serve, we simply require certain of our fellow-creatures to spend double the necessary time working for us in a mill. That is, supposing we get the full value out of our two common coats when we have them · the evil is greater if we fail to do so, and, to gratify our selfishness or caprice, require three instead of two. And the question arises,—Is it *kind* or *just* to require from others double the needful quantity of such labour as we would not choose to undergo ourselves? That it is not *Christian* so to do, may be learned by any one who will think out to their far-reaching consequences the words of our Lord ‘Therefore ALL THINGS WHATSOEVER ye would that men should do to you, do ye even so to them.’

"Now the use of the sewing machine has been all in favour of the 'three-coat' system, indefinitely multiplied and variously recommended; and the consequent absorption, year by year, of larger numbers of persons in mechanical toil, toil of the hands only—numbing to the brain, and blighting to the heart, or maddening to both

"So far as the question of clothing is concerned, I would venture to sum up our duty under present circumstances, broadly, as follows." [It can't possibly be done better —J. R]

"Always demand the best materials, and use no more of them than is necessary to dress yourselves neatly or handsomely, according to your station in society. Then have these materials made up by hand, if possible under your own supervision, paying a just price for the labour For such ornament as you need to add, remember that it must be the expression, first of your delight in some work of God's, and then of the human skill that wrought it This will save you from ever tampering with the lifeless machine-work, and though you have little ornament, it will soon be lovely and right.

"Above all, never buy cheap ready-made clothing of any kind whatsoever; it is most of it stained with blood, if you could see it aright. It is true you may now buy a 'lady's costume,' made up and trimmed by the sewing machine (guided by a human one), for the sum of two shillings and fourpence (wholesale), *but you had a great deal better wear a sack with a hole in it"* [Italics mine —J R] " It may be worth while hereafter to define with some precision what is the best value in various kinds of goods Meantime, should it be suggested that machine sewing is good enough for common materials, or for clothes that you intend to wear only a few times, and then throw aside, remember you have no business to buy any but good materials, nor to waste when you have bought them; and that it is worth while to put solid hand work into such."

("I use the word 'value' for the strength or 'availing of a thing towards life.' See Munera Pulveris, p. 10.")

IV. With respect to the next following letter—one which I am heartily glad to receive—I must beg my readers henceforward, and conclusively, to understand, that whether I print my correspondence in large type, or small, and with praise of it, or dispraise, I give absolutely no sanction or ratification whatever to any correspondent's statements of fact, unless by express indication. I am responsible for my own assertions, and for none other; but I hold myself bound to hear, and no less bound to publish, all complaints and accusations made by persons supposing themselves injured, of those who injure them, which I have no definite reason for supposing to be false or malicious, and which relate to circumstances affecting St George's work. I have no other means of determining their truth, than by permitting the parties principally concerned to hear them, and contradict them according to their ability, and the wish with which my present correspondent's letter closes, to be delivered from evil speaking and slandering, (she seems not quite clearly to understand that the prayer in the Litany is to be delivered from the guilt of these,—not from their effects,) may, so far as these affect her own family, be much more perfectly accomplished by her own statement of their true history, than by any investigation possible to me of the facts in question. But, as far as respects the appeal made by her to myself, my answer is simply, that, whether made by patents, ingenuities, or forges, all fortunes whatever, rapidly acquired, are, necessarily, *ill* acquired; and exemplary of universal ill to all men. No man is ever paid largely for ingenuity; he can only be paid largely by a tax on the promulgation of that ingenuity.

Of actual ingenuities, now active in Europe, none are so utterly deadly, and destructive to all the beauty of nature and the art of man, as that of the engineer.

And with respect to what my correspondent too truly urges—the shame of our ancient races in leaving their houses abandoned—it does not make me look with more comfort or complacency on their inhabitation by men of other names, that there will soon be left few homes in England whose splendour will not be a monument at once of the guilt of her nobles, and the misery of her people.

"Dear Mr Ruskin,—We have only just read the September number of Fors Clavigera My husband is the Ned G—— referred to in the letter you quote from E L. Said he, 'It (*i e*, the letter) is not worth notice.' I replied, 'In itself perhaps not, but I have known Mr Ruskin in his writings many years, and I shall write him to put before him the actual facts, and request him to withdraw these misstatements' The whole letter is written on the supposition that Mr Green is an *iron king*, or *iron lord*. No such thing he is an *engineer*—quite a different affair, the maker of a patent which is known all over the world as the 'Fuel Economiser' He consequently never had a forge, and is indebted to the use of his intellect and the very clever mechanical genius of his father for their rise in life, and not merely to *toiling half-naked Britons*, as stated The picture of the forge, with its *foul smoke and sweltering heat and din*, is drawn from some other place, and is utterly unlike the real workshops of E Green and Son—costly, airy, convenient, and erected to ensure the comfort of the workpeople, having a handsome front and lofty interior.

" As to smoke, the whole concern makes no more than, if as much as, an ordinary dwelling-house ; while we suffer too much at Heath from the town smoke to add to the dense volumes. We have no whistle—some other place is meant, we were never possessed of a 'devil,' American or English, of any sort. Mr. Green derives no pecuniary benefit from Wakefield, and but for the attachment of his father and himself to their birthplace, would long ago have conducted his operations in a more central spot

"Several other grave charges are brought against Mr. Green—one so serious that I am surprised to see it printed viz, *that he rules his people with an iron hand.* That may go with the rest of the 'iron tale.' Your correspondent is either very ignorant or wilfully false. No such assertion can be for a moment sustained, after inquiry is made among our people; nor by any one in the town could an instance of such be proved.

"As to the Scotch estate, Mr. Green does not possess one.

"The history of *Robin the Pedlar* is equally a work of E L 's imagination, although no false shame as to a humble descent has ever been shown or felt What! you taunt a man because he and his father have risen above the state in which they were born by use of the intellect God gives them? Fie! What sort of encouragement do you give to the working men to whom you address these letters, when you insinuate that *one sprung from the people* has no right to dwell in a hall or drive a carriage; and broadly hint he is no *gentleman*, no *scholar*, and *has nothing to boast of but his money?* Come here, and see if Ned G—— is the sort of man you picture; see the refinement visible in his idea of art, and which he has tried to impress on others by his example, and then ask yourself whether you have done well to lend the sanction of your name to decry, as a mere vulgar parvenu, one who has done his best to keep a high standard before him.

"As to living at Heath Hall, I ask, Is it a crime to spend your money in preserving to posterity a beautiful specimen of the house of the smaller gentry in Queen Elizabeth's time, which you only enjoy during a few years' lease? A little longer neglect, and this fine old house would have become a ruin when we took it, ivy grew inside, and owls made their nests in what are now guest-chambers

"No *squire* has lived here for a century and a quarter, and the last descendant of the *venerated Lady B*——, (Dame Mary Bolles, that is), utterly refused to reside near so dull a town as Wakefield— preferring Bath, then at the height of its glory and Beau Nash's; even before his time the hereditary squires despised and deserted the lovely place, letting it to any who would take it. Now it is repaired and restored, and well worth a visit even from Mr. Ruskin—who, if he is what I believe him, will withdraw the false imputations which must cause pain to us and surprise to those who know us. That last little stroke about bribery betrays E. L.'s disgust, not at the successful man, but at the Blue Tory. Well! from envy, malice, and all uncharitableness, from evil-speaking and slandering Good Lord deliver us!

" Yours very truly,

" MARY GREEN."

(I make no comments on this letter till the relations of Dame Mary Bolles have had time to read it, and E. L. to reply.)

V. The following account, with which I have pleasure in printing the accompanying acknowledgment of the receipt, contains particulars of the first actual expenditure of St. George's moneys made by me, to the extent of twenty-nine pounds ten shillings, for ten engravings* now the property of the Company. The other prints named in the account are bought with my own money, to be given or not given as I think right. The last five engravings—all by Durer—are bought at present for my proposed school at Sheffield, with the Melancholia, which I have already; but if finer impressions of them are some day given me, as is not unlikely, I should of course withdraw these, and substitute the better examples—retaining always the right of being myself the ultimate donor of the two St. Georges, in their finest state, from my own collection. But these must at present remain in Oxford.

* The printseller obligingly giving an eleventh, "Pembury Mill," For thus directing that the first art gift bestowed on the Company shall be Turner's etching of a flour mill.

London, *October* 5, 1875.

JOHN RUSKIN, ESQ.

			£	s	d.
St G 1	. .	Apollo and the Python, by Master of the Die	1	0	0
,, 2		Raglan Castle	3	10	0
,, 3	. ..	Solway Moss . ..	4	0	0
,, 4	...	Hind Head Hill ...	1	10	0
,, 5, *a*, *b*, *c*	Three impressions of Falls of the Clyde (£2 each) . .	6	0	0
,, 6.	...	Hindoo Worship . ..	2	0	0
,, 7		Dumblane Abbey	3	10	0
,, 8		Pembury Mill			
,, 9	...	Etching of the Severn and Wye ...	2	10	0
,, 10	.	Tenth Plague (of Egypt)	2	0	0
,, 11.	...	Æsacus and Hesperie ..	3	10	0

			29	10	0

(The above Prints sold at an unusually low price, for Mr. Ruskin's school.)

J. R 1	.	Sir John Cust	0	10	0
,, 2.	...	Lady Derby . . .	5	0	0
,, 3 4	.	Two Etchings of Æsacus and Hesperie (£4 each) .	8	0	0
, 5. 6.	...	Two Holy Islands (£2 6*s* each) . .	4	12	0
,, 7		Etching of Procris	4	4	0
,, 8	...	Holy Island	2	6	0
,, 9	...	The Crypt	4	4	0
,, 10	...	The Arvernon	8	8	0
,, 11.		Raglan Castle	7	0	0
,, 12.		,, ,, ...	6	0	0
,, 13.	...	,, ,, ...	6	0	0
,, 14	..	Woman at the Tank	7	17	6
,, 15	...	Grande Chartreuse	8	8	0

			101	19	6
Discount (15 per cent)	. .. .	10	1	0

			91	18	6

								£	s	d
			Brought forward	...	. .	. .		91	18	6
St G 16	...		Knight and Death	...	...	. .	. .	18	0	0
,, 17	...		St. George on Horseback	...	. .	. .		3	10	0
,, 18	...		,, ,, Foot	...	...	. .	. .	7	0	0
,, 19	...		Pilate ...	. .	...	. .	...	. .	2	0	0
,, 20	...		Caiaphas	. .	.	...	...	. .	3	0	0

$£$125 8 6

My dear Sir,—It is delightful to do business with you. How
I wish that all my customers were imbued with your principles.
I enclose the receipt, with best thanks, and am

Yours very sincerely and obliged.

JOHN RUSKIN ESQ.

Of course, original accounts, with all other vouchers, will be
kept with the Company's registers at Oxford. I do not think
it expedient always to print names, which would look like
advertisement.

Respecting the picture by Filippo Lippi, I find more difficulty than I expected On inquiring of various dealers, I am
asked three shillings each for these photographs. But as I on
principle never use any artifice in dealing, most tradesmen think
me a simpleton, and think it also their first duty, as men of
business, to take all the advantage in their power of this my
supposed simplicity, these photographs are therefore, I suppose,
worth actually, unmounted, about a shilling each; and I believe
that eventually, my own assistant, Mr. Ward, will be able to supply
them, of good impression, carefully chosen, with due payment
for his time and trouble, at eighteenpence each; or mounted,
examined by me, and sealed with my seal, for two shillings and
sixpence each. I don't promise this, because it depends upon
whether the government at Florence will entertain my request,

made officially as Slade Professor at Oxford, to have leave to photograph from the picture.

At present holding it of more importance not to violate confidence* than to sell photographs cheap, I do not even publish what I have ascertained, since this note was half written, to be the (actual) trade price, and I must simply leave the thing in the beautiful complexity of competition and secretiveness called British Trade ; only, at Oxford, I have so much personal influence with Mr. Davis, in Exeter Street, as may, I think, secure his obtaining the photographs, for which, as a dealer combined with other dealers, he must ask three shillings, of good quality; to him, therefore, at Oxford, for general business, my readers may address themselves ; or in London, to Miss Bertolacci, 7, Edith Grove, Kensington ; and, for impressions certified by me, to Mr. Ward, at Richmond, (address as above), who will furnish them, unmounted, for two shillings each, and mounted, for three And for a foundation of the domestic art-treasure of their establishment. I do not hold this to be an enormous or unjustifiable expense.

---

* Remember however that the publication of prime cost and the absolute knowledge of all circumstances or causes of extra cost, are inviolable laws of established trade under the St George's Company

FORS CLAVIGERA.

STARS IN THE EAST.

I CANNOT finish the letter I meant for my Christmas
Fors ; and must print merely the begun fragment—and
such uncrystalline termination must now happen to all
my work, more or less, (and more and more, rather than
less,) as it expands in range. As I stated in last letter,
I have now seven books in the press at once—and any
one of them enough to take up all the remainder of
my life. ' Love's Meinie,' for instance, (Love's Many, or
Serving Company,) was meant to become a study of
British birds, which would have been occasionally useful
in museums, carried out with a care in plume drawing
which I learned in many a day's work from Albert
Durer ; and with which, in such light as the days give
me, I think it still my duty to do all I can towards
completion of the six essays prepared for my Oxford
schools :—but even the third of these, on the Chough,
though already written and in type, is at pause because

I can't get the engravings for it finished, and the rest—
merely torment me in other work with the thousand
things flitting in my mind, like sea-birds for which
there are no sands to settle upon.

' Ariadne ' is nearer its close ; but the Appendix is a
mass of loose notes which need a very sewing machine
to bring together—and any one of these that I take in
hand leads me into ashamed censorship of the imper-
fection of all I have been able to say about engraving ;
and then, if I take up my Bewick, or return to my old
Turner vignettes, I put my Appendix off again—'till
next month,' and so on.

' Proserpina ' will, I hope, take better and more har-
monious form ; but it grows under my hands, and needs
most careful thought.   For it claims nothing less than
complete modification of existing botanical nomenclature,
for popular use ; and in connexion with ' Deucalion ' and
the recast ' Elements of Drawing,' is meant to found a
system of education in Natural History, the conception of which I have reached only by thirty years
of labour, and the realization of which can only be
many a year after I am at rest.   And yet none of this
work can be done but as a kind of play, irregularly,
and as the humour comes upon me   For if I set myself
at it gravely, there is too much to be dealt with ; my
mind gets fatigued in half an hour, and no good can
be done ; the only way in which any advance can be
made is by keeping my mornings   entirely quiet, and

free of care, by opening of letters or newspapers ; and then by letting myself follow any thread of thought or point of inquiry that chances to occur first, and writing as the thoughts come,—whatever their disorder ; all their connection and co-operation being dependent on the real harmony of my purpose, and the consistency of the ascertainable facts, which are the only ones I teach ; and I can no more, now, polish or neatly arrange my work than I can guide it. So this fragment must stand as it was written, and end,—because I have no time to say more.

COWLEY RECTORY, 27*th October,* 1875

My Christmas letter this year, since we are now definitely begun with our schooling, may most fitly be on the subject, already opened in Fors 12th, of the Three Wise Men.

'Three wise men of Gotham,' I had nearly written ; the remembrance of the very worst pantomime I ever saw, having, from the mere intolerableness of its stupidity, so fastened itself in my memory that I can't now get rid of the ring in my ears, unless I carefully say, ' Magi,' instead of ' wise men '

Such, practically, is the principal effect of the Sacred Art employed by England, in the festivity of her God's birthday, upon the minds of her innocent children, like me, who would fain see something magical and pretty on the occasion—if the good angels would bring it us, and our nurses, and mammas, and governesses would allow us to believe in magic, or in wisdom, any more.

You would not believe, if they wanted you, I suppose, you wise men of the west? You are sure that no real magicians ever existed; no real witches—no real prophets;—that an Egyptian necromancer was only a clever little Mr. Faraday, given to juggling; and the witch of Endor, only a Jewish Mrs. Somerville amusing herself with a practical joke on Saul; and that when Elisha made the axe swim, he had prepared the handle on the sly—with aluminium? And you think that in this blessed nineteenth century—though there isn't a merchant, from Dan to Beersheba, too honest to cheat, there is not a priest nor a prophet, from Dan to Beersheba, but he is too dull to juggle?

You may think, for what I care, what you please in such matters, if indeed you choose to go on through all your lives thinking, instead of ascertaining. But, for my own part, there are a few things concerning Magi and their doings which I have personally discovered, by laborious work among real magi. Some of those things I am going to tell you to-day, positively, and with entire and incontrovertible knowledge of them,—as you and your children will one day find every word of my direct statements in 'Fors Clavigera' to be; and fastened, each with its nail in its sure place.

A. In the first place, then, concerning stars in the east. You can't see the loveliest which appear there naturally,—the Morning Star, namely, and his fellows,—unless you get up in the morning.

B If you resolve thus always, so far as may be in your own power, to see the loveliest which are there naturally, you will soon come to see them in a supernatural manner, with a quite—properly so-called—' miraculous' or ' wonderful' light which will be a light in your spirit, not in your eyes And you will hear, with your spirit, the Morning Star and his fellows sing together ; also, you will hear the sons of God shouting together for joy with them , particularly the little ones,—sparrows, greenfinches, linnets, and the like

C. You will, by persevering in the practice, gradually discover that it is a pleasant thing to see stars in the luminous east ; to watch them fade as they rise ; to hear their Master say, Let there be light—and there is light ; to see the world made, that day, at the word , and creation, instant by instant, of divine forms out of darkness.

D. At six o'clock, or some approximate hour, you will perceive with precision that the Firm over the way, or round the corner, of the United Grand Steam Percussion and Corrosion Company, Limited, (Offices, London, Paris, and New York,) issues its counter-order, Let there be darkness ; and that the Master of Creation not only at once submits to this order, by fulfilling the constant laws He has ordained concerning smoke,—but farther, supernaturally or miraculously, enforces the order by sending a poisonous black wind, also from the east, of an entirely corrosive, deadly, and horrible quality, with which, from him that hath not, He takes away also that light he hath ; and changes the sky during what remains of the day,—on the average now three days out of five,*—into a mere dome of ashes, differing only by their enduring frown and slow pestilence from the passing darkness and showering death of Pompeii.

E. If, nevertheless, you persevere diligently in seeing what stars you can in the early morning, and use what is left you of light wisely, you will gradually discover that the United Grand Steam Percussion and Corrosion Company is a company of thieves ; and that you yourself are an ass, for letting them steal your money, and your light, at once. And that there is standing order from the Maker of Light, and Filler of pockets, that the company shall not be thieves, but honest men ; and that you yourself shall not be an ass, but a Magus.

F. If you remind the company of this law, they will tell you that people "didn't know everything down in Judee," that nobody ever made the world , and that nobody but the company knows it.

But if you enforce upon yourself the commandment

---

* It is at this moment, nine o'clock, 27th October, tearing the Virginian creeper round my window into rags rather than leaves.

not to be an ass, and verily resolve to be so no more,
then—hear the word of God, spoken to you by the only
merchant city that ever set herself to live wholly by
His law.*

" I willed, and sense was given to me.
I prayed, and the Spirit of Wisdom was given to me.
I set her before Kingdoms and Homes,
And held riches nothing, in comparison of her."

That is to say,—If you would have her to dwell
with you, you must set her before kingdoms ;—(as, for
instance, at Sheffield, you must not think to be kings
of cutlery, and let nobody else in the round world make
a knife but you ;)—you must set her before homes ;
that is to say, you must not sit comfortably enjoying
your own fireside, and think you provide for everybody if you provide for that :—and as for riches—you
are only to *prefer* wisdom,—think her, of two good
things, the best, when she is matched with kingdoms
and homes ; but you are to esteem riches—*nothing* in
comparison of her. Not so much as *mention* shall be
made "of coral, nor of pearls, for the price of wisdom
is above rubies."

You have not had the chance, you think, probably,
of making any particular mention of coral, or pearls, or
rubies ? Your betters, the Squires and the Clergy,
have kept, if not the coral, at least the pearls, for their

---

* See Fourth Morning in Florence. ' The Vaulted Book.'

own wives' necks, and the rubies for their own mitres ; and have generously accorded to you heavenly things,— wisdom, namely, concentrated in your responses to Cate- chism. I find St George, on the contrary, to be minded that you shall at least know what these earthly goods are, in order to your despising them in a sensible manner ; —for you can't despise them if you know nothing about them.

I am going, under His orders, therefore, to give you some topazes of Ethiopia,—(at least, of the Ural moun- tains, where the topazes are just as good,)—and all manner of coral, that you may know what co-operative societies are working, to make your babies their rattles and necklaces, without any steam to help them, under the deep sea, and in its foam ; also out of the Tay, the fairest river of the British Isles, we will fetch some pearls that nobody shall have drawn short breath for : and, indeed, all the things that Solomon in his wisdom sent his ships to Tarshish for,—gold, and silver, ivory, and apes, and peacocks,—you shall see in their perfection and have as much of as St. George thinks good for you : (only remember, in order to see an ape in per- fection, you must not be an ape yourself, whatever Mr. Darwin may say ; but must admire, without imi- tating their prehensile activities, nor fancy that you can lay hold on to the branches of the tree of life with your tails instead of your hands, as you have been practising lately).

And, in the meantime, I must stop writing because I've to draw a peacock's breast-feather, and paint as much of it as I can without having heaven to dip my brush in. And when you have seen what it is, you shall despise it—if you can—for heaven itself. But for nothing less !

My fragment does not quite end here ; but in its following statements of plans for the Sheffield Museum, anticipates more than I think Atropos would approve ; besides getting more figurative and metaphysical than you would care to read after your Christmas dinner. But here is a piece of inquiry into the origin of all riches, Solomon's and our own, which I wrote in May, 1873, for the 'Contemporary Review,' and which, as it sums much of what I may have too vaguely and figuratively stated in my letters, may advisably close their series for this year.

It was written chiefly in reply to an article by Mr Greg, defending the luxury of the rich as harmless, or even beneficent to the poor. Mr. Greg had, on his part, been reproving Mr Goldwin Smith—who had spoken of a rich man as consuming the means of living of the poor. And Mr. Greg pointed out how beneficially for the poor, in a thousand channels, the rich man spent what he had got

Whereupon I ventured myself to inquire, " How he got it ? " and the paper went on thus,—' Which is indeed the first of all questions to be asked when the economical relations of any man with his neighbour are to be examined.'

Dick Turpin is blamed—suppose—by some plain-minded person, for consuming the means of other people's living. " Nay," says Dick to the plain-minded person, " observe how beneficently and pleasantly I spend whatever I get !"

"Yes, Dick," persists the plain-minded person, " but how do you get it ?"

"The question," says Dick, " is insidious, and irrelevant."

Do not let it be supposed that I mean to assert any irregularity or impropriety in Dick's profession—I merely assert the necessity for Mr. Greg's examination, if he would be master of his subject, of the manner of *Gain* in every case, as well as the manner of *Expenditure.* Such accounts must always be accurately rendered in a well-regulated society.

" Le lieutenant adressa la parole au capitaine, et lui dit qu'il venait d'enlever ces mannequins, remplis de sucre, de cannelle, d'amandes, et de raisins secs, à un épicier de Bénavente. Après qu'il eut rendu compte de son expédition au bureau, les dépouilles de l'épicier furent portées dans l'office. Alors il ne fut plus question que de se réjouir , je débutai par le buffet, que je parai de plusieurs bouteilles de ce bon vin que le Seigneur Rolando m'avoit vanté."

Mr. Greg strictly confines himself to an examination of

the benefits conferred on the public by this so agreeable festivity, but he must not be surprised or indignant that some inquiry should be made as to the resulting condition of the épicier de Bénavente

And it is all the more necessary that such inquiry be instituted, when the captain of the expedition is a minion, not of the moon, but of the sun, and dazzling, therefore, to all beholders. "It is heaven which dictates what I ought to do upon this occasion," * says Henry of Navarre, "my retreat out of this city, before I have made myself master of it, will be the retreat of my soul out of my body." "Accordingly, all the quarter which still held out, we forced," says M. de Rosny, "after which the inhabitants, finding themselves no longer able to resist, laid down their arms, and the city was given up to plunder. My good fortune threw a small iron chest in my way, in which I found about four thousand gold crowns."

I cannot doubt that the Baron's expenditure of this sum would be in the highest degree advantageous to France, and to the Protestant religion. But complete economical science must study the effect of its abstraction on the immediate prosperity of the town of Cahors ; and

* I use the current English of Mrs Lennox's translation, but Henry's real saying was (see the first—green leaf—edition of Sully), "It is written above what is to happen to me on *every* occasion" "Toute occasion" becomes ' Cette occasion" in the subsequent editions, and finally "what is to happen to me" (ce que doit être fait de moi) becomes "what I ought to do" in the English

even beyond this—the mode of its former acquisition by
the town itself, which perhaps, in the economies of the
nether world, may have delegated some of its citizens to
the seventh circle.

And the most curious points, in the modes of study
pursued by modern economical science, are, that while
it always *waives this question of ways and means* with
respect to *rich* persons, it studiously pushes it in the
case of *poor* ones ; and while it asserts the consumption
of such an article of luxury as wine to take that
which Mr. Greg himself instances) to be economically
expedient, when the wine is drunk by persons who
are *not* thirsty, it asserts the same consumption to be
altogether inexpedient, when the privilege is extended
to those who *are*. Thus Mr. Greg dismisses, at page
618, with compassionate disdain, the extremely vulgar
notion "that a man who drinks a bottle of champagne
worth five shillings, while his neighbour is in want of
actual food, is in some way wronging his neighbour ; "
and yet Mr. Greg himself, at page 624, evidently remains under the equally vulgar impression that the
twenty-four millions of much thirstier persons who spend
fifteen per cent of their incomes in drink and tobacco,
are wronging their neighbours by *that* expenditure.

It cannot, surely, be the difference in degree of refinement between malt liquor and champagne which causes
Mr. Greg's conviction that there is moral delinquency
and economical error in the latter case, but none in the

former ; if that be all, I can relieve him from his embar-
rassment by putting the cases in more parallel form. A
clergyman writes to me, in distress of mind, because the
able-bodied labourers who come begging to him in winter,
drink port wine out of buckets in summer. Of course
Mr. Greg's logical mind will at once admit (as a consequence of his own very just argumentum ad hominem
in page 617) that the consumption of port wine out of
buckets must be as much a benefit to society in general
as the consumption of champagne out of bottles , and
yet, curiously enough, I am certain he will feel my
question, " Where does the drinker get the means for his
drinking ?" more relevant in the case of the imbibers of
port than in that of the imbibers of champagne. And
although Mr Greg proceeds, with that lofty contempt
for the dictates of nature and Christianity which radical
economists cannot but feel, to observe (p. 618) that
" while the natural man and the Christian would have
the champagne drinker forego his bottle, and give the
value of it to the famishing wretch beside him, the radical
economist would condemn such behaviour as distinctly
criminal and pernicious," he would scarcely, I think,
carry out with the same triumphant confidence the con-
clusions of the unnatural man and the Anti-Christian with
respect to the labourer as well as the idler ; and declare
that while the extremely simple persons who still believe
in the laws of nature, and the mercy of God, would have
the port-drinker forego his bucket, and give the value of

it to the famishing wife and child beside him, " the radical
economist would condemn such behaviour as distinctly
criminal and pernicious "

Mr. Greg has it indeed in his power to reply that
it is proper to economize for the sake of one's own
wife and children, but not for the sake of anybody
else's.   But since, according to another exponent of the
principles of Radical Economy, in the ' Cornhill Magazine,'
a well-conducted agricultural labourer must not marry
till he is forty-five, his economies, if any, in early life,
must be as offensive to Mr. Greg, on the score of their
abstract humanity, as those of the richest bachelor about
town

There is another short sentence in this same page
618, of which it is difficult to overrate the accidental
significance

The superficial observer, says Mr. Greg, " recollects a
text which he heard in his youth, but of which he never
considered the precise applicability—' He that hath two
coats, let him impart to him that hath none.' "

The assumptions that no educated Englishman can
ever have heard that text *except* in his youth, and that
those who are old enough to remember having heard
it, " never considered its precise applicability," are surely
rash, in the treatment of a scientific subject.   I can
assure Mr. Greg that a few grey-headed votaries of the
creed of Christendom still read—though perhaps under
their breath—the words which early associations have

made precious to them ; and that in the bygone days, when that Sermon on the Mount was still listened to with respect by many not illiterate persons, its meaning was not only considered, but very deliberately acted upon. Even the readers of the ' Contemporary Review ' may perhaps have some pleasure in retreating from the sunshine of contemporary science, for a few quiet moments, into the shadows of that of the past ; and hearing in the following extracts from two letters of Scott's (the first describing the manner of life of his mother, whose death it announces to a friend ; the second, anticipating the verdict of the future on the management of his estate by a Scottish nobleman) what relations between rich and poor were possible, when philosophers had not yet even lisped in the sweet numbers of Radical Sociology.

" She was a strict economist, which she said enabled her to be liberal ; out of her little income of about £300 a year, she bestowed at least a third in well-chosen charities, and with the rest, lived like a gentlewoman, and even with hospitality more general than seemed to suit her age ; yet I could never prevail on her to accept of any assistance. You cannot conceive how affecting it was to me to see the little preparations of presents which she had assorted for the New Year, for she was a great observer of the old fashions of her period—and to think that the kind heart was cold which delighted in all these arts of kindly affection."

" The Duke is one of those retired and high-spirited men who will never be known until the world asks what became of the huge oak that grew on the brow of the hill, and sheltered such an extent of ground. During the late distress, though his own immense rents remained in arrears, and though I know he was pinched for money, as all men were, but more especially the possessors of entailed estates, he absented himself from London in order to pay, with ease to himself, the labourers employed on his various estates. These amounted (for I have often seen the roll and helped to check it) to nine hundred and fifty men, working at day wages, each of whom on a moderate average might maintain three persons, since the single men have mothers, sisters, and aged or very young relations to protect and assist. I ndeed it is wonderful how much even a small sum, comparatively, will do in supporting the Scottish labourer, who in his natural state is perhaps one of the best, most intelligent, and kind-hearted of human beings ; and in truth I have limited my other habits of expense very much since I fell into the habit of employing mine honest people. I wish you could have seen about a hundred children, being almost entirely supported by their fathers' or brothers' labour, come down yesterday to dance to the pipes, and get a piece of cake and bannock, and pence apiece (no very deadly largess) in honour of hogmanay. I declare to you, my dear friend, that when I thought the poor fellows who kept these children so neat, and well taught, and well behaved, were slaving the whole day for eighteen-pence or twenty-pence at most, I was ashamed of their gratitude, and of their becks and bows But after all, one does what one can, and it is better twenty families should be comfortable according to their wishes and habits, than that half that number should be raised above their situation."

I must pray Mr. Greg farther to observe, if he has condescended to glance at these remains of almost prehistoric thought, that although the modern philosopher will never have reason to blush for any man's gratitude, and has totally abandoned the romantic idea of making even so much as one family comfortable according to their wishes and habits, the alternative suggested by Scott, that *half* " the number should be raised above their situation," may become a very inconvenient one if the doctrines of Modern Equality and competition should render the *other* half desirous of parallel promotion

It is now just sixteen years since Mr. Greg's present philosophy of Expenditure was expressed with great precision by the Common Councilmen of New York, in their report on the commercial crisis of 1857,* in the following terms :—

" Another erroneous idea is that luxurious living, extravagant dressing, splendid turn-outs, and fine houses, are the cause of distress to a nation No more erroneous impression could exist. Every extravagance that the

* See the ' Times' of November 23rd of that year

man of 100,000 or 1,000,000 dollars indulges in, adds to
the means, the support, the wealth of ten or a hundred
who had little or nothing else but their labour, their
intellect, or their taste.　If a man of 1,000,000 dollars
spends principal and interest in ten years, and finds himself beggared at the end of that time, he has actually
made a hundred who have catered to his extravagance,
employers or employed, so much richer by the division
of his wealth.　He may be ruined, but the nation is
better off and richer, for one hundred minds and hands,
with 10,000 dollars apiece, are far more productive than
one with the whole."

Now that is precisely the view also taken of the matter
by a large number of Radical Economists in England
as well as America ; only they feel that the time, however short, which the rich gentleman takes to divide his
property among them in his own way, is practically
wasted ; and even worse, because the methods which
the gentleman himself is likely to adopt for the depression of his fortune will not, in all probability, be conducive to the elevation of his character.　It appears,
therefore, on moral as well as economical grounds, desirable that the division and distribution should at once
be summarily effected ; and the only point still open
to discussion in the views of the Common Councilmen
is to what degree of minuteness they would think it
advisable to carry the subsequent *sub*division.

I do not suppose, however, that this is the conclusion

which Mr Greg is desirous that the general Anti-Christian public should adopt ; and in that case, as I see by his paper in the last number of the ' Contemporary,' that he considers the Christian life itself virtually impossible, may I recommend his examination of the manners of the Pre-Christian ? For I can certify him that this important subject, of which he has only himself imperfectly investigated one side, had been thoroughly investigated on all sides, at least seven hundred years before Christ ; and from that day to this, all men of wit, sense, and feeling have held precisely the same views on the subjects of economy and charity in all nations under the sun. It is of no consequence whether Mr. Greg chooses the experience of Bœotia, Lombardy, or Yorkshire, nor whether he studies the relation of each day to its labour under Hesiod, Virgil, or Sydney Smith. But it is desirable that at least he should acquaint himself with the opinions of some of these persons, as well as with those of the Common Councilmen of New York ; for though a man of superior sagacity may be pardoned for thinking, with the friends of Job, that Wisdom will die with him, it can only be through neglect of the existing opportunities of general culture that he remains distinctly under the impression that she was born with him.

It may perhaps be well that, in conclusion, I should state briefly the causes and terms of the economical crisis of our own day, which has been the subject of the debate between Mr. Goldwin Smith and Mr. Greg.

No man ever became, or can become, largely rich merely by labour and economy. All large fortunes (putting treasure-trove and gambling out of consideration) are founded either on occupation of land, usury, or taxation of labour. Whether openly or occultly, the landlord, money-lender, and capital-holding employer, gather into their possession a certain quantity of the means of existence which other people produce by the labour of their hands. The effect of this impost upon the condition of life of the tenant, borrower, and workman, is the first point to be studied;—the results, that is to say, of the mode in which Captain Roland *fills* his purse.

Secondly, we have to study the effects of the mode in which Captain Roland *empties* his purse. The landlord, usurer, or labour-master, does not, and cannot, himself consume all the means of life he collects. He gives them to other persons, whom he employs in his own behalf—growers of champagne; jockeys; footmen; jewellers; builders; painters; musicians; and the like. The diversion of the labour of these persons from the production of food to the production of articles of luxury is very frequently, and, at the present day, very grievously, a cause of famine. But when the luxuries are produced, it becomes a quite separate question who is to have them, and whether the landlord and capitalist are entirely to monopolize the music, the painting, the architecture, the hand-service, the horse-service, and the sparkling champagne of the world.

And it is gradually, in these days, becoming manifest to the tenants, borrowers, and labourers, that instead of paying these large sums into the hands of the landlords, lenders, and employers, that *they* may purchase music, painting, etc. ; the tenants, borrowers, and workers, had better buy a little music and painting for themselves! That, for instance, instead of the capitalist-employer's paying three hundred pounds for a full-length portrait of himself, in the attitude of investing his capital, the united workmen had better themselves pay the three hundred pounds into the hands of the ingenious artist, for a painting, in the antiquated manner of Lionardo or Raphael, of some subject more religiously or historically interesting to *them ;* and placed where they can always see it. And again, instead of paying three hundred pounds to the obliging landlord, that he may buy a box at the opera with it, whence to study the refinements of music and dancing, the tenants are beginning to think that they may as well keep their rents partly to themselves, and therewith pay some Wandering Willie to fiddle at their own doors ; or bid some grey-haired minstrel

> " Tune, to please a peasant's ear,
> The harp a king had loved to hear."

And similarly the dwellers in the hut of the field, and garret of the city, are beginning to think that, instead of paying half-a-crown for the loan of half a fireplace, they had better keep their half-crown in their pockets till they can buy for themselves a whole one.

These are the views which are gaining ground among the poor ; and it is entirely vain to endeavour to repress them by equivocations. They are founded on eternal laws ; and although their recognition will long be refused, and their promulgation, resisted as it will be, partly by force, partly by falsehood, can only take place through incalculable confusion and misery, recognized they must be eventually ; and with these three ultimate results :— that the usurer's trade will be abolished utterly ,—that the employer will be paid justly for his superintendence of labour, but not for his capital ; and the landlord paid for his superintendence of the cultivation of land, when he is able to direct it wisely ;—that both he, and the employer of mechanical labour, will be recognized as beloved masters, if they deserve love, and as noble guides when they are capable of giving discreet guidance ; but neither will be permitted to establish themselves any more as senseless conduits, through which the strength and riches of their native land are to be poured into the cup of the fornication of its Babylonian ' City of the Plain.'

So ends my article, and enough said for 1875, I think. And I wish you a merry Christmas, my masters ; and honest ways of winning your meat and pudding.

NOTES AND CORRESPONDENCE.

I am busy, and tired, this month ; so shall keep my making up of accounts till January. The gist of them is simply that we have got £8000 worth of Consols , and we had a balance of £501 7s. at the bank, which balance I have taken, and advanced another hundred of my own, making £600, to buy the Sheffield property with ; this advance I shall repay myself as the interest comes in, or farther subscription. and then use such additional sums for the filling of the museum, and building a small curator's house on the ground. But I shall not touch any of the funded sum , and hope soon to see it raised to £10,000 I have no word yet from our lawyer about our constitution. The Sheffield property, like the funded, stands in the names of the Trustees

I have accepted, out of our forty subscribers, some eight or nine for Companions, very gratefully. Others wish well to the cause, but dislike the required expression of creed and purpose. I use no persuasion in the matter, wishing to have complete harmony of feeling among the active members of the Society.

E L.'s courteous, but firm, reply to Mrs. Green's letter reaches me too late for examination In justice to both my correspondents, and to my readers, I must defer its insertion, in such abstract as may seem desirable, until next month.

I. Letter from a clergyman, now an accepted Companion. The extract contained in it makes me wonder if it has never occurred to the Rev. Dr. Mullens that there should be immediately formed a Madagascar Missionary Society, for the instruction of the natives of England —

" My dear Sir,—*Apropos* of your strictures on usury which have from time to time appeared in ' Fors,' I have thought you would be interested in the following extract from a recent work on Madagascar, by the Rev. Dr. Mullens, of the London Missionary Society.

"After describing a ' Kabáry,'—a public assembly addressed by the Queen,—in the Betsileo* province, he goes on to say: ' Having expressed in a clear and distinct voice her pleasure in meeting her people once more, the Queen uttered several sentences usual to these assemblies, in which she dwelt upon the close and affectionate relations subsisting between them and herself "You are a father and mother to me having you, I have all. . . . And if you confide in me, you have a father and a mother in me. Is it not so, O ye under heaven ? " To which, with a deep voice, the people reply, " It is so." Passing at length to the subject specially before her, the Queen said, " My days in the South are now few; therefore I will say a word about the Schools. And I say to you all, here in Betsileo, . . . cause your children to attend the Schools My desire is, that whether high or low, whether sons of the nobles, or sons of the judges, or sons of the officers, or sons of the centurions, your sons and your daughters should attend the Schools and become lovers of wisdom." The Prime Minister, then, in the Queen's name, addressed the assembly on the subject of usury,—a great evil among poor nations, and only too common in stages of society, like that in Madagascar,—and said, "Thus saith the Queen *All the usury exacted by the Hovas from the Betsileo is remitted*, and only the original debt shall remain ! " '

" I am, dear Sir, faithfully yours,

" JOSEPH HALSEY."

* I can't answer for Madagascar nomenclature

II. Useful letter from a friend —

" You say when I agree in your opinions I may come, but surely you do not exact the unquestioning and entire submission of the individual opinion which the most arrogant of churches exacts.* With your leading principles, so far as I am yet able to judge of them, I entirely and unreservedly agree. I see daily such warped morality, such crooked ways in the most urgent and important concerns of life, as to convince me that the axe should be laid to the root of the tree. Mainly I am disgusted—no more tolerant word will do—with the prevalent tone of thought in religious matters, and the resulting tortuous courses in daily work and worship. What a worse than Pagan misconception of Him whom they ignorantly worship—

" ' Ille opifex rerum, mundi melioris origo '—

is shown by the mass of so-called religious persons ! How scurrilously the Protestant will rail against Papist *intolerance—* making his private judgment of Scripture the infallible rule,—

" ' Blushing not (as Hooker says) in any doubt concerning matters of Scripture to think his own bare Yea as good as the Nay of all the wise, grave, and learned judgments that are in the whole world. Which insolency must be repressed, or it will be the very bane of Christian Religion.'—(Ecc. Polity, Book II.)

" I believe the St. George's Company contains the germ of a healthy and vigorous constitution. I see that you are planting that germ, and fostering it with all deliberation and cautious directness of advance , but what Titanic obstacles ! It seems to me the fittest plant of this age to survive, but in the complexities of the struggle for existence, its rearing must be a Herculean labour. Yet wherein is this age singular? When was there any

---

* By no means ; but *practical* obedience, yes,— not to *me* but to the Master of the Company, whoever he may be ; and this not for his pride's sake, but for your comfort's

time whose sentence we might not write thus : 'L'état agité par les brigues des ambitieux, par les largesses des riches factieux, par la vénalité des pauvres oiseux, par l'empirisme des orateurs, par l'audace des hommes pervers, par la faiblesse des hommes vertueux,' was distracted and disintegrate ?

"When I can get better words than my own I like to use them—and it is seldom I cannot. In the selfish pleasure of writing to you I forget the tax on your time of reading my vagaries ; but I feel a kind of filial unburdening in writing thus freely. Will that excuse me ?

"Always sincerely and affectionately yours,

"James Hooper."

Wood *versus* Coal.—Subject to such correction as may be due to the different quantity of carbon contained in a load of wood as in a ton of coal, the product of the coal-field is seven times as much [of fuel] per mile, as that of the forest. To produce a yield of fuel equal to that obtainable from the known coal measures of the world, if worked with an activity equal to that of our own, seven times the area of cultivated forest is required. But the actual area, as estimated, is not seven, but twenty-seven times that of the coal measures It is thus four times as important, regarded as a source of fuel But while the life of the coal-field has been taken at 150 years, that of the forest, if rightly cared for, will endure as long as that of the human family. A wealth such as this is not to be measured in tons of gold.— *Edinburgh Review*, p. 375, Oct., 1875.

"I think Sheffield is more likely ' Schaf-feld ' than Sheaf-field. 'Sheep-fold,' the sheltered hollow with moors all round it. I know a place called ' Theescombe,' meaning 'theaves-combe,' or 'young lambs-combe.'"—*Note by a Companion.*